The Vil'

# The Village in Revolt

## The Story of the Longest Strike in History

**Shaun Jeffery**

HIGDON PRESS

HIGDON PRESS

First published in Great Britain in 2018 by Higdon Press

A CIP catalogue record for this book is available from the British Library

ISBN 978–1–5272–2225–0

Typeset by RefineCatch Limited, Bungay, Suffolk
Printed and bound in Great Britain by Clays Ltd, Elcograf S.p.A.

# Contents

# List of Illustrations

# The Higdon Timeline

| | |
|---|---|
| 21 August 1869 | Thomas George Higdon born, in the parish of East Pennard, Somerset |
| 13 December 1864 | Anne Catherine Schollick born, in Poulton-cum-Seacombe, Cheshire |
| 4 July 1896 | Tom and Annie are married in the Holy Trinity Church, Clifton, Gloucester |
| 14 April 1902 | Commencement of teaching positions at Wood Dalling County School, Norfolk |
| 22 October 1902 | Tom assaults local farmer, Mr Gamble, for repeatedly taking children out of school to do farm work |
| 2 May 1904 | The Clerk to the School Managers writes to the Norfolk Education Committee to inform them that they and the Higdons are barely on speaking terms |
| 1 December 1908 | First enquiry at Wood Dalling examining the tensions between the Higdons and the school managers |
| 19 March 1910 | The *Norwich Mercury* records Tom and Annie's election at the Wood Dalling parish elections |
| 17 July 1910 | Second enquiry, after further friction between the school managers and Annie Higdon |
| 2 August 1910 | Annie Higdon is asked to send in her resignation '. . . as the most prejudicial form of removal' |

| | |
|---|---|
| 24 October 1910 | Tom Higdon receives a month's notice to terminate his employment |
| 30 November 1910 | Under pressure, Annie expresses 'sincere regret for my lack of discretion in addressing some of the managers' |
| 17 December 1910 | In light of Annie's apology, the committee endeavours to transfer the Higdons to Burston |
| 31 January 1911 | The Higdons arrive in Burston during the evening, on foot, after walking from Diss railway station |
| 1 February 1911 | The Higdons commence teaching positions at Burston Council School, Norfolk |
| 11 October 1912 | The government inspector of schools gives a good and improving report after only one year with the Higdons in charge |
| 13 March 1913 | Tom tops the poll at the Burston parish elections. Reverend Charles Tucker Eland comes bottom |
| 29 November 1913 | Annie receives a letter from the Norfolk Education Committee referring to a letter from the school managers asking if they '. . . will kindly remove Mrs Higdon to a sphere more genial' |
| 23 January 1913 | Rev. Eland writes to the Norfolk Education Committee making false allegations against Annie's treatment of two Barnardo's children |
| 23 February 1914 | First (afternoon) of the Education Committee's enquiry into the allegations made against Annie |
| 27 February 1914 | Second (afternoon) of the Education Committee's enquiry into the allegations made against Annie |

| | |
|---|---|
| 28 March 1914 | Annie is given three months' salary in lieu of notice and Tom one month's in lieu of notice, with their employment to terminate on 31 March 1914 |
| 1 April 1914 | The Higdons' dismissal takes effect. Later in the day sixty-six out of seventy-two children go out 'on strike' |
| 3 June 1914 | The Higdons leave the school house after the eviction notice expires |
| 1 April 1915 | First anniversary celebrations; the children recreate their march around the village, with tea in the afternoon. At night the parents hold a 'social' and the Higdons are presented with gifts |
| 20 February 1916 | First of a series of London public meetings organised by the NUR held at Kentish Town Public Baths. The Higdons and some twenty striking children are present |
| 1 April 1916 | Two years after the start of the strike, the Burston School Strike and Evicted Glebe Tenants National Committee is formed |
| 18 February 1917 | The National Committee meet in the Burston Crown and set the date for the grand opening demonstration of the new 'Strike School' for 13 May 1917 |
| 26 February 1917 | Both the vice president and president of the NUT visit Burston to hear evidence in a new inquiry against the allegations made against Annie |
| 13 May 1917 | The new 'Strike School' is declared open by Violet Potter, the leader of the striking children |
| 10 April 1919 | Tom is defeated in the parish elections, which were mainly split down party lines. Tom's labour group loses out in the post-war wave of conservatism |

| | |
|---|---|
| 17 August 1939 | Tom George Higdon passes away from bowel cancer |
| February 1940 | After twenty-five years the Strike School closes; the remaining children are transferred to the Council School |
| 24 April 1946 | Annie Katherine Higdon dies in a retirement home in Swainsthorpe, near Norwich |

# Foreword

Britain in the spring of 1914 was a very different place from that often pictured in the golden-age memories of a later generation. The women's militant struggle for the vote was reaching a point where the 'Cat and Mouse Act' was imprisoning women, force feeding them, releasing them for medical reasons and then taking them back into prison once they had recovered. Perhaps more importantly, these women, once a minority, were gaining support throughout the country. In Ulster an armed insurrection was brewing with thousands of Ulster people signing 'The Solemn League and Covenant', pledging to fight rather than accept Home Rule. Many signed in their own blood. In the Curragh Camp outside Dublin, English cavalry officers said they would refuse to ride against their Ulster brothers, a move supported openly by many in the Conservative Party, including, at least tacitly, the leader of His Majesty's Opposition.

Nor was the south of the country quiet. In 1913 there was a transport strike in Dublin which was one of the most bitter and angry in Irish, if not British, history, and which had led to the creation of the Irish Citizens Army led by James Connolly and Jim Larkin, with widespread support from the Irish Transport and General Workers Union. It was to be the ICA which marched with the Irish Volunteers at Easter 1916.

In mainland Britain things were, in the eyes of some, if anything, worse. Labour held forty-two seats in the House of Commons (ten years earlier it held only two) and although most of these men were moderate reformers, some were not. More worrying for those in power was an extra-parliamentary movement from within the trades unions. After a series of setbacks in the 1890s organised labour had begun to grow again. Central to this were three great and powerful unions, The Workers Union (now Unite), The Miners Federation of Great Britain (now the NUM) and The National Union of Railwaymen (now RMT) – the Triple Alliance.

The years 1911–12 had seen a series of strikes which involved more men and women in industrial action than at any time in British history before or since. The strikes, especially those of the South Wales coalfields, were marked by a level of violence, including military firing on crowds of strikers, which had not been seen since the 1830s. Many working-class people were prepared to take lessons from this, and some saw the Triple Alliance as a weapon to seize power. Even outside this minority more and more were embracing a vision of a Socialist Commonwealth.

Behind the spectacular, and too often forgotten, chapter in our history are the stories of countless struggles, in factories, mines, shops and farms, which turn up again and again in the local records of these years. But one that moves beyond them is the story and the struggle told in this book – that of the villagers of Burston in Norfolk, their school teachers and the farm workers unions against the petty (and not so petty) actions of the local elite in trying to control every aspect of their lives. It led to what we are proud to call 'the longest strike in history', lasting from 1914 to 1939.

To some the story of the Burston Strike School will be familiar, especially those who join us on the village green each September. To others it will be a discovery. To both groups I say: read this book. It will tell you more about Burston, the strike and, above all, those who led it, nurtured it and kept the vison alive both in Norfolk and elsewhere. In 1921 South Norfolk returned the first rural Labour MP, George Edwards. Edwards was a firm supporter of the school and Burston was the centre of his campaign. A small victory but a very important one.

Shaun Jeffery, who has written this book, is not an academic (although his standards of research would shame many of my ex-colleagues); he is a horticultural worker. He grew up in a small market town on the Norfolk/Suffolk border. Today, he works on a contractor basis as a landscape gardener, but over the years has been employed on urban parks, at wholesale plant nurseries; market gardens, estates and farms. He still occasionally works on farms, hedge planting or pruning fruit trees.

Once he began working he joined the then Transport and General Workers' Union. Within the TGWU he was allocated to the Rural, Agriculture and Allied Workers' (RAAW) trade group of the London and Eastern region. From there he was elected onto the national committee of the sector. For some fifteen years he has served the interests of land workers through his involvement in the constitutional structures of the union that has now evolved into the Food, Drink and Agriculture sector of Unite. He is Secretary of the Burston Strike School Trustees.

I first went to Burston in 1974. I was an ex-Ruskin student working on my book *Poor Labouring Men*. When I and my partner moved permanently to Norfolk in 2010 I was proud and delighted to be asked to be a Trustee of the School.

Alun Howkins
*Professor Emeritus in Social History, University of Sussex.*

# Introduction

## The School of Freedom

'A cottage roof or two, a line of trees in the distance, was all that could be seen of the South Norfolk village of Burston, from the station.'[1] The Great Eastern Railway special charter train from London Liverpool Street had, at 12:15, arrived ahead of time. It had only become known on the Friday that the train had been granted, or otherwise perhaps a thousand or more people would had travelled down along with the 250 men of the National Union of Railwaymen, two bands, eighteen banners, Mr W. Carter of the National Union of Railwaymen (NUR), John Scurr the Labour politician and trade union official, and suffragette leader Sylvia Pankhurst. As the train thundered across the Norfolk countryside making good speed to its small rural destination, the passengers were in high spirits as they sang revolutionary songs and talked of Russia. The Romanovs had long gone into oblivion, and the first All-Russia Congress of Soviets of Workers and Soldiers was soon to open. The hope of the workers across Europe was high.

This was not the first big demonstration that had come to make the village of Burston world famous, but after a long and often bitter struggle, it was to be a joyous day of celebration. The weather on Sunday 13 May 1917 was most favourable—almost unseasonably hot for the time of year. And so, it was under a near cloudless sky that the NUR leader and Treasurer of both the Burston School Strike and Evicted Glebe Tenants National Committee, Mr W. Carter, began to marshal the disembarked passengers into the adjoining lane.

As the men of the Bethnal Green NUR band were taking the covers off their brass instruments, eighteen or twenty great painted silk banners, gorgeous in brilliant red, green, blue and purple, and gleaming gold and silver, were being unfurled and hoisted high. The NUR banners were not to have the day all to themselves as the National Agricultural Labourers' Union had sent two banners along, as had branches of the National Vehicle Workers' Union. Their huge size seemed to dwarf everything around them, even the old trees.[2]

As the procession began to take shape, parties with their banners still to be unfurled came walking down the road to join the visitors: contingents from Norwich and the surrounding district, and Londoners who had reached Burston the night before. The people assembling that day had come from as far away as Liverpool, Coventry and Yorkshire. They included representatives of Friendly Societies, Miners' Lodges, and Socialist Societies, as well as trade unions. And all had done so to praise and show gratitude to the little Norfolk village and its fighters for freedom against rural tyranny.

And then came the people of Burston: the children wearing their clean white Sunday clothes, and the women, many bent over after years of life and toil in hard conditions, but all smiling, hurrying towards the assembling visitors. In twos and threes, they came along to join the procession. When ready, on Mr Carter's call, the march to Crown Green, centre of the village and home of the new 'Strike School', began. And joyously they marched along the country lane; the bands played revolutionary airs, and with just the lightest of breezes the big banners swayed, and the bearers staggered a little to control them as they guided them away from the branches of overhanging trees.

'Close to the Green, and standing at the church gate after giving the morning service, the procession met the rector, Rev. Charles Tucker Eland.'[3] A man of such reverence for established orthodoxy that his own vindictive actions had brought on the revolt in the village and had drawn the solidarity of the labour movement from across the country to his parish. His eyes diverted downward as the children greeted him with lusty hoots when they passed. Perhaps his own thoughts were on repentance. But for the most part, on first glimpse of the man who placed himself firmly in opposition to the empowerment of the agricultural labourers, curiosity just stuck the marchers dumb. John Scurr thought that 'He looked a poor soul and one could only feel a great pity for him that he so lowered the dignity of man and was so petty'.[4] Later, the procession would reform and proceed to the rectory, where the 'The Red Flag' was sung, followed by cheers for the victims of his pettiness.

From the church, the procession soon reached the village green and all Eland's manoeuvrings were swiftly forgotten. For many in attendance, this was the first time that they had shown their support by travelling to Burston. And now, standing at the edge of the green, they could witness the old carpenter's shop that first housed the Strike School, and whose tenant, the blind Ambrose Sandy, had been forced to give up his glebe land and leave the village.

Standing close by was the temporary wooden structure which was erected for the scholars when they were obliged to leave the carpenter's shop, and which was still used to educate the children into the following year. And there, bounded on one side by the churchyard and in front of the village green— which would afford a fine playground for decades to come— was the 'Strike School'. The 36ft. by 24ft. structure, all new and sharp-cut, with its windows yet unglazed and woodwork yet unpainted, but with its Bath stone front already graven with the names of the societies that had subscribed towards its erection: miners' lodges, NUR and other trade union branches, branches of the Independent Labour Party, and British socialist organisations from England, Scotland and Wales.[5]

Each stone had been engraved with the names of the societies that had contributed funds, while along the top ran the bold inscription, 'BURSTON STRIKE SCHOOL 1917'. Co-operative societies, miners' lodges, railwaymen, Independent Labour Party branches, educational societies and individuals were all there, the stones firmly fixed together providing a solid front for the new village school and for what would become a permanent record of the British Labour movement. As the war raged in Flanders and after many delays and difficulties incidental to the building in war time, the first real workers' elementary school had been provided by the workers themselves.

As John Scurr, representing George Lansbury, stepped on to the green,[6] he was met with warm handshakes from Mr and Mrs Higdon, the two teachers at the heart of the rebellion. Thomas George Higdon was the son of a yeoman farm labourer from Somerset, and his wife Annie Katherine, more affectionately known as Kitty, was the daughter of a foreman-shipwright from Cheshire. They had first arrived in Norfolk in 1902 to take up a joint teaching position at the county school in Wood Dalling, but after friction with the school managers there, they were forced into taking up the offer of a transfer to Burston in the January 1911.

The Higdons were a most devoted couple, and unusual in many ways—not least because of their high-level qualifications: Mrs Higdon was the Headmistress and her husband the Assistant Master. They might have looked like any average man and woman, yet to those that met them, they both possessed a tremendously generous soul and great spirituality which meant they never compromised their belief in, and commitment to, social justice and equality.

On return to the common green from the march to the rectory, a public meeting was held at which the audience was estimated to be about 1,200. Mr Robert Green, a member of the Agricultural Labourers' Union Executive and Chairman of the National Burston Committee, presided, supported by Mr W. Carter, the future MP for West Bromwich Mr F.O. Roberts, Mr E.B. Reeves, JP of Norwich, and John Scurr, to whose original inspiration the strike school was due.

It had been due to Mr Carter's untiring efforts that NUR contingents on three occasions in November 1915, at the sod-turning, and now at the opening of the new school, had gathered en masse in Burston. He gave a brief financial statement showing that the income of the fund to the present was £1,248.3s.1d. with expenditure of £990.16s.10d. The school was to be opened and furnished debt free. Of this sum, the miners' lodges had contributed £300, the NUR £160, the Co-operative Society

£139 and the Independent Labour Party £50. As he was speaking a further two £1 notes were handed up from the audience.[7]

Mr Frederick O. Roberts followed, and said the agitation that had been raised in connection with the Burston matters would not cease with the opening of the school, for it was equally necessary that the former tenants of the glebe lands should be reinstated in their holdings, and that the campaign to secure this was now being arranged.

Following on, addresses were given by Sylvia Pankhurst, Mr and Mrs Higdon, Sam March (General Secretary of the Vehicle Workers' Union), Mr W. Holmes (National Labour Party organiser), Mr J. Sutton of Burston, Mr J. Corbett (National Union of Teachers [NUT], Manchester), Mr G.F. Johnson, NUT, Norwich), and Mr Mabberley of Coventry.

Then, finally, on being given a pre-arranged signal, the young Violet Potter stepped forward to declare the new school open. Some three years before at the age of thirteen, when the Higdons were dismissed, she had organised her fellow pupils at the Council School to go on strike in support of their teachers. Now, the strike leader was rightly to have the honour to lead the first people inside.

The crowd was so large that she could not see over their heads. But she had prepared her words the night before: 'With joy and thankfulness I declare this school open . . . To be forever a school of freedom.' And on that cheers went up from the assembled crowd. Violet opened the doors and headed inside, followed by Mr and Mrs Higdon, 'some members of parliament', as she knew them, and then members of the National Union of Railwaymen.[8]

As they marched inside the deep-voiced Robert Green recited a little poem that he had composed for the occasion:

> Now the Shrine of Freedom's open,
> See its doors unfolded wide;
> Now's the time of Strike School children,
> Haste ye to take your place inside.[9]

And from inside, the soft accompaniment of 'The Red Flag' began, and how sweetly the words must have risen in the air, sending their message of hope and defiance to the world. As they went inside, alongside the doors another engraved tablet recorded for perpetuity just why they had all come to be there:

MR.T.G.HIGDON AND MRS.A.K.HIGDON

WERE UNJUSTLY DISMISSED FROM THE

COUNCIL SCHOOL OF THIS VILLAGE ON

THE 31ST DAY OF MARCH

1914.

THIS BUILDING WAS ERECTED BY PUBLIC

SUBSCRIPTION, TO PROTEST AGAINST THE

ACTION OF THE EDUCATION AUTHORITIES

TO PROVIDE A FREE SCHOOL, TO BE A CENTRE

OF RURAL DEMOCRACY AND

A MEMORIAL TO THE VILLAGERS' FIGHT FOR

FREEDOM

Finally, at 6 o'clock, the procession of London supporters reformed and the visitors made their way back to the railway station. The special charter train returned them home at 6.50pm,[10] at the close of a day that all agreed had marked a new era for the countryside.

# Chapter 1

# Down the Great Western Line

A train journey out of London down the Great Western line to reach the West of England. The traveller recounts, after quitting Middlesex, of passing through a magnificent stretch of country, constituting some of the most fertile parts of England. The month is May, and the best time for judging of the wonderful richness of soil of the fine old county of Somerset. At that season the extensive pasture lands which stretch almost interruptedly from Bristol to Bridgwater are literally clothed with the beautiful buttercup, the presence of which in large numbers is well known to indicate the most fertile lands. They bound the land in such profusion that they give more than a golden hue to the fields.

The opening of Francis George Heath's investigative account, *The "Romance" of Peasant Life in the West of England* (1872), describes a pleasant journey through a pastoral idyll, but nothing on that journey into the lives of the Somersetshire agricultural labourers—not even the anticipated wretched existence to come—would actually prepare him for the hardship and human misery he would record.

'It has been truly said,' Francis Heath laments as he enters deeper into exposition, 'and the saying is a very common one, that one-half of the world does not know how the other half lives.'[1]

For the first time in his life, as he would witness with his own eyes, 'wretchedness and squalor are not confined, as is too commonly supposed, to our great cities'.[2]

The 'romance' of peasant of life was always just that.

'It would be found that in Somersetshire the labourer is worse off than in Wiltshire, and considerably worse off than in

Dorsetshire and Devonshire.'[3] The 1843 Royal Commission reporting on the employment of women and children in agriculture concluded: 'The average wages during the whole year, paid in money, appeared to be rather lower than in Wiltshire, but the labourer has an allowance of cider, three pints daily, considered to by both master and labourer as worth about 1s or 2s 3d. per week.'[4] The report was quietly shelved. In 1870, a second commission would find no change in the dreadful conditions of the Somerset labourers. The summer of 1872, when across the country the agricultural labourers were themselves ready to sever the umbilical ties to their abject situation, was still a time to come.

Heath was an odd representative of the toiling masses—but not the first to speak out before the rise of Arch's 'National Union'. A respectable civil servant with a great love of flora and fauna—and a published pteridologist (expert on ferns)—he liked to ramble around the countryside. Later, he would become a pioneer of the Open Space Movement, securing the enlargement of London's Victoria Park, and assisting in the preservation of Epping Forest and the acquisition of Burnham Beeches between 1872 and 1879. In Romance of Peasant Life, he claimed that he 'had long believed from my previous knowledge that in no county in England could the labourer in agriculture be in a worse condition than in the county of Somerset'.[5] Only at the age of twenty-eight would he see through his beloved ferns to the human destitution.

'As far as the eye can reach, on every side, stretch rich pasture lands';[6] from the very opening account, his recorded journey contrasts the lyrical poetry of the surrounding natural world with that of the inhuman conditions of the labourers he encounters. 'Even on the hill-sides the pastures extend, only broken here and there by thickets of trees, the dark invisible green of which lends a sombre majesty to the scene.'[7] Rich lands, but not for those that work on them.

I stopped and accosted an old labourer, and made some pertinent enquiries about himself. He told me he was seventy-seven years of age, and had worked as a farm

DOWN THE GREAT WESTERN LINE

labourer in that part of the country nearly all his life. He was then receiving 7s. a week, out which he had to pay 1s.6d. a week for his cottage. He had received somewhat better wages when younger; but I could not help thinking it hard that a hale old man (for my informant had all the appearance of being one) could not, after sixty years of hard toil, obtain little more for food and clothes than a miserable pittance of 5s. 6d. a week.[8]

As he rambled across some of the richest and most productive land in the whole of the county—from the Vale of Wrington and Taunton Deane into the parish of Banwell, and villages like Stoke St. Gregory and Montacute—Heath was confronted with the living, but often barely human, stories that were contained in the 'Blue Books'; the evidence books of the Royal Commissioners.

John P_____ (the inhabitant of this "cottage"), his wages were 5s. a week. Out of that he paid his master £2 10s a year rent for his "cottage," and 10s. a year more for the privilege of running his pig.

George H_____, seventy years of age, piece workers, 1s.6d. a day. A family of ten persons, ranging in age from sixteen downwards.

Abraham B_____, earned 10s. a week, raised recently from 9s. Rent of cottage 1s.3d.[9]

On the ground it was low wages, dilapidated housing and children living in near starvation that provided the not so exquisite scenery away from the buttercups.

Heath's determined efforts to uncover for himself the truth of how the other half lived began on the streets inhabited by the 'luxurious Londoners'. As he was walking one day down Upper Thames Street, not far from London Bridge, a placard in a shop forcibly attracted his attention. Inside the shop's plate-glass frontage were arranged for show some of the most beautiful specimens of sculptures rendered in marble and alabaster that he had ever seen.

The notice had attracted quite a crowd, who were gathered around, earnestly perusing its contents. It was signed in bold by 'One from the Plough'. Heath decided to go inside and speak to the proprietor. The shop was that of a stonemason—a Mr George Mitchell of Montacute, Somerset.

The eyebrow-raising placard in question referred to the case of 'John_____, 'a fine young English labourer, strong and in full vigour, who living in one of the richest and most productive counties in England, had received as payment for twelves months' toil in the fields just thirty-two pounds. Out of that sum six persons—the father, the mother and four children—had to be housed, fed and clothed'.[10]

Mitchell was not putting this man's case forward as an illustration of the miserable lot of one, but of the many thousands of his class left back in his native Somersetshire.

The placard had originally been a letter written by Mitchell to the Pulman's Weekly News at Crewkerne, and George Mitchell was the 'One from the Plough'. By 1872 he had become a regular correspondent to the local Somerset press, lamenting the suffering of the agricultural peasantry. 'At the foot of the letter, in larger type, was this paragraph: "It is a well-known fact that three-fourths of the farm labourers of Devon and Somerset are only receiving eight shillings a week; and some of them have as many as fourteen children."'[11]

This was startling stuff to a man like Heath. And like Mitchell, he was now tethered to the cause of the agricultural labourer.

If Heath had come to the labourers' cause out of curiosity, George Mitchell did so through birth. Born 6 February 1826 on a pallet of straw in the upstairs room of his parents' broken-down cottage in Montacute, George was the fourth son of Amelia Mitchell. His father, Joshua Mitchell, worked in the quarry at nearby Ham Hill, and spent much of his earnings on drink. An experienced quarryman could earn double that of an agricultural labourer, but he had developed a taste for cider when working as a farmhand and was often unable to provide for his family.

As a boy of five, George had begun 'crow scaring' at nearby Windmill Farm. Rising as early as 4 o'clock on summer mornings, and not returning till dusk, he would trudge the fields in all weathers. He would often return home soaked to the skin from long hours in the rain and was thrashed unmercifully by farmers at work; other boys and girls were constantly beaten in the fields. Their parents were unable to intervene, not only because their own jobs depended on the farmers having the labour of their children, but also because the magistrates were always on the farmers' side.

The family seldom tasted meat. Often there were times that there was just not enough food to go around. Out in the fields, with hunger gnawing at young George, 'he foraged for whatever he could eat. If he was lucky a turnip, beans, peas or acorns might be found. Searching in the hedgerows, he would come across snails, which he roasted for his lunch or tea'.[12] Unsurprisingly, shortly after his nineteenth birthday, George resolved to escape his harsh world. And the route out was his father's trade of stonemasonry.

In time, he made his way to London, where he prospered and became a successful marble merchant. Mitchell had escaped from rural poverty, but the bonds were not completely broken either. He remained all too acutely aware of labourers' suffering, and the bitterness from his early days drove him to be a zealous and forceful advocate in the historic task of organising the farm workers. The 'One from the Plough' could not forget, nor could he leave well alone. By the end of his days he had ruined his health and lost a fortune in pursuit of the labourers' cause.

'When I embarked on this great movement I really had not the slightest idea that it would have made the progress it has achieved in so little time,'[13] Joseph Arch happily confessed at another mass meeting of farm workers in South Warwickshire. The agitation among the farm labourers had begun in the February of 1872, and the numbers on strike were increasing daily, reported the *Western Gazette* in early April. 'Neither masters nor men show signs of yielding,' the paper declared.

What had happened over the previous weeks had fully convinced Arch that if the agricultural labourer, 'ignorant as he may be, downtrodden as he has been—is only shown the right way, he will very soon begin to see and think for himself'.[14] His own conviction was still tempered by a sense of pleasant surprise, but during the first few weeks of the foundation of the National Agricultural Labourers' Union (NALU) Arch was feeling truly happy to be engaged in the noble movement. George Mitchell was not too far behind.

Much has been written about the labourers' uprising, and Joseph Arch was certainly the right man for the occasion. Born in 1826, the same year as Mitchell, he too had been nurtured in the grinding, pitiless poverty of the countryside. He, though, had been gifted with three years of education before becoming an experienced agricultural labourer—only beginning work at the age of nine, crow scaring. Skilled in his trade and an eloquent speaker due to his experience as a lay Primitive Methodist preacher, Arch was a natural leader and was now ready to reap the harvest.

Arch had long been aware of the servile state of the labourers, and saw that their only hope lay in 'combination', but he quietly went on with his work until the men themselves were ready to move. The movement did not begin with the agitation of the Warwickshire men; or with Arch standing on a pig tool under the Chestnut tree at Wellesbourne on 14 February 1872; or when Mrs Arch opened the door of their cottage in Barford to those brave men whose names are sadly not preserved in history; but with those who were looking to combine and thought that only Joe must lead them. The sickles had already been sharpened.

By the end of the 1860s, not since the days of the Martyrs of Tolpuddle had the dissatisfaction among the labourers at their low wages and conditions of employment been so high. A few responded to the situation by a reversion to the old-fashioned method of arson, but the number of stack fires caused by malevolence rather than accident was not great. In general, dissatisfied labourers preferred to register their discontent by voting with their feet and leaving the land altogether. But some could be found to whom neither of the above solutions seemed acceptable. Instead, for the first time, they decided to imitate the urban workers and try to form trade unions.

As early as 1866, a short-lived agricultural union, the Agricultural Labourers' Protection Association, had been established in Kent, while in June of the same year a similar attempt was made around the village of Great Glen, near Leicester. In 1867, a further attempt was made to set up a union based in the town of Buckingham, a union which sought to organise workers in both Buckinghamshire and Northamptonshire. In addition, the 1867 Reform Act had excluded agricultural workers and their families from voting in elections, and a strike of Labourers in the Buckinghamshire village of Gawcott, which had been called in connection with this union, even aroused the attention of the national press.

The coverage evoked a reaction from labourers in a number of Buckingham villages, giving rise at Great Missenden to the establishment of the Agricultural Labourers' Protection Union. Then, in Ivinghoe on 20 May, two hundred men met in a field opposite the new Wesleyan chapel to form a committee to discuss the subject of wages. But in the face of determined opposition from the employers the nascent movement faded away.

Next, in the spring of 1868, the West Country was roused with the first attempt to establish a national union of agricultural labourers. Again, the impetus did not come from the labourers but from middle-class well-wishers such as Canon Girdlestone, who in 1863 was transferred from Lancashire, where the labourers' lot was considerably better, to the village of Halberton, North Devon. In 1872, while Francis George Heath was in the West of England, he would accept an invitation from Canon Girdlestone to visit him at the Halberton rectory.

On 28 March 1868 a conference was called, and trade union leaders Robert Applegarth and George Potter were invited. It was a noble effort, but the labourers' response was too weak, and it came to nothing. By the end of the 1860s, all tentative steps to form agricultural trade unions either came to little, due to lack of leadership and effective organisation, or rapidly disappeared in the face of vigorous opposition from farmers. But fresh impetus came in 1871 with the passage of the Trade

THE VILLAGE IN REVOLT

Union Act, and the next serious attempt was made to establish an agricultural union in Herefordshire in 1871.

The North Herefordshire and South Shropshire Agricultural Labourers' Improvement Society largely came about because of Thomas Strange, a Primitive Methodist school teacher from the parish of Leintwardine. This example was then followed elsewhere; during the winter of 1871–72, a small union, the Staffordshire Agricultural Labourers' Protection Society, was set up in the Warwickshire–Staffordshire border area. Yet again it came to nothing due to the power of the farmers over the labourers, particularly their power to evict workers from tied cottages should they resort to industrial action, or even have the free-thinking idea of joining a union.

The upsurge of bitterness and discontent at this time existed long before Joseph Arch and his union officially appeared on the scene. What Arch and other leaders like Mitchell were able to do was to lead and unify these workers against the harshness of their daily living conditions.

It was with mounting concern that the *Western Gazette* reported on 19 April 1872 that 'the wave of agricultural dissatisfaction and agitation of increased wages has reached Suffolk, which county must now be numbered with those where farm labourers had already begun to revolt'.[15] The farmers and Chambers of Agriculture were increasingly concerned. 'The men demand more. The men have communicated with other parishes and the movement is spreading.'[16] During the following week, the same newspaper, conveying the situation in Herefordshire, carried the news that Arch had lately addressed a large meeting of labourers employed in the Ross district, at the close of which a branch of the union was formed.

On Wednesday 19 May, Arch was speaking at Hoxne, eight miles south-west of Diss. This was to be one of the first meetings attended in an area that would provide a bedrock of support throughout the entire lifespan of the NALU. Chairing the meeting from the back of a farm wagon was Mr. Wingfield, Secretary of the Diss branch; delegates had travelled from Cambridge, Essex, and across Norfolk and Suffolk. Arch delivered a lengthy address on all matters of concern to the labourer, including education. The press at the time had been carrying comment from, among others, Mr. Merewether, the MP for Northampton, who had said that all the education a labourer wanted was to be able to read signposts. Arch was to commend the government that was committed to making changes so all children should be educated.

After no more than four months, the union now had no fewer than sixty-four branches with 4,695 members. With the wind in their sails, the first National Congress of Agricultural Labourers was held in Leamington on 29 and 30 May.

George Mitchell was watching these unfolding events attentively, with a keen but—fair to say—wary eye; 'at first I had laboured under a prejudice against trades unions, but was gratefully surprised to find that they were not the personifications of evil, with neither horns, hoofs or tails, and that most N.A.L.U delegates were mostly Methodist local preachers and teetotallers.'[17]

Mitchell resolved to bring the union to the West Country, and on 3 June 1872 the National Union arrived in Somerset. 'A meeting of Agricultural labourers, presided over by Mr. George Potter, the trade unionist, was held on Tuesday, and passed off very quietly.'[18] Both the *Western Gazette* and Pulman's Weekly News reported on the evening:

> The audience consisted chiefly of decently-clad labourers, with their wives; glovers from Yeovil and Stoke-sub-Hamdon; and a sprinkling of middle-class people living in the neighbourhood . . . Mr. Potter took the chair, upon the motion of one his friends, and spoke at length upon the hardships of the agricultural labourers' lot, picturing it in its darkest colours, insisting up in the necessity of organisation, and upon the right of the labourer—the producer of wealth—to a greater share than he has at present. The only way to get this is by an agricultural union, and if the labourers of Montacute would combine, he would guarantee that within twelve months they would have 12s, if not 15s. a week: and would be delivered from the land of bondage (cheers).

Mr George Mitchell, marble merchant, of Brompton Road and Upper Thames Street, London, detailed his experiences when he was a ploughboy in Montacute, earning 4s a week. He said he remembered when he was a labouring man was expected to maintain himself and family on 6s a week, and called several aged labourers to corroborate his statement on the platform. He had been working from four o'clock in the morning until ten at night, and because he refused to work later, his master treated him as he would a dog, and called him a lazy fellow.[19]

After more personal testimonies from labourers, Jacob Bool then proposed:

It is resolved that this meeting deeply sympathises with the long depressed condition of the agricultural labourer of Somerset, and approves of the establishment of a branch of the National Agricultural Union, at Montacute, for the purpose of improving the condition of the labourer, and this present pledge themselves to become members, and to use their influence to induce others to do so likewise.[20]

The motion was carried.

The chairman announced that a branch had been formed that afternoon. Fifty-eight labourers afterwards entered their names as members of the union and paid their deposits that day—within eighteen months the Montacute branch would to grow to some five hundred members.

Fifteen miles away, in the midst of the deprivation and what would rapidly develop into NALU heartland, Thomas George Higdon had been born in an agricultural dwelling in Huxham, East Pennard, on the evening of 21 August 1869. East Pennard was a village and civil parish containing the hamlets of Stone, Parbrook and Huxham. Thomas's father Dennis, an agricultural labourer, had moved into Huxham Mead Cottage a few years before, after leaving neighbouring village of Wraxall to work on a farm owned by the Richards. Born in East Pennard, he had married Tom's mother, Ann Hardwick from Castle Cary, in 1858.

From the limited record left of their existence, Tom's parents owned nothing, and were typical members of the agricultural peasantry. At the age of seventy-eight, Dennis (b.1833) was still employed as a farm labourer in Huxham.

Even less is recorded about Ann Hardwick (1833–1915). Still, at least the small cottage, which is now a holiday let, survives. At the time of Tom's birth, it was an increasingly overcrowded cottage; already living there, along with his parents, were his two brothers, William (John) (b.1862) and Frank (b.1867), and one sister, Mary (Anne) (b.1864). Shortly they would be joined by Dennis's brother John, a farm labourer from the parish.

# Chapter 2

## The Schollicks' Rise

One friend with whom Mrs. Annie Higdon maintained a connection in adult life was Mr G.T.C. Giles, an elementary school head teacher from Acton and the first Communist president of the NUT. Their enduring friendship came about through a member of the Potter family of Burston whom Giles had employed to keep house in London. Giles got to know the Higdons and when his first wife died, he sent his school-aged son to the Strike School. At first he boarded with the Higdons, and then the Potters. Later in life Annie Higdon developed a proclivity for fresh air and liked to keep the windows of their cottage open, even in the depths of winter. After a few weeks of that first winter, the young Mr Giles moved into new lodgings.

Annie was a strong character from the start, and she got more self-centred as she got older. 'When she didn't want to answer a question, she would suddenly talk about something else: the stars, or the flowers. She'd say, "Oh look at that beautiful honeysuckle!" or "Oh, aren't the roses lovely this year!"'[1] In later years, Giles tried to persuade her to take on an assistant, but she would not even contemplate this: 'She just wouldn't listen. We drove around in a trap for hours and got nowhere! She just avoided the issue. We went for miles! It was her school you see.'[2]

Despite the obstinacy, the friendship endured for some twenty-five years. But despite these years of friendship, Mr. Giles knew nothing of Annie Higdon's origins. 'She was always very close. She never told you anything about her affairs, her family, or anything like that. I think her father was a doctor. She was certainly from a different class than the labourers. She had no inhibitions about talking to the upper classes.'[3]

The reasons for this long concealment seem obvious at first glance. Anne Katherine Schollick, born 13 December 1864 in Poulton-cum-Seacombe, Wallasey, Cheshire, had been accustomed to a comfortable middle-class upbringing. Her husband was a labourer's man not gifted the opportunity of a level of formal education that his own abilities warranted. She, on the other hand, had been well educated, and could speak multiple languages and play numerous musical instruments; she had been trained to sing and her knowledge of literature and the arts was superior to that of most rural schoolmistresses. It was not uncommon at the time for a married couple to take charge of a rural school, but it was that the wife, because of higher academic qualifications, was the head teacher and her husband the assistant master. She was not a daughter of a labourer, and yet she found herself at the heart of two rural communities, and engaged in bitter political struggles on the side of the agricultural labourers against the ruling landowner–church establishment of the day. Socially, politically and morally, Annie Katherine Higdon was on the side of the workers.

With deeper consideration, however, Annie's apparent level of secrecy is more puzzling, for she was by nature neither a respecter of class nor an inverted reactionary. Both she and Tom Higdon subscribed to extreme egalitarian attitudes, acquired more from the Chapel than the Church. Annie's conventional middle-class education had done nothing to discourage the blooming of an unconventional woman who saw the social norms of the day as being the thinly veiled methods of control that they were—and paid them no respect. Wherever she went, her kindness and generosity of spirit endeared her to communities, and in particular the children who belonged to them.

Annie didn't believe that background should limit the life chances of any child, and perhaps no one at the time was much bothered to ask about her own background. But silence breeds rumour, and rumour distorts as it drifts through time. Her origins were misty, but she was not the daughter of a doctor from Somerset; the doctor in the family was uncle Thomas

James Schollick (b.1835) who went on to reside in London and become the coroner of Croydon. But she had fallen in love with Thomas Higdon in the country lanes of East Somerset. Another rumour said that her family had been Austrian aristocrats who fled to England for political reasons at the beginning of the nineteenth century. Inaccurate, but the degree of misfire is understandable.

Etymologically, Schollick is an unusual name—of German origin—that is a dialect variant of the German word Schell, itself a nickname for a wild or obstreperous person. Given the woman, who could, as it happens, speak German, how appropriate the name.

Anne Katherine was the seventh child of Samuel Schollick, shipwright-foreman from Poulton-cum-Seacombe. Her ancestors had lived in Colton, Lancashire for two centuries, earning their living in carpentry and domestic service. But by the time of her birth, the Schollick family had been on the move, and on the up for twenty years.

Annie's great grandfather, Thomas Schollick (1742–1825), was from Colton village. The parish consisted of large areas of forestry, which gave employment to a number of parishioners. Others found employment in farming, the iron industries at Backbarrow, Nibthwaite and Rusland, and in the manufacture of bobbins, gunpowder, baskets, hoops and laundry blue. Thomas, however, appears to be the first in the family to turn his hand to carpentry as a profession. He was also a prolific producer of offspring, fathering thirteen children—most of whom reached adulthood. One of these children, James Schollick (1785–1859) died before his granddaughter Annie was born. With only six children, he was not quite up to his old man's stride, but two of his girls survived to marry tradesmen, and one of the boys, Samuel (b.1822), was Annie's father.

In the 1820s James Schollick moved into the nearby parish of Egton-cum-Newland, eventually retiring as a house carpenter to Oak Bank Cottage. Originally founded as a township-chapelry, Egton-cum-Newland lies on the estuary of the Leven, and later on the Ulverston and Lancaster railway. It was in this parish that his six children, including Annie's father Samuel, were born and christened. Samuel began his apprenticeship with his father, as his father had before him. As Samuel learned his father's and grandfather's trade in Egton, his brother, Edward Jones Schollick (b.1824), decided to forego carpentry and entered into domestic service. It would not be long before things got very interesting for the Schollicks of Lancashire.

Aldingham village lies on the coast looking across to Morecambe Bay. Believed to once be a mile long, legend claims that storms and tidal waves washed away many of the original cottages and that the church was once the centre of the village. Inside the church, to the left of the altar, is a stone commemorating the life of Reverend John Stonard, a man whose existence, or rather, whose death, irrevocably changed the lives of the Schollicks.

Reverend Dr John Stonard was born in Surrey in 1769, ordained in 1794, and became rector of Aldingham in 1814. Throughout his life Rev. Stonard was an exceptional scholar and left behind a number of theological works. If that did not provide enough recognition, he was tutor for some time of William Pitt, who later became Prime Minister.

When Stonard went to Aldingham he took with him his two sisters—neither sister happened to marry, and both died before their brother John. The Stonard family were extremely rich and owned a large part of the borough of Lambeth in London. Their father had made a fortune dealing in the supply and sale of starch. Thanks to the considerable family silver—or rather the family starch—the bachelor reverend was able to develop a reputation for charity as strong as his scholarship.

Stonard's kindness and decency is supported by none other than Queen Victoria. Her Majesty had been on a trip to the Furness Abbey ruins in 1848 and decided to call in to see the rector on her way home. A letter written by her lady in waiting, Lady Augusta Bruce, describing the afternoon is still extant in the Royal Collection, Windsor Castle, and provides a touching reflection of the parson-gent. Close at hand during the occasion, as he was every day, was Reverend Stonard's twenty-three-year-old butler—footman Edward Jones Schollick.

The last years of Rev. Stonard's life saw two noticeable achievements added to his legacy; he was awarded the North Lonsdale Agricultural Society's prize for the best field of mangold wurzels (and not for the first time) and he commissioned the building of Aldingham Hall. The large building stands opposite the church, but has no connection with the earlier lords of the manor. To commemorate the visit of the Queen, a carving depicting Victoria's head was placed in the red sandstone on the left arch of the entrance porch. It took four years of building works to complete the magnificent new Sir Matthew Digby Wyatt hall, but Stonard never saw it finished; he died in early 1849. Instead, Aldingham Hall became the home of the new lord of the manor, the twenty-four-year-old, now former, manservant, Edward Jones Schollick.

Without any descendants or surviving family, Reverend Stonard had bequeathed his entire estate to the young Schollick. Clearly, the young man was held deep in the affections of the old clergyman; it could be for no other reason than because Edward had saved Stonard's life after he got into difficulties crossing the Morecambe Bay sands after attending an ecclesiastical meeting in Lancaster. But, quite oddly, in a court case of 1861, Edward said he had been adopted by John Stonard. There is nothing to support this claim; perhaps Edward was getting bored of sniffy questioning over his right to inherit, but the statement was made in the law courts. If it was true that he had been adopted, it must have been a little surprising for his biological father, James Schollick, who lived until 1859 surviving the reverend by ten years.

From footman to gentlemen at the age of twenty-four Edward had not just jumped up the social ladder but had overshot the top rung and carried on over the moon. The Stonard estate was a significant bequest; it included not just Aldingham Hall, but land at Scales, Newbiggin and North Scale on Walney. The Scales estate was rough grazing pasture on the edge of Birkrigg Common, but most importantly, and in 1861 almost fatally for the newly qualified Dr Thomas James Schollick, it included a limestone quarry. After the inheritance, one thing life which never lacked for the Schollicks was drama.

Once the estate had been settled, Edward married his sweetheart, Margaret Jackson. Unlike Stonard, Edward and his brother Samuel had not been the recipients of a formal education, but neither lacked creative imagination. Edward was a fine painter in oils and had painted the reverend's portrait before his death. If he had lacked an appreciation of the importance of education before, he must surely have had it instilled in him by the scholarly Stonard. Perhaps the adopting theologian tutor had subsequently educated his bright young servant. We do not know, but Edward did carry on in his benefactor's philanthropic footsteps, giving generously to everyone around him, and particularly to educational causes.

The Westmoreland Gazette and Kendal Advertiser's report on the marriage of Edward Schollick in September 1849 shows how his philanthropy was evident on his wedding day:

At Ambleside, on Wednesday, the 12 inst . . . by the Rev. the Chancellor of Carlisle, D.D, Edward Jones Schollick, Esq. of Aldingham Hall, to Margaret, youngest daughter of Thomas Jackson, Esq., of Waterhead. The bridegroom, instead of following the old but much abused custom of throwing money to the crowd assembled at the chapel gates, left, in the hands of the Rev. S. Irton Fell. M.A. minster of the chapel, five pounds, in aid of the funds of the National, Infant and Sunday Schools, and also sent by the clerk a donation to be distributed amongst the boys attending the Free School.[4]

Edward's immediate ongoing concern was the completion of Aldingham Hall. The hall was built at the request of the wealthy Stonard, but a modern-day discovery of some information on the reverse of a picture hanging in the church vestry revealed that it was actually Schollick who was responsible for the hall as it is. He had the old one demolished and the new one built on higher ground, so it is Edward Schollick's hall—not Stonard's—that one can still see today. It cost over £30,000, a huge amount of money in 1849, but it still stands and today is used as a residential care home.

It's fair to say that Edward Schollick probably couldn't believe the turn of events; neither, one imagines, could the rest of his family, those who had worked until quite recently with him in service, nor the born money that the newly elevated gentleman would come to associate with. But Edward never forgot his family origins or his bloody good luck.

Growing up in Egton-cum-Newland parish, the young Schollicks would not have been too far away from the sea, Ulverston Canal, and shipbuilding. When opened in 1796 the Ulverston Canal was heralded as the 'shortest, straightest and broadest' in England—but it was never the great money-earner that its subscribers had hoped for.

Nevertheless, it was there, in February 1851, that Samuel Schollick began shipbuilding at Greenodd, at the shipyard that had previously been owned by the Ashburners. Between 1849 and 1851, the records show that Samuel had gone from being a carpenter to a fully fledged shipbuilder, 'employing eleven men and three apprentices'.[5] From that time onwards, the Schollicks were on the rise.

Samuel's brother had the money to invest and a willingness to help, but his family would be given the means to achieve, and not just handouts to live on. The youngest brother, Thomas James, then twenty-one, would be given the educational advantage that the older Schollicks had all been deprived of. He was sent to Durham to be a boarding scholar and to receive private tutoring. The career path to his becoming Dr Thomas James Schollick, surgeon and apothecary in London, had begun.

To help Samuel Schollick, and possibly to make what he thought would be a wise investment, Edward purchased the Ashburners' shipyard and left it to Samuel to run as foreman. The first—and as it turned out, only—vessel built by that yard was the 'Edward and Margaret', a ninety-tonne schooner built for E.J. Schollick. Eight shares were sold but Edward held on to the other fifty-six.

However, the railway arrived sooner than expected; the canal was to be cut in two by the Ulverston and Lancaster railway, which crossed the waterway by a series of six elegant arches known locally as the Six Bridges. Schollick's Shipyard, still a partnership between brothers, was relocated from Low Yard to Canal Foot. Again, it appears that the Schollicks managed to produce only one ship together: the Thrifty, which was launched on 3 August 1854. Perhaps the ship's name was ironic, given the contraction of the local industry at the time.

For unknown reasons the brothers' partnership was dissolved in early 1855. Historians of the industrial heritage of South Ulverston claim that the partners fell out: not an uncommon ending in business, but it's a presumption not based on discernible evidence. Perhaps Samuel had matured sufficiently in his own business confidence—and means—to want to go it alone. Maybe Edward had reached the end of his patience at how Samuel managed the yard? Whatever the reason, Edward paid Samuel £200 and advertised that the yard was under his sole control;

> E.J. Schollick of Aldingham Hall, Ulverston: Begs to intimate to the public, that the Shipbuilding business as the Canal Foot, Ulverston, is now given up, and that as Samuel Schollick, his late foreman and agent is no longer in his employ, he will not be responsible for any debts he may incur . . . E.J. Schollick will be glad to treat with any one, for the Timber, Patent Slip, Tools &c. laying in the Timber-yard, and for the unfinished Schooner.[6]

As partings of the waves go, it was more of a gentle ripple.

This was far from the conclusion to the Schollicks' foray into shipbuilding. And, perhaps as an indication of failings on Samuel's part, Edward employed John Wilson (who had worked at the yard) as foreman and set about building a small fleet. Under Wilson eight schooners were turned out, six of which were named after Edward Schollick's children. Edward went on to father eleven children in total; four died young and are buried in Aldingham churchyard. All the children were christened with the middle name of Stonard in honour of the reverend and his generous financial legacy to the family.

Although Edward Schollick subscribed to every public appeal in the parish and gave generously to the church (continuing in the vein of Rev. Stonard, and also like a man who never forget his own good luck and original deprivations), it was not enough to stop him from falling out with the wardens at Aldingham Church. A dispute arose over the number of pews allotted to his household, and he was to take it all the way to Carlisle Consistory Court (the case where he claimed to have been adopted by Reverend Stonard). He lost.

Things at this time were going more positively for the youngest brother, Thomas James; between September 1859 and December 1860 he passed his final medicine exams at St. Bartholomew's, London. As for Samuel, he remained working out of Canal Foot and was advertising as late as 1860 for ship carpenters for yacht and boat building. Evidently, either the work or skilled men were not available or better offers abounded from elsewhere, as by 1861 he relocated to Thornton, Fylde, Lancashire and continued there as a ship and boat builder. From then on he was a regular attendee at the monthly Improvement Commissioners meetings, acting under the Fleetwood Improvement and Market Act. The carpenter was still doing alright.

Samuel Schollick's final refuge was to be the bustling and expanding coastal town of Seacombe. The opportunities in Thornton-le-Fylde had proven limited, so he relocated the family to neighbouring Poulton-cum-Seacombe, Wallasey. By the early 1860s the household had swelled to include four young children and a general servant and, though still comfortably middle class, it was proving ever harder to maintain expectations.

In December 1851, Mr R. Rawlison, Superintending Inspector to the General Board of Health, published his report of a preliminary inquiry into the sewerage, drainage, and supply of water, and the sanitary condition of the inhabitants of the township of Poulton-cum-Seacombe, in the parish of Wallasey. And it made for grim reading:

In the company of Mr * I inspected some parts of the district and found many instances of defective drainage, as of overcrowding. Some of the courts & cottages are in the most wretched state possible. In no town in England is there more actual filth and all that may produce is decease than in certain portions of the comparatively rural village of Seacombe; the ravages of fever & cholera bear the truth of the statement.[7]

The report was a catalyst to improvement works. In 1857, under Wallasey Improvements, 'power was given to the Local Board of Health to construct Gas and Water Works—to acquire Ferries—to levy rates and raise Money'.[8] It all helped ameliorate conditions, but the efforts were being restrained by the township expanding as an industrial and shipping hub, leaving Victorian Seacombe looking like it was straight out of a Dickensian novel.

Beyond a few plush terraces of houses lay a shanty town of dank, overcrowded, poorly constructed houses, industrial sweatshops, brothels and common lodging houses. A network of open ditches and cesspools criss-crossed the town and the main streets had been formed with defective material, imperfectly cleansed. Many of the back streets, lanes, courts and yards had no form of pavement and were allowed to fester in a filthy state. Disease was commonplace—unsurprising, since the sewers and drains were too few, and the ones that did exist were either imperfect in their construction or inefficient in use. Many rooms were without adequate ventilation; slaughter-houses were situated in improper places (in the midst of inhabited houses); and the town was full of seafarers. Travelling the globe, if not necessarily all to exotic worlds, the seafarers would return with a variety of infections.

The necessity of work may well have meant that the brutalities and squalor of the surroundings were invisible to Samuel, or more likely he had little choice. For ten years he had only known work in ship and boat building, and any yard meant grime and stench, but increasingly he was having to get hands on to keep his wife and family in appropriate middle-class fashion.

# Chapter 3

## Sickles and Seaside

Little is known about the early childhoods of Tom Higdon or Annie Schollick apart from the 'where' and 'with whom' extracted from census returns and parish records. No diaries, letters, articles or school reports are known to have survived. Tom appears to have resided in Huxham, East Pennard, in the same agricultural dwelling from his birth in 1869 to 1899. As the Royal Commissions (1843 and 1870) pointed out, life for agricultural labourers in this part of Somersetshire was as poverty stricken as it got. Being the son of a yeoman farmer, in an almost full-to-bursting cottage, his upbringing was always going to be materially tough.

Nevertheless, it was a happy household, and Tom never harboured any personal bitterness towards his family for having the lot of a labourer's child. What angered Tom as he matured into adulthood was seeing the labourer deliberately kept down in almost sub-human conditions, while the landed gentry-farmer class and the established Church lived like kings at their expense.

Despite the typical difficulties, the Higdons were a close-knit family and remained so throughout their lives. Tom's parents lived in Huxham Mead Cottage until their deaths, and only for a brief interlude did his sister Mary Anne (commonly referred to as Polly) move away to Gloucester for work. After a short period she would return, and finally saw out her days there in 1951.

Tom's brother Frank remained Huxham-bound until the end of the nineteenth century, and then only went as far away as nearby Street. The oldest, William, resided there throughout the 1870s, and only moved fifteen miles away, to Langport, in the following decade. It was the Higdons' youngest, Tom who, after marriage and in search of suitable employment, found himself any distance from East Pennard. Even then, and throughout the rest of his life, he kept in close contact with everyone, writing letters or sending postcards to his mother, visiting when the holidays allowed.

In many ways Tom was born just at the right time. In Victorian England it was expected that a child would contribute to the household; and on a small farm both sons and daughters would help with weeding the crops, haymaking and harvesting. In many rural areas, this often-unpaid juvenile labour continued beyond 1914. But initially, it had been 'concerns raised over the use of child labour in the new textile mills, and to ensure that they received a little schooling, that a series of Factory Acts was passed'.[1] The 1844 legislation prohibited the 'employment of any child below the age of eight in a textile factory'.[2] Between the ages of eight and thirteen every child was supposed to attend school for three hours a day and from 1874, the minimum age was raised to ten. But agriculture and domestic service, which had always been major employers of juvenile labour, were not included.

The 1867 Gangs Act attempted to bring a little control over the use of child workers in agriculture, save for those recruited into public gangs. The act was supposed to ensure that 'no child under eight years old might be employed [though they could still work privately for individual farmers]: no woman or girl might be employed on a gang in which men worked; gang-masters must be licensed [by the magistrates], and might only employ women or girls if a fully licensed gang-mistress went with the gang'.[3]

But the act did not prevent children over the age of eight from becoming gang members, and the Assistant Commissioners on the Royal Commission of 1867 found that as a consequence of the act many public gangs just transformed themselves into private ones. This necessitated the need for further regulation to protect the young, but it 'was left to the education legislation of the 1870's and beyond to tackle this by establishing a minimum employment age of ten, and laying down that unless children could pass a leaving examination as specified in local by-laws, they must remain at school until fourteen'.[4]

In addition, although the 1867 Reform Act had excluded agricultural workers and their families from voting rights, the extension of the franchise to all male householders living in towns, it did contribute to an upsurge in interest in elementary education. If the great unwashed were to be empowered, then 'their education was an "imperative necessity"'.[5] And so the Elementary Education Act (1870) was passed, 'in order to give every child a school place, in a building of reasonable quality and with a qualified head teacher'.[6]

Up to the late 1860s education—if a child received any at all—was likely to be delivered by the voluntary sector or various religious and philanthropic bodies, particularly those associated with the Church of England. In the wake of the Education Act, the Church and other voluntary providers were allowed six months to make good any shortfalls in accommodation identified by a national survey of school facilities; 'thereafter a new rate aided school could be set up, under the aegis of a board of locally elected ratepayers'.[7]

On a national scale, the 1870 legislation led to the building of many new schools. One of the initial problems in extending education provision into rural areas, was the complete absence of the required infrastructure to house teaching. Many communities lacked any existing school, or if fortunate enough and it did, it was likely to be in a substandard condition. A nationwide wave of school building was begun; 'the overall principle of design remaining much what it had been a quarter of a century earlier, when voluntary providers were advised that a barn or a warehouse would offer a suitable model for a school. Children were taught within one large room, perhaps subdivided by a partitions or curtains, but with little genuine separation between the different classes.'[8]

The new East Pennard Council School was one such institution to be opened as part of the wave of educational expansion. At the 1875 'election' for the new five-member East Pennard School Board (five delegates, uncontested) those appointed included: the Rev. A. Goldney, Vicar; E.B. Napier, Esq, JP; and Messrs George

Richards, Joseph Board and James Dredge. The fact that the local parson, the squire, and a number of farmers from the parish constituted the school managers was typical. The makeup of the boards tended to reflect the social stratification of the time—so usually, no labourer involvement. Originally, there had been considerable Anglican opposition to the establishment of school boards, as they were perceived as a threat to the voluntary supply of education and the Church's influence over it. But resistance was brief, and the Church soon embraced being involved. Mistakenly, many local parsons would come to believe that a seat on the local school board was their automatic right.

If the older Higdon children received any formal education, it was only to the minimum level. By the time of the 1881 Census, Frank Higdon, then aged thirteen, was working as an agricultural labourer. William and Mary, the oldest two siblings, were already in work and domestic service. School was often little more than a daily routine of unremitting grind in the three Rs, with constant repetition and rote learning. Individual initiative was crushed, as teachers endeavoured to meet the conditions of the 'Code' (from 1862, the notorious Revised Code imposed a 'payment by results' system that determined the government grant element of a school's funding), and discipline was severe. But the typical farmer still considered that degree of education a waste; what schooling should do, if it had to be provided, was to prepare the next generation for the work of their forefathers.

At least Tom Higdon did receive what the Education Act intended: a school place, in a new building, with a certified head teacher. Tom did not leave behind any reminiscences of being put to work at the tender age of six or nine, like Mitchell and Arch, but he did grow up in a world where that was the case for others. As a child he would have helped out around the cottage, in the family vegetable patch, and at times on Huxham Farm. During harvest it was universal practice that children would help gather in the crops alongside their parents. Most parents would had been put to work as children themselves, and so were quite happy for their own children to do so as it meant an extra few shillings in the pocket.

For the Higdons, it was George Richards—school board manager, churchwarden and owner of Huxham Farm—on whom their livelihood depended. Dennis Higdon lived in Huxham Mead Cottage and worked on the Richards farm for over fifty years. His daughter, at some point, was in service to them, and his sons (and occasionally his brother) all worked on the farm. Even throughout the times of agricultural depression Dennis maintained his employment, while others did not. It is, then, highly doubtful that Dennis was ever a prominent union agitator, or even a member of the NALU. On many farms, even the slightest whiff of interest in the union was enough to have the farmer come threaten their eviction from both work and home. Nevertheless, even if he was never a paying union member, living in East Pennard at the time he could not fail to be aware of the union from its earliest days.

When the agitation of the Warwickshire labourers began, industrial action spread rapidly to other counties. Some farmers in parts of Somerset rushed to increase pay by a shilling a week, even before George Mitchell organised the founding meeting and branch. The National Agricultural Labourers Union may have been new, but the movement was growing fast in both size and influence. Once more, it seemed, the labourers were beginning to stir from their slumbers and, 'throughout the summer of 1872 as the N.A.L.U gained strength, handbills, advertising meetings fluttered like confetti across the West Country'.[9] The next meeting in Somerset was organised at Chard, on 14th June, where Joseph Arch was promoted to speak. In the end Arch couldn't attend, and it was left to George Potter, Rev. S. Walmsley of the Free Methodist Church, and the 'One from the Plough'. But on 14 August the 'apostle of the movement' was addressing a meeting of enthusiastic labourers in Yeovil (alongside Mitchell and Potter), before moving on to Sherbourne in Dorset. The Yeovil meeting ended in the moonlight with the Montacute drum and fife band playing such stirring tunes as 'Britons never shall be Slaves'.[10]

Next, Whit Monday 1873 was chosen by Mitchell for what would be the first mass rally of agricultural labourers and NALU supporters. He had formulated the plan over the winter and then chosen the natural amphitheatre called the Frying Pan, on Ham Hill, some two miles from Montacute for the event. Mitchell was able to use his knowledge of advertising to 'spread the word throughout the farming communities of the west country. Posters were pasted on hoardings, trees, and many a barn [until torn down by the opposition]. Hand bills were produced in their thousands',[11] and spread across the surrounding parishes. They implored the men to bring their families, to 'demand the franchise and decent wages—no surrender!'[12]

Mitchell couldn't have chosen a better day: it was bright and clear from dawn and, unusually, the quarry would stand idle. For one day the sound of blasting and sawing would not echo out across the surrounding landscape. In the vicinity of the Frying Pan tents had been raised, and stalls and refreshment stands erected. Men and their families travelled from miles to rally on the hill. Some of the earliest to arrive—two hundred men, their wives and children from Dorset—turned up at South Western Railway Station. Once they had disembarked a procession was formed and they marched into town. Many of them wore the promotional hand bills in their hats. In Yeovil, residents lined the street to wave and cheer the labourers as they passed by. Many carried their club flags and banners (with bunches of stinging nettles tied on). Later, these men connected up with the Montacute contingent, who were marching behind their own drum and fife band to Stroke under Ham. From West Somerset they came from places like Chinnock, and from the north, Glastonbury and Langport. As their brothers had done, when they arrived at Martock Station they formed a procession, unfurled banners and marched to the hill, this time to the sound of the Curry Silver Band. By 4pm it was estimated that twenty thousand had marched up the steep hill. From its height, looking out from east to west stretched open fields—a scenic landscape that shrouded some of poorest labourers in the country. They had all come to hear Mitchell, Arch and Potter speak, and were told that things could change and life improve, but only if they remained loyal to the union and fought collectively.

It had been solely through Mitchell's organisation, and defrayment of all expenses, that the rally had occurred at all. The day proved a great success, and nobody left disappointed, except maybe any farmer that had come to spy on the proceedings. For the next twelve years, on every Whit Monday, the countryside would come alive to the sound of NALU songs, drum and fife bands, and speakers, as thousands of agricultural labourers gathered to rally at Hall Hill.

During their first two years in Seacombe, the Schollicks also left limited trace of their existence. The young family settled in their new residence at 7 Tower View—one of the leafy parts where small cottages with big gardens nestled against the few terraces. Samuel was engaged full time as a shipwright. Whether his role was ever 'shipwright-foreman/agent/manager', as he'd been at 'Schollick's Shipyard' remains unclear, but it is unlikely. It was a time that the boatbuilders were coming to town full of high hopes and investment; for twenty years they did much that was memorable and then, quite suddenly, they closed their yards forever, and they were left to tumble into decay. But the grass and moss had yet to reclaim the docksides, and the Schollicks had arrived during the boom, when launchings were occasions for the flying of flags and the granting of special holidays for children at school.

The end of the business partnership with his brother did not bring an end to the trappings of middle-class family life. The shipwright was not any tradesman to begin with; they were the backbone of any dockyard organisation, and were the highest paid workmen—a craft above. 'Both in the private yards and Royal yards shipwrights would refuse to work with a man who had not completed an apprenticeship.'[13] Thus, this system not only guaranteed thorough training, but also provided established shipwrights with a valuable 'perk' in the form of extra income and assistance in their work by having apprentices in their service.

The tools of a working shipwright were similar to those of the carpenter (often, wrights would be referred to as ship carpenters). However, as the wright worked in oak rather than soft wood, and with large timbers, the tools were heavier. He used an adze—a long-handled tool much like a gardener's hoe. The transverse axe-like blade was used for trimming timber. The auger was used to bore holes into which the treenails were driven, and the shipwright had the choice of some ten sizes ranging from 2 down to ½ . A mall, basically a large hammer with a flat face and a long conical taper on the other end, was used for driving the treenails. Shipwrights also used two-man cross-cut saws as well as a single handsaw. Good sawing saved much labour with the adze. Other tools used were heavy axes and hatchets for hewing, and hacksaws and cold chisels to cut bolts to length. Iron nails of all sorts and sizes, as well as spikes, were available. Nails were used in particular to fasten the deck planks. In other words, to be a shipwright you needed to be in robust health to work.

With the birth of Anne Katherine, Samuel Schollick's household was one of seven children, a wife and a house servant. They might not have been living beyond their means, but Samuel had to constantly strive so his children could do better, particularly the four girls. If in the future the girls were to marry the best that they could, it would require Samuel to provide the best social advantages he was able. To attract the right suitor, a young lady of the time had to be seen at the right dances, in fine dresses. And for that they would need dancing classes, music lessons and all the other educational conditioning that money could buy and the state did not provide. It had always been possible for an individual to elevate themselves socially from nothing (George Mitchell was one example), but for both boys and girls, if you could buy that step up then it was a whole lot easier.

By her teenage years, Annie could speak French and German; she could play the organ and violin, sing beautifully, and her drawing was quite proficient. Perhaps she even attended a local 'ladies' seminary to refine her etiquette and speech. It was the thing one did at the time, and though later in life she may have been silent on her origins, she couldn't hide her polished middle-class mannerisms. Whether the older Schollick children, born in Lancashire, had been gifted with the same level of educational attainment is unknown. The Schollick boys went on to be clerks on the railways, and one a school board officer; all respectable enough positions. But Annie did benefit from private tuition and extra tutoring at home. In the early 1870s, the household received an extra mouth to feed when the recently widowed maternal grandmother, Nancy Anderson, came to stay. Mrs Anderson was a retired schoolmistress.

To outward appearances life was fine, and certainly better than for most of the populous living down the unpaved backstreets where the sewers ran open, but the family finances had already been stretched to breaking in the mid-1860s. Then, Samuel had taken a position at Thomas Vernon's new boat yard, which opened in Seacombe in 1865. But on 11 January, as Samuel worked on the new ship Achilles, 'some planking intended for the ceiling of the lower hold, was being hurriedly passed below, came loose and smashed into his leg, just about the ankle, causing a nasty compound fracture'.[14] With his lower leg a mess, and obviously in great pain, he was taken home. Although he received some surgical aid, the day after, The Liverpool Mercury had to report that 'he still lies in a precarious condition, and it is feared that he may have to undergo amputation. He has a wife and seven children entirely dependent on his exertions'.[15]

In the end Samuel's foot was saved, but he would not be able to work for nearly two years. Naturally aggrieved over the accident, his frustration became directed towards the Liverpool Shipwrights Association. For fifteen months Samuel had been on the sick list of the society; six months on full pay, and nine months on half pay. According to the rules, he thought they should also pay a sum of £3.17s.6d., for incurred medicine expenses. The Liverpool Shipwrights Association begged to differ, and so a 'curious action against' the society was made in July 1867.[16]

The case was simple enough. With Samuel invalided at home, two or three surgeons appointed by the society had visited him for care. He had asked Dr. Jennette, one of the surgeons who attended him, for medicine; the doctor agreed but then failed to see about it. Once the greater part of the cost had been incurred, Dr. Jennette told him that he could get the medicine at his practice. In defence, the society argued that the claim was not at all recognised by the rules. Each member paid 3s.3d. per annum to a surgeon, who would be appointed by the society to give medicine and medical attendance, but because the complainant 'lived in Cheshire', the bone setter had appointed Dr. Jennette to attend—and that Schollick chose to get his prescriptions made up at a druggist's instead of through the appointed doctor's establishment. Samuel, they argued, had not followed the small print.

A day of argument in court ensued. Mr. Anderton, Samuel's solicitor, stated that his client had paid his money, had no say in the appointed surgeon, and that the society was responsible. Mr Tobin, speaking for the society, claimed otherwise; 'the society has to supply the medicines through the surgeon and in this case the surgeon did not do so, although he was aware that he was getting them from other parties.'[17] The bench decided that the claim should be paid by the society, subject to an examination of the account, and the case was adjourned for that purpose.

The case was won, but it was not the last time that Samuel Schollick and the Liverpool Shipwrights Association would become legally entangled. Vernon's yard was closed two years later, and soon after the Schollicks shifted a short distance to Victoria Terrace, just off the main Victoria (now Borough) Road.

# Chapter 4

# Cometh the Nomads

Richard Eland was never to quite share his own son's interpretation of scripture. He was pleased to see young Charles Tucker do well in his studies, just as any father would be, and he was far from discouraging of intellectual inquiry. He would be happy, too, with his interest in following in the 'family business', which for a hundred years had provided the Elands with divine purpose. But for Richard, or rather more for his son, the points of division between the pair would grow to become insurmountable. Many thought it a relief that he died before witnessing his son's rigorous opposition to the Nonconformists, whose chapel he came to regard as a citadel of evil.

His son would die notorious and hated. The villagers of Burston would remember the Reverend Charles Tucker Eland as a strict churchman raised in the Victorian tradition. By then he was in his early fifties and enjoyed the settled convictions of middle age. 'His attitude towards his parishioners was conditioned by his belief that God "made them high or lowly and ordered their estate", and his purpose was to instil into them the understanding that respect for authority on Earth was a fit preparation for the paradise of the life to come.'[1] His own dominion was to extend over the local wildlife, and he was anointed (behind his back) the sporting parson because of his taste for hunting, shooting and fishing.

The 'little man with big consequences'[2] was never to be held in high regard or warm affection in his Burston parish. Reverend Eland assumed that he had inherited the undisputed right to lead the community, and the local farmers, almost instinctively, provided him with support. Preaching condemnation against those who chose to worship away from his shadow, he would acquire the reputation of a 'narrow-minded Church bigot and despotic parish priest'.[3] Certainly, all Nonconformists were sighted in his crosshairs, which some might have found surprising had they known that he was descended from a long family line of Wesleyan ministers.

Reverend Eland's paternal great-great-grandfather, John Eland (b.1756), had become a Wesleyan in York in the 1770s, thus making the Eland family early adopters of the revivalist ideas.

The contemptible religious zealots of their day were a reaction against a perceived apathy in the Church and excited much finger wagging and sneering monikers within it. With an evangelical message of salvation, Wesley developed his own styles of worship and activities to reach the previously unreached. He frequently visited the sick and the poor, as well as prisoners, and exhorted his followers to practise both a personal and a social piety, as individuals and as a denomination. No longer would tipping one's hat at the Sunday service lead to salvation; his followers were empowered to speak out and act on behalf of those whom Jesus called 'blessed', and the 'blessed' were everywhere.

Charles Tucker's grandfather, Richard Eland (the first), was a Yorkshire lad born in Hutton Rudby (North Riding) in 1787. It was this Richard Eland that first devoted his life to the Wesleyan mission. His wife, Sarah, bore him seven children before her death in 1831. In the early 1820s, and following his qualification as a minister, he was to make the move from Yorkshire to Cambridgeshire and begin his rotations around the eastern circuits. Though the family often found themselves living in Huntingdon, his children were born in such places as Luton and Eaton Bray, Bedfordshire; Blackley and Daventry, Northampton; and the first born, Richard Eland, in St. Ives, 1822. One consequence of his years of theological study and apprenticeship was that, at the age of thirty-five, he was quite a late starter in the fatherhood stakes, and not exactly hands on. A further six children were born over the next nine years, but two did not live to be christened.

Early Methodism was a radical reforming tendency that cut across Church convention and scoffed at the bloated bellies of its elders with a self-satisfied smile. Armed with an evangelical zeal, the Wesleyans were not afraid to be a wet towel in the face of those that—as they saw it—had engorged themselves and fallen from the path of righteousness. From the very beginning they did not shy away from their detractors and instead incorporated the intended mockery aimed at them, by calling themselves by the term their detractors had applied to them: Methodists. Such was the radicalism of these early days that they allowed women authority in church leadership, and women preachers emerged from the sense that the home should be a place of community care and should foster personal growth. These Methodist women formed a community that cared for the vulnerable, extending the role of mothering beyond physical care into that of faith. However, the sun was soon set on the dawn bloom of gender empowerment, and after 1790 the Methodist churches became more structured and more male dominated.

By the age of forty-seven, Richard Eland found himself to be a busy circuit superintendent in Newport Pagnell, and a widower with five young children. One can fairly assume that the practicalities of caring for his budding family were significant in his decision to remarry just a few months after the burial of his first wife. Lucy Essington, a forty-one-year-old spinster, was the next Mrs Eland, and the immediate inheritor of an instant family and motherhood duties.

The Wesleyan Church employed a connexional system employing a combination of itinerant and local preachers. Both their organisations included an array of local, circuit, district and connexional officials and committees. Richard Eland's final tour of circuit duty would see the minister relocate to Market Harborough, Leicestershire, where he subsequently retired and, eventually, died in 1866.

Richard Charles Tucker Eland jr., to give him his full name, was the first son of Richard Eland, and was to have no less a nomadic career than his father. Thanks to his father's missionary enthusiasm, which he apparently inherited, he was to live in three different counties before the age of ten, and receive schooling in an additional two, before enrolling as a student at the Wesleyan Theological Institution, Southern Branch, Richmond—his father's former college. The three years he spent as a scholar in London (1843–6) would not be the last tricyclical that his family would have to live through.

It was as a theology student that he met Adelaide Billingham, who he went on to marry in 1850. The newlywed couple were soon on their way to Swanage, Wareham, Dorset, where Richard was a figure of increasing respectability. Although the Methodists engaged many lay preachers and officials, the Wesleyan 'clergy' derived their income from the Church and had a vested interest in ensuring a more conservative policy. By the mid-1850s, Wesleyan Methodism was increasingly middle class, and its congregations were more likely to be from a lower middle class.

The Hereford Times of 3 September 1853 was one to carry the Wesleyan Minister Station appointments for the districts (1853–4), and Richard Eland jr. was now heading on to Gloucester. It would prove a definitive move for the future Charles Tucker Eland, who was to be born there in 1856, shortly before the family relocated once more. Though the life of a minister and his family had become materially comfortable, the constant rotation around the circuits was unsettling for the family. All the Eland children—however unwillingly—had no choice but to up sticks with each appointment. Barely had they found time to settle into school, make new friendships and alliances, integrate into the neighbourhood, and begin to think of the new residence as home, than the removal process was once more initiated. And unlike his father, Richard Eland jr. took no retirement before his death in 1884; further appointments before his passing would include Portsea Island, Hampshire; Stourbridge, Worcestershire; Bilston, Wolverhampton; and Southwark, London.

The Eland ministerial dynasty left little mark of their years of dedicated service apart from the next generation of Wesleyans. The exception was the reported correspondence first published in the Bristol Times (May 1853), and later reproduced in the Leicester Journal, over the re-baptism of a child. John Wesley's expressed views on baptism were essentially in line with those of the Anglican Church. The early Methodists believed that it was in our acts of worship, the sacraments in particular, that God's presence was most fully felt. The sacraments, it was believed, had the power to transform, and so they continued with the adopted Anglican practice of infant baptism being the normative expression of the sacrament.

Despite this, opinions on the issue of baptism were not entirely uniform; there were Methodists who questioned its power and purpose as applied to children, with opposition from the established Church to Nonconformists also getting in on the act. Richard Eland was not impressed to read that the Curate of Newent had re-baptised an infant that had previously been baptised by a Wesleyan. A long correspondence ensued, played out in the national press as he 'most respectfully' demanded a justification for the action. It was clear that the Rev. Howard I. Parry was not a man to budge, either in giving a Methodist baptism credence, or in being forthcoming with a satisfactory answer to the inquiry.

Upon receipt of Parry's note, Eland wrote to the Vicar asking him whether he was of the same opinion as his curate on the matter. The Vicar of Newent was forthcoming, with lavish terseness: 'I am resolved to perform my duties as my own judgements shall dictate, and do not intend rendering account of my actions to any human authority but to the ordinary to whom I am responsible.'[4] Next it was on to the bishops of the diocese. 'Trusting that his lordship would so interfere as to come some guarantee that, for the future, the validity of the public baptism of the Wesleyan Methodists shall be unquestioned, and receive no kind of iteration at the parish church.'[5] The Bishop of Gloucester and Bristol, finally, was more lucid in explaining the actions of the junior clergyman, who had considered the baptism of the child that had taken place at the Wesleyan chapel no valid baptism. But Eland had the bit between his teeth and had had no intention of letting things rest until he had gone as far as he could with the issue; and there was only one place left to go— the Archbishop of

Canterbury: 'I offer no opinion on the subject, it being one in which I have no jurisdiction or authority; and as you are already aware of the decision of the Privy Council in the case of Mastin v. Escott, which turned on some of the points in question.' Correspondence ended, and little was achieved but a degree of bemusement in the reporting of the whole affair. It had been a mild difference of opinion, and a need by one man to attain justification; but perhaps it was a slight reveal as to where one of his sons inherited a dogged persistence in the pursuit of satisfaction.

Throughout the last decades of Richard Eland's life, his son Charles Tucker was to remain a scholar and then, during the Bilston, Wolverhampton, placement, a student of theology into the 1880s. John Wesley first visited Bilston in 1745, and the early pioneers suffered much victimisation from the Anglicans of the town. Although over a hundred and fifty years had passed, and Wesleyan Methodism had become the acceptable face of Nonconformism, Charles Tucker was determined to cut loose from the influence of his father and the weight of generations of dead Wesleyans.

# Chapter 5

## Fall and Resurrection

The upheaval in the fields was always likely to be eventually thwarted by the concerted efforts of the farmers, or the end of the boom in agriculture. The first of a succession of bad harvests occurred in 1875; for three years the springs were bleak and the summers wet—mould, rot and blight ravished their way through the crops—while disease and poorer pasture affected livestock. Yields declined, animals died and prices slumped, and with them, farming was knocked flat. The year 1879 turned out to be the most disastrous farming year in living memory—it rained throughout, and 'the harvest blackened in the fields'.[1] Between 1871 and 1881, 120,000 labourers left the land for good,[2] and with them the burning fires of revolt, though not completely extinguished, had been severely dampened.

'Up until the year 1877 the "National" union held its membership well; in that year it had 55,000 members',[3] but at the start of the next decade the figure had fallen to 15,000. Arch and Mitchell continued to travel the country, arguably with even more intensity, and the labourers still rallied in their thousands on Ham Hill. But the union was 'soon riven with feuds, brought about mostly by the new anxieties, by the growing sense of weakness, by the sting and smart of defeats'.[4] Somersetshire and Norfolk, though reduced in strength, remained bunkers of support during the rear-guard action of rural trade unionism.

Life for the Higdons appears to have tottered by just as it always had: like the gentlest of breezes. The sweep of history can seem to float right over the smallest communities, leaving the people, as much as the country lanes or village pond, pretty unmarked. It doesn't, of course; it just plays its hand more covertly—change creeps in, surrounds and assimilates incrementally. Dennis Higdon was working the same farm, and 13-year-old Frank was soon to join him full time. William, was there too, but his days as a labourer were soon to finish for good. But young Thomas, an eleven-year-old scholar, was benefiting from the changes brought in by the Education Act, and showing himself to be an intelligent and capable pupil.

But sometimes change can be seismic and rapid. For two decades the shipwrights in Seacombe had crafted such magnificent vessels like The Sunbeam that sailed the world and set records. But almost as quickly as the owners had originally rushed in to set up their yards, they closed them down and departed for good. For four years after 1879 there was no boat building at all in Seacombe. In part, larger yards elsewhere, working to new methods and greater mechanisation, were taking over. The industry was later recommenced on Vernon's old site in 1883, but it was a momentary last hurrah—1887 marked the final end of boatbuilding in Seacombe altogether.

On 4 July 1879 Jane Schollick, Anne Katherine's mother, was buried. Though the four oldest Schollick children had already left the family home, it still left four others under the age of sixteen and two borders for Samuel to maintain. In the best of times this would have been a hard enough task, but being a shipwright in a town with no ship building would be an even taller order. Samuel had been sensible enough to make some investments in property that undoubtedly would have eased the difficulty, but his own actions were soon to place the family under great stress. On 27 July 1818 Samuel Schollick and John Muir, a boatman with five previous convictions for felonies and being drunk, were admitted to bail. Their crime was 'stealing eighteen hams and a tierce, the property of the Liverpool Underwriters' Association, at Poulton-cum-Seacombe on the 15 July 1881'. On 4 August both were arrested and tried. Samuel was sentenced to six months' hard labour to be served at HMS Knutsford prison, and the term was to commence the same day.

Aside from any social embarrassment, the removal of the head of the household, albeit for only months and not years, was still to have profound repercussions in Annie's life. With Samuel unable to work it fell to the oldest remaining sibling to leave Seacombe for gainful employment. Work was required and acquired fast, but there were few options open to a teenage woman, no matter how educated. There was one, however, and shortly after Samuel was imprisoned, sixteen-year-old Anne Katherine Schollick made her to Wales, to begin a life of teaching.

Whether the position was obtained through public advertisement or, more likely, through personal family connections is not conclusively known, but Annie had become a governess at Pistyll Hall, Domenichino, St Asaph, Denbighshire, Wales. At the time, the Gothic-style building (with views over the Dee Estuary, Wirral Peninsula and beyond) formed part of the Pentrehobyn Estate in the tranquil and unspoiled rural village of Nercwys. The owner, Edwin D. Elliot, had made his money as an annuitant and from farming 43 acres. And a governess was much in need, as along with Edwin's youngest son who had just been born, there were another six children ranging from two to ten years old in the house.

Eventually, Annie would go on to train as an elementary school teacher and become a fully certified head teacher. Tom Higdon was never to have that opportunity, or he was never able to take up the opportunity. He would only become a certificated teacher by want of a Local Oxford Senior Certificate, and receive his training as a former pupil-teacher.

The pupil-teacher scheme had originated in the 1840s and was launched for carefully selected elementary school pupils, aged thirteen or over, 'who fulfilled certain scholastic, moral and physical conditions'.[5] The stimulus of the 1870 Education Act meant that, by the end of the following decade, there had been a near trebling (from 12,467 to 31,422) in the number of certificated teachers, and a more than doubling (14,612 to 32,128) of pupil-teachers.[6] Later legislation then raised the minimum starting age to fourteen and reduced the training period to four years from five. The scheme was not without official criticism but it remained one of the few ways in which brighter pupils from poorer backgrounds could receive some form of secondary education.

Tom was bright, aged fourteen in 1883, and from a poor background. Pupil-teachers like him would have been apprenticed to a selected head teacher for the four years. During this time, they would spend much time in private study and receive tuition from the head out of school hours. They would be examined annually and be paid £10 per annum for boys during the first year, with girls receiving about two thirds of this. On completion of their apprenticeship the pupil-teacher would receive a certificate which would enable him or her to sit the examination for the 'Queens's Scholarship', which would qualify the holder for a place in a training college with a maintenance grant of £25 for men, £20 for women. If they could not afford to delay working, or did not wish to, they could take up a position in a grant-aided elementary school as an 'Uncertificated Teacher'.

As Tom only ever lived in Huxham until the married Higdons left for London, he probably participated in the pupil-teacher scheme at East Pennard Council School. It appears that he did not sit the scholarship exam, or that he did pass and either could not afford to go to a training college or other circumstances prevented him. Equally, he took up no uncertified teaching position after the completion of his four-year apprenticeship. Perhaps there were no posts available in the parish or in the near vicinity as, quite oddly, he appears wedded to Huxham until the age of thirty. But then, the hand of tragedy was not far off, as the close-knit Higdon family were to suffer their own hard loss in 1887, just as Tom completed his pupil-teacher training.

William John Higdon (b.1862) was the first-born child of Dennis and Anne. Nothing survives of him except his grave and the knowledge that his childhood was spent in Huxham rather than Wraxall, where he had been born. At the age of nineteen he married his sweetheart, Melita, and by 1881 the newlyweds had moved into 24 Queen St, Keinton-Mandeville,

Langport, Somerset. His years of agricultural labouring were now already over; perhaps it was only out of economic necessity, but William had become a boot maker. Financially it was a wise choice; by the time of his death six years later, he had done well enough to have to pay inheritance tax (the tax was first introduced in 1796 and by 1857 was applied to any estate with a value over £20).

Melita and William had no more than three years of married life together before she was dead at the age of twenty-two. The records are incomplete, so there is uncertainty whether it was by accident, or perhaps, given her age, the all too common occurrence of dying in childbirth. If that was the case, no child born survived long enough to have their own short existence recorded. The only certainty is that less than four years later, William was buried on 14 March 1887, back in East Pennard. Perhaps disease or an accident also befell the twenty-five-year-old William as it did his wife. Or possibly, with a broken heart he aided his own demise.

Whatever lay behind William's death, it was unexpected, premature and had a lasting resonance for the Higdons. Tom was eighteen at the time, but sixteen years later, after being in Norfolk for little more than a year, he would have a sixteen-page extended poem published by Jarrod & Son's Ltd of Norwich. Called 'To the Departed', apart from the publishers' mark on the last page and an image of All Saints Church, East Pennard on the cover, there is no further information. The copy that Tom sent to his mother in Somerset survives, and is simply inscribed 'To mother, with best love from Tom'.[7] There was no need for him to write more; each line speaks directly of his own family sorrow.

The poem is an evocation on death and loss, written in a direct and personal form. Any reader would not fail to realise that the lines had come from the heart and painful personal experience. The seventh stanza opens 'Here I my brother mourn . . .',[8] the eighth, 'Oh, cruel Death, that this my brother stole',[9] and the thirtieth, 'And I for him as for a brother mourn'.[10]

In the opening of another verse, Tom even states how it has been nigh on twenty years since death took such a good soul.

At one point he takes you into the churchyard of All Saints, and on a walk around the gravestones, to 'witness death's work'. There are other unnamed Higdon relatives' graves. Perhaps the most revealing part lies in the opening stanzas, where the lines are reflective and questioning, and dripping with guilt over whether they had done enough by their lost brother.

In time, both William's parents and sister would also be laid to rest at All Saints Church. It was where all the Higdon children were baptised, and if they had stayed in the parish, then it's most likely that Tom and Frank would have been buried there too. But what is certain is that both Tom and Frank became Methodists (Nonconformist churches rarely had their own burial grounds, so followers would still be buried in the parish church cemetery), and like Arch, Mitchell and most of the NALU leadership, also Primitive Methodist lay preachers.

Primitive Methodism started as a revival-reaction to the Wesleyan moves towards respectability and denominationalism, from around 1810. It was a more decentralised and democratic church, with its social base drawn from among the poorest sections of society. The 'Prims' were most likely to be small farmers, servants, mill workers, colliers, agricultural labourers and the like. It exalted its poor congregations by glorifying plain dress and speech; its chapels were characterised by relatively plain design—all an alternative to the increasingly middle-class Wesleyan Methodists and the upper class-controlled Church of England, which were not at all democratic in their governance.

The Primitive Methodist movement made a virtue out of their difference, and their chapels were used extensively for meetings of the farm labourers' unions during the building of the first 'National'. It is where many of its leaders, like Arch and Mitchell, honed their oratorical skills. The fact that the two young Higdon labourers, growing up through the 1870s and 1880s, would come to be drawn to both the union and Methodism is unsurprising.

From time to time the rest of the Higdon family may also have found their way to the chapel. In Huxham there was an overlapping of identities of farmers and churchmen involved in the Wesleyan chapel and its social activities. Although there is no mention of the founders of Methodism visiting East Pennard, John Wesley did travel through rural Somerset on a number of occasions. But Wesley preferred to work in the larger town and actually expressed a poor opinion of farmers, considering them to be the most discontented of people.

Irrespective of that, Wesleyans were in the area as early as 1810. At that time meetings were often held in private houses, and a meeting house licence survives for Huxham from 1840, suggesting that it had been a Wesleyan cause for some years before. A chapel was recorded to be in existence in East Pennard by the 1870s, and on 7 June 1881 the foundation stones of neighbouring Parbrook Chapel were laid. In August 1882, the Huxham Wesleyan Sunday school was started, and its first anniversary was celebrated with a public tea in the school and chapel (to which about a hundred persons sat down). 'In the evening addresses were given by Rev. A. Taylor, Pearson and Doctor Brennard, and other friends. Chaired by Mr. J. Day of Stone House. The chapel was nicely decorated for the occasion, and suitable hymns were sung by the children and teachers.'[11]

Each August, the Sunday school would hold an annual outing to Burnham, where the children, teachers and friends would spend the day by the sea. Possibly less endearing to the labourers of East Pennard, was the chapel's use for temperance meetings; 'A Gospel Temperance Blue Ribbon Meeting was held in the Wesleyan chapel on Thursday, Oct. 25th. A public tea was provided in the school room. At 5 o'clock, to which upward of 50 persons sat down.'[12] So far, so good. At the after meeting, chaired by Rev. W.E. Francis (congregational) of Glastonbury and supported by Dr. Brennard of East Lydford, 'The chairman in his opening remarks, spoke of the difficulties in the way of temperance work in the agricultural districts through men being partly paid in cider.—Dr. Brennard spoke warmly on the great evil of strong drink, and touched on local option reforms . . . It was decided to start a band of hope in connections with the Sunday-school'.[13] At the close of the meeting The *Western Gazette* could not report that three cheers had been given as it had for the organisers of that year's seaside excursion.

Rural industrial life had been quiet for years, but 'When from 1885 onwards the trades unions of unskilled labourers were formed, and the Dock Strike ended in a great victory, life awoke again on the land'.[14] The strike of 1889 proved to be a definitive mark in the sand for the end of a long period of depression and decline, and the revival of trade union organisation among the farm workers. But while the fortunes of the NALU were in the doldrums, it was not an absolute wilderness of victories in the interests of the labourers.

Arch and others had always seen the extension of the franchise as 'a vital step towards winning for the labourers' fundamental rights and opportunities union power could never obtain for them'.[15] The 1867 Reform Act had excluded countryside residents from the vote, but the campaign to extend the franchise never stopped. Long before it was official policy of the new union, Arch had accepted invitations to speak on the issue at meetings organised by the Electoral Reform Association in London during the winter of 1872. The meetings were presided over by Joseph Chamberlain, the audiences consisting mainly of Liberal Party activists, and they concluded with the 'passing unanimously a resolution demanding the same voting rights for rural areas as the towns'.[16]

By the end of 1884 victory was finally in sight. It had been an arduous struggle, and the dying contortions of those that opposed the Franchise Bill in the House of Lords meant that campaigning went on to the last. But the endgame was at hand. In July and August, Great Franchise Demonstrations were held in London and Manchester. In September, at that year's Trades Union Congress, Arch was chosen to move a resolution condemning the Peers for rejecting the Reform Bill. Joseph Chamberlain had also initiated a countrywide campaign, with the war cry of the 'Peers against the People' that culminated in another Great Franchise Demonstration, this time held in Stroke-on-Trent on 6 October. It was reported by the union's paper that month that there had been 794 meetings in favour of the bill, and 195 for the House of Lords' position. All these pressures helped convince the Conservatives to make concessions, after which the reintroduced Franchise Bill passed its third and last Commons' reading and then sailed through the House of Lords without a vote taken.

On 6 December 1884 the Representation of the People Bill (known informally as the Third Reform Act) received its Royal Assent at long last. All men paying an annual rental of £10 or all those holding land valued at £10 now had the vote. It did not establish universal suffrage, although the size of the electorate was widened considerably, to over 5.5 million (but all women and 40 per cent of adult males were still without the vote).[17] Arch described in his autobiography what a monumental achievement it was:

> Next to the famous year of the start of the Union, the year which saw the agricultural labourers enfranchised was the greatest of my life. We had the vote at last: we were now politically active and existent, and there were those amongst us who intended to use that existence to the utmost or our power in pressing for our best interests.[18]

The year had ended on a historic high, and because of the agitations around the bill, upwards of 3,000 new members had joined the NALU, and the union paper had also increased its circulation to a proportional degree. Many on the executive committee felt a physiological shift was occurring 'by which the masses of the people are quietly turning over in their minds questions of great magnitude'.[19] Key for 1885 would be the need to seize the moment and build on the fruitful gains of the year now passed. But the improvements on the union's membership would not be sustained.

However, with the vote now extending into the countryside, increasing the size of the electorate, the political front now opened up as a potential arena for greater success. In February 1885, a large number of printed addresses to the 'old and new electors' of the Crewkerne, Yeovil and Chard divisions in Somersetshire appeared. George Mitchell was announcing his acceptance of an invitation that had been sent to him to contest the newly formed division at the next general election. The *Western Daily Press* carried his pledge that, if elected:

He would be a voice in the House of Commons for the advocacy of an alteration of the laws that have oppressed the people, and amongst other things, in favour of "a restoration of all lands that have been taken away from the poor;" an immediate alteration of the land laws "so that land may be bought and sold as easily as an ox or an ass or any other things;" an abolition of the game laws, "and all other cruel and idle sport," an immediate alteration in the constitution of the House of Lords, and a searching inquiry into the system of perpetual pensions.

In the ensuing 1885 General Election, Mitchell's parliamentary career never left the starting blocks, but Arch was returned as the Liberal Party MP for North West Norfolk, the first agricultural labourer to enter the House of Commons. The Gladstone government was short-lived, and split by division over Irish Home Rule; an election was held in June 1886 where Arch narrowly lost his seat. But you can't keep a good labourers' man down, and he was successfully re-elected to the same constituency in 1892, when he was one of twelve labouring class MPs in Parliament.

After the bill and the General Election, the issue of land reform was taken forward with continuing gusto. Mitchell organised a mass meeting of close upon 3,000 labourers in November 1886 at Montacute, where Arch and Mitchell shared the platform to urge reform in the Land Acts.

Incidentally, as the *Nottinghamshire Guardian* reported, the long running sore that was a dispute between the two leaders over the use of some union funds from the sick benefit, arose at the meeting. There had been constant strife over the use of sick club funds since 1877. Mitchell, as one of the union's trustees, disagreed over whether funds could be used from the fund to pay for union expenses. After much internal 'debate' and publicly exchanged words, it finally boiled over in 1887 and went all the way to court.

In the end the judge granted the union's petition that the disputed funds should be released and vested in them, and made an order that the vesting of the funds should be undertaken by three new trustees. Arch was vindicated, and Mitchell had to pay his own costs. Leaving aside the deteriorated state of personal relations, with accusations flying about between the leaders of the union, farmers and other opponents made considerable hay from them. Undoubtedly, in 'later years attempts to win farm workers for trade unionism were hampered by memories among the villagers of these reports about the misuse of union funds'.[20]

All of the executive leadership was glad to see the back of 1887, but more positive signs were coming out of Norfolk, where the organiser from North Creake, 'Zacharius Walker had been conducting a mini-revival of his own, recruiting 600 new members over the past five months'.[21] Arch was soon on his way back to the county, where in the NALU's North Walsham and Diss District, he addressed four large and enthusiastic meetings in a row. At the meetings large numbers of men joined the union, and in some cases then went on to start their own local branches.

In this second revival of the union, what became an annual demonstration was held in the New Buckenham district— Arch would come and speak at both an afternoon and night meeting. Although just a boy at the time, Josiah Sage had vivid memories of the occasions, when The New Buckenham and Carleton Rode bands would head up two processions from either side of the village, and march to the central square before heading to the platform ready for the meeting.

The NALU was then far from dead. It may have been dismembered in many counties, but there was still a beating heart. When the executive committee travelled to Cambridge for its first meeting of 1888, they were to hear reports of stirrings similar to those in Norfolk, where in and around Aylesbury, 'the branch delegate had enrolled 56 new members in one branch alone'.[22] One indication of a potential upswing to come (yet a problem for the NALU) was that other unions were appearing on the scene. The Workers' Union was a newly formed general labourers' union that did some organising in Staffordshire, North Shropshire, South Cheshire and Norfolk, and 'in the course of one year founded forty branches with some 2000 members. The Navvies Union, also had gained a membership in Norfolk over the previous two of three years, and in 1888 these men organised a strike at St. Faith's, a village some four miles from Norwich.'[23]

Before his return to Parliament in the 1890s, Arch stood as a Radical candidate for Wellesbourne in the County Council elections, and was narrowly elected on Thursday 24 January. It was a personal triumph of sorts, but he had to deplore the fact that countrywide there had been 'all too few working men candidates in the field'. One of those that did stand, and lost, was Zacharius Walker, in the Burnham Division of Norfolk.

But it was in the late summer of 1889 that the glowing embers ignited into an industrial wildfire that proved a turning point in the history of trade unionism. It was only one year after the successful 'Match girls' strike, and more recently the city had been in 'ferment because the capital's newly organised gas workers had gone on strike for an eight-hour day'. Ben Tillett was the General Secretary of the tiny Tea Operatives & General Labourers' Association when a strike began on 13 August. A few labourers at the South West India Docks went out on the demand of four hours' continuous work at a time and a minimum rate of sixpence an hour—and an end to the so-called 'dockers tanner'. The Dock companies refused the demand, and were confident that they would be able to starve the men back to work.

Originally only five hundred casuals marched out, but the dispute spread rapidly, and after another day the strike had spread to the neighbouring docks. In a week half of East London was out. Ben Tillett was active in the Socialist movement and was able to persuade several friends, including John Burns and Tom Mann, to help rally support. Both Burns and Mann were tried and tested militants from the Amalgamated Society of Engineers, and together they systematically organised the mass of dockside labourers who queued up in their thousands to join Tillett's union. Many of those involved were recipients of poor relief and were desperately in need, and 'when it was announced that relief tickets were to be distributed some thousands of them gathered before the door of the dingy little coffee tavern where Tom Mann and his helpers, having just received the relief tickets from the printers, were preparing to issue them'.

The dockers marched through the city and held daily meetings at Tower Hill. They carried with them not just their industrial banners but, to represent the typical docker diet, totem poles crowned with stinking fish heads and rotting onions. However, the employers refused to budge and the government turned a blind eye, and before long the strikers' relief funds had diminished to perilously low levels. The employers then attempted to bring in blackleg labour. But the tactic was not decisive because the dispute extended over haysel and harvest, when the countryside workers were fully occupied. The supply of blacklegs was not there as it would have been over winter. And then, without warning, some £30,000 started to pour in from all over Australia. The strike was sustained long enough for the Dock Companies to begin to recognise where the public sympathy lay, and to feel the concentrated pressure of the newspapers, clergyman, ship-owners and merchants. The employers were compelled to 'concede on practically the whole of the men's demands'.

After the successful strike, the dockers formed a new general labourers' union. Ben Tillett was elected General Secretary and Tom Mann became the union's first President. Joseph Arch and the NALU's leadership could now see how the recent upsurge in their membership was part of a wider pattern of activity and growth among unskilled workers. They also realised there would never be a better time than this for the farm labourers to combine once more and win back what they had once won but then lost through indifference.

It was also no coincidence that over the winter of 1889 militant activity by working class children, supported by their parents, became evident in many schools. In the year that the National Union of Elementary Teachers dropped 'Elementary' from its title, a wave of school strikes began in Hawick, Roxburgh at the beginning of October and then spread throughout the Scottish Lowlands into Tyneside, London, Bristol and Cardiff. Sporadic school strikes had occurred before, but because teachers and school managers were anxious to minimise any negative impact of their reputations, they often refused to acknowledge their existence. But this wave was a widespread defiant gesture against excessive authoritarianism, corporal punishment and a centralised structure of schooling that was increasingly taking control of education from the local community. Their rapid diffusion meant that the strikes could not be ignored, and so they aroused widespread public interest and concern.

# Chapter 6

## Another Grand Time

'The rich expanse of embryo corn fields, the pasture land, the green slopes and gentle undulations with its sparkling brook, its many hedgerows, and its clumps of trees was black and dreary about the region of Huxham.'[1] It was a raw morning for the funeral; the nipping East wind was sufficient to pinch everybody with cold and turn any exposed visages a shade bluer. The biting February weather merely added to the solemnity of the occasion. Nor did the fact that the internment was due to take place at ten o'clock act as any deterrent to the large numbers of people who resolved to attend. 'It was a village enchanted into silence and stone,'[2] the local paper waxed, unusually lyrically, and at length, for a burial report.

It was a melancholy opening to 1890, but the biggest drama to hit Huxham in a generation had just occurred; the murder–suicide of James and Emma Gosling. The tragedy was such a sensation that large numbers flocked to the village to satisfy their morbid curiosity, and it caused journalists to generate some truly overblown and romanticised reporting.

> It was a picturesque domicile in which this labourer and his wife and family lived . . . Indeed that is the case with all the cottages in Huxham which enclose its industrious population of some hundred divided souls, representing a bold peasantry, their country's pride, who can enlighten visitors from the populous towns how pastoral housekeeping is done upon ten shillings a week.[3]

Well, not quite.

James Gosling was a farm labourer with a wife and family of seven sons and one daughter, living in a cramped cottage on a mere ten shillings a week. Two days before their funeral, Gosling had bloodily killed his wife on the roadside at midnight and then returned home and killed himself. The newspapers failed to ask why he might have 'struck his wife from the list of the living', and missed the intense hardships that lay behind the ivy-clad walls. But James Gosling had been driven mad by dire circumstance. The lot of the labourer was not a picturesque one; ten shillings and some cider was not a living wage for a family in 1890. The heady days when farmers in East Somerset had raised wages by a shilling a week in a desperate attempt to prevent the NALU from establishing a foothold were long passed. At its best, the contraction of the union had seen stagnation in the material interests of the labourers; in many areas of the country pay had fallen back to pre-1872 levels.

The Higdons attended the Gosling funeral, following the sleek coated pair of black horses that pulled the plumed cortege. They were likely to have been graveside to see the bearers discover, when attempting to lower the body of James Gosling, that the grave had not been dug wide enough, and an unfortunate delay occurred while pick and spades were set to widen the aperture. The only Higdon absent was Mary Anne, who was now living at 31 Hill Street, Bristol, Gloucestershire and working as a tailoress. Apart from domestic service and dress making, there were few occupations open to women at the time, particularly those with a limited education. Whether it had been through choice or necessity, she had moved further away from Huxham than any of her male siblings had so far managed.

The other profession that afforded women a career was teaching, although it was one that 'was so poorly paid that few people were prepared to undertake the employment who were "not incapacitated by age of infirmity for manual labour"'.[4] The need to improve the general education standards of teachers had become so apparent that in 1846, the government drew up its programme for pupil-teacher training. The scheme was not without its hardships and stresses for the participants, but the arrangement at least 'afforded both men and women of relatively humble backgrounds a chance to enter a respectable profession with modest prestige'.[5] Yet, such bright, qualified men could earn higher salaries in business or industry, and the gender pay inequality meant that many hard-pressed school managers (especially in rural areas) found women increasingly attractive. 'In the mid-1890's there were still over 1,200 country headmistresses who were paid under £50 a year, and even the advent of local education authorities after 1902 did not eliminate gender pay differences,'[6] and, well into the new century, elementary teaching remained the preserve of the children of skilled artisans, shopkeepers and labourers, who were themselves products of the same school system.

Annie Schollick had been born to parents from the 'lower orders', yet unexpected circumstances had gifted her with a far superior education than she would have otherwise expected to receive. In part it was thanks to her father that she had a culturally refined intelligence and a middle-class missionary zeal for education; yet she had to leave home and become a governess on the back of his conviction and imprisonment. Annie, from the very beginning, was fundamentally shaped by the age she was living in, and constantly out of sync with it.

Yet, despite of her own enhanced childhood education, she began her career in teaching as an unqualified governess. Nevertheless, the first children in her care had grown and prospered, and the position reached its natural end, as it always would. She might have loved the rural agrarian setting, but as events would prove, she would always go wherever the new teaching opportunity lay. Next it was onto Westbourne, Sussex to work as an elementary teacher in a Church of England school.

It was in Sussex that Annie was to undergo her formal teacher training and become fully certified. From the time of their meeting, and then latterly marrying Tom Higdon, she held the senior teaching positions because of her superior qualification. Tom never expressed any sense of inferiority over it, but was always rather immensely proud and admiring of his wife. For Annie, teaching was an absolute passion; for Tom, education was a means by which greater social equality and justice could be realised—that labourers, like himself, could rise up and overturn centuries of servitude if only they were better educated. And it was to be through becoming a teacher that Tom Higdon would leave his own personal servitude to the land behind.

No government inspector was ever to give Annie Schollick a bad report in an annual assessment, but because of a growing general concern at the time over the standard of pupil-teachers and former pupil-teachers, amendments to the scheme were made. Later, two of the larger school boards, London and Liverpool, began to gather pupil-teachers into external classes for their education. This practice spread rapidly and by the 1890s, most pupil-teachers were being educated in Pupil-Teacher Centres. It was through an Oxford University regional centre, probably Bristol, that Tom Higdon was able to acquire his Oxford Local Senior Certificate.

The new decade had been entered into on a wave of personal change and political optimism. The Schollick family, driven by employment opportunities, was now dispersed across the country. Of Annie's two surviving brothers, Alfred Smith was back living in Lancashire and was working as a bookkeeper, while James Heaton had moved to Nottingham to work as a railway clerk. Only one sister was left in Seacombe, along with father Samuel who, though still giving his occupation as ship and boat builder, had retired when the industry was laid to permanent rest in 1887. The fortunate Edward Jones Schollick had emigrated to South Australia (with less of a fortune), and Uncle Thomas James had become the coroner of Croydon.

In the same period, Charles Tucker Eland was a clerk in Holy Orders and was not to leave Runnymede Street, Egham behind until 1897 when he was appointed to the Vicarage of Butley, Suffolk. Prior to the appointment he had been the Curate in Egham Parish Church, and it was there on 10 November 1891 that he married Mary Elizabeth Collingwood.

Mary Elizabeth's father, John Nelson Collingwood, had been the owner of a new and second-hand bookseller, stationer, binder, music and print seller, and account-book manufacturer on the High Street, Epsom. A specialist in 'Bibles, Prayer Books, Church Services and Altar Books in every variety of binding',[7] he also had a sideline in tea as the 'appointed agent for the sale of Horniman & Com's pure uncoloured tea for Epsom, Ewell, and surrounding villages'.[8] Then in his early thirties, Eland had first met his future bride in her father's shop. By the time of the wedding both John Nelson Collingwood and Charles Tucker's father Richard were deceased. Mary Elizabeth was to have the register signed by her brother, who shared the same name, and Eland by his mother, Adelaide.

Within a week of the dockers' victory, Arch was back in Norfolk where he addressed six meetings in a row, and was 'accompanied by his "old and tried friend" Zacharius Walker, whose Herculean recruiting efforts over the next two or three years would be held up as shining example to union members everywhere'.[9] During 1890, Arch visited Norfolk and Suffolk at least once a month and sometimes more often. The 'second uprising of farm labourers' was underway, and Norfolk was at its leading edge. The union's paper, *The English Labourers' Chronicle*, carried a succession of headlines that conveyed that new positive movement; but as had always been the case, the NALU did not have the labourers' ears and subscriptions all to itself.

'The Dockers' Union was also active in the countryside, sending organisers out into Oxfordshire and Lincolnshire,'[10] and a great number of new unions formed in the first years of the 1890s. In May, arguably the most important, the Eastern Counties Labour Federation, with its centre in Ipswich was established. In a year it could claim 3,000 members, and by the spring of 1892 it had spread 'over Essex, Suffolk and Cambridge, and had 10,047 members in 174 branches'.[11]

In May 1890 the NALU's Annual Council was held in Norwich, where it would be 'reported that the total Union membership had bottomed out at 4,254 the previous December and that nearly 5,000 new recruits had been enrolled within the past four months'.[12] By the following year the 'National' had over 12,000 members in Norfolk alone.

Over in Somerset, George Mitchell was once again putting his all into resuscitating union organisation, but this time not under the fluttering banner of the NALU. 'The agricultural labourers of West Somerset appear to be determined to reorganise their trade union, and on Saturday the first of series of meetings were to be held in the top room of a large warehouse at Westport.'[13] The main object of the meeting, the *Western Times* made clear, was to 'increase the wages and regulate the hours of labour of the farming population'.[14]

The occasion was a grand affair, like from the 'good ole' days, where streams of labourers could be seen making their way to the meeting from the surrounding villages. From all directions, bands could be heard in the distance, and on drawing closer, each was seen to have been heading a torchlight procession. After the election of officers, letters of support were read out from people expressing sympathy with the movement, including, albeit brief, a letter from Gladstone. It ended with the following motion being moved and seconded:

> This meeting of agricultural labourers of Somerset is of opinion that their class is suffering greatly through oppression and neglect; therefore, all present pledge themselves to contrive to joining the Somerset and West England Agricultural Labourers' Union for the purpose of defending themselves and homes against injustice, and further, after hearing the proposed rules and officials, hereby agree to adopted the same, and to use every legitimate means of making the organisation a success, by forming branches in every parish in the county, having a view the extension of the organisation into the adjoining counties of Dorset, Wilts, Devon, and other adjoining counties.[15]

During the subsequent months the union's foothold in Somerset was re-strengthened; its presence, as in parts of Norfolk, had never completely disappeared. With the efforts to reorganise the labourers' bearing fruit, Mitchell, a man with a nose for the historic opportunity, was to announce in May 1892 the return of the mass demonstration at Ham Hill. It had been Whit Monday 1885 that last hosted a mass rally of labourers—before the long years of depression and struggle set in. And Mitchell was reaching high, with invitations to speak being sent to Prince George of Wales, Gladstone, the Bishop of Bath and Lord Roseberry. All, for one reason or another, politely declined the offer. One who did not decline, and whose presence offered, as it turned out, a nice historical bookend, was Mr Francis George Heath, the author of *The "Romance" of Peasant Life in the West of England* (1872). Mitchell was not to know at the time, but the 1892 rally would be the last one organised; a final wave of the arm before the head went below the waters for good.

This was not 1890; two years on and agriculture was beginning to feel a pinch, and Tom Higdon's own exit from his occupation as a labourer was not be too far behind. In March 1892, within the 'Butlers, Coachmen, Gardeners' classifieds of the *Western Daily Press*, appeared: 'A young man, strong, steady and industrious requires situation in Garden, Farm or Stable.' The situation did not materialise and in April the same young man was seeking work as a 'Single or Under Gardener'. If Tom Higdon was advertising for gardening work, then things were getting tight on Huxham Farm.

The difficulties already being faced then became a full-blown agricultural crisis the following summer due to a persistent drought and a bad harvest. Wages fell, unemployment increased, and the year was unhelpfully capped off by a hard winter seldom experienced. Where, as in Norfolk, the unions put up resistance against the cuts, it ended in defeat. Men found it difficult to pay the few pence required as subscription and 'in the winter of 1893–4 most of the unions found that their membership was already going down again. And those which had been called into life by the dock labourers were "practically defunct"'.[16]

The NALU's *Chronicle*, the paper that had chartered the progress of the movement for the past twenty-two years, was last published on 8 September 1894. By the end of the year, the union's 'total registered membership had fallen to 1,100 and its funds to a trifling two pounds'; there was nothing that could be done to save it or the other labourers' unions. In Norfolk, Primitive Methodist and former member of the union George Edwards, joined forces with Arch and Walker in one last attempt to defend the labourers' interests, but after a brief moment in the sun, the NALU limped on a little further before being official dissolved in 1896.

But for the labourers there were still bright spots of hope. The 1892 election had returned a Liberal majority into the House of Commons, and Joseph Arch was back in Parliament. Though his parliamentary career never burned as brightly as it did when he was the inspirational leader of the farm workers, he was to speak several times during the Commons' Reading of the Parish Councils Bill. One of the most important measures of the new government was to be the extension of democratic self-government by the creation of district and parish councils. 'The Bill, which in the main provided for councils to be set up in every parish with a population of 300 and over, put the obtaining and control of allotments in the hands of the council, and gave the new bodies the right to appoint trustees for Parish Charities.'[17]

The landed gentry in the House of Lords did their utmost to sabotage the entire bill, in an unsurprising 'last-ditch bid to preserve all they could of their traditionally dominant role in village life'.[18] But with the bill back in the Commons, the government soon made good most of the wrecking, and on 5 March the Local Government (England and Wales) Act 1894 was given Royal Assent. As with the 'labourers' leader' who spoke repeatedly in favour of democratisation, many supporters of the rural labourer expected the Act to lead to the final solution to all their difficulties.

It was not on the Higdons' arrival in Norfolk that Annie was to take on her first job as a school head, but rather Mrs Schollick, headmistress, first arrived in Somerset. An opening appeared in the winter of 1892, in the irregularly shaped parish of East Lydford, for the now fully certified teacher. The parish had suffered from a severe influenza epidemic; within a week of the old year there had been no fewer than five deaths (this was in a parish whose population peaked at 194 in 1841). But it was worse than that; the press had to report in January that the parish had 'sustained a heavy loss in the death of Mrs. Young, the schoolmistress'. She had held the post for fifteen years, and was given the credit for raising the standard of the school to a very high state of efficiency. 'She had also played the harmonium at the church for many years, and her services in this and many other ways will be very much missed.'[19] Mrs Schollick had a lot to live up to.

'The parish of East Lydford, lies 5 miles east of Somerton, extending about 1½ mile from north to south, and from east to west. The course of the Foss Way forms the whole of its north-western boundary; its northern boundary is marked by the river Brue and a small stream, and the southern by the river Cary.'[20] But most importantly, the schoolhouse was just four miles away from Huxham.

Annie was now back in a rural community where the principal income of the manor came from leasing summer and winter pasture, and tenant arable farming. The contrast with the landscape to North Wales was striking, yet back living in the countryside, surrounded by nothing but a rolling agricultural fabric, provided a familiar continuity. As a young governess, Ms. Schollick had liked to take long walks out around the country lanes, both with the children in her care, and also to escape the stresses of the work in those rare moments of freedom.

Yet the reality of the rural idyll was as much a romantic invention for the schoolmistress as it was for the broad-shouldered labourer working twelve hours a day (or more) in the open fields for ten shillings a week. As a result of the Education Act (1870), thousands of small schools opened in parishes across the country, and the difficulties faced by the female mistresses were neither rare nor did they escape the attention of more distant observers. The *Supplement to The Cheltenham Chronicle*, 18 March 1893, would provide a precise summation of the phenomena to its readers:

## VILLAGE SCHOOLMISTRESSES.

There are certain female workers, isolated in position, not great in numbers and unable to make their hardships known by combining together, whose case, to say the least, is a pitiable one. We allude to the trained schoolmistresses who govern the smaller village schools in the country. It is doubtful whether any set of women suffer greater hardships. There are in England alone between five and six thousand village schools in which the average attendance is very greatly under sixty. These teachers have been duly certificated—that is to say, they have passed through a two years' course at some Government training college after their apprenticeship as pupil-teachers. In their training they have had to work hard in order to obtain their certificates; consequently they are all fairly educated, and are supposed to have acquired some taste for literature and intellectual pursuits. When these schoolmistresses have passed their Government examination, they are drifted off to rural schools, with thirty or forty children around them, to teach all the subjects which are put down in the Government curriculum. Formerly reading, writing and arithmetic were all taught, but this would not now enable the children to pass the examination of the Government inspector, nor would it obtain for the school the Government grant. Without which a board cannot go on. It is said that some of these women are working for less than £40 a year, that there are over 500 whose annual stipend is under £45, and 700 whose salaries range between £45 and £50 per annum—that is to say, 10 per cent. of the women in charge of English schools are fulfilling their laborious duties for less than 20s a week. With this sum the teacher must find herself in food, washing, dress (and she is bound to look respectable), and pay something for the additional books which are necessary to keep herself au courant with her work. She must have someone to take care of her home, for she cannot cook her own food and teach in school at the same time. In many cases she has to pay for her own lodgings. In remote villages there is no mental relaxation whatever. Often there are but few books to be obtained. The condition of a lone teacher during the long winter evenings is almost too painful to contemplate. How greatly it could be lightened by the sympathy of those who are more fortunately situated is easy to contemplate.[21]

How painful Annie found the long winter evenings in East Lydford is open to question. The only certainty is that taking over from Mrs Young was not without its challenges. Perhaps it was because Mrs Young had become a fixture in the parish,

ANOTHER GRAND TIME

overseeing a generation of local scholars, or maybe it was simply
because she was married, but a group of local boys began to
harass the new schoolmistress and her female assistant. The
two young, unmarried women, one with a funny foreign name
and a cultured accent, were thought to be easy targets for a bit
of cheeky banter.

With the boys becoming persistent goaders, Annie used what
would become her preferred weapon of defence and resorted to
the law. The boys were reported and brought before the local
magistrates. On the day, Annie and Caroline Waters, the
assistant mistress, presented their evidence calmly and without
theatrics that, simply, the defendants were near the school house
just after school time (Sunday), making a great disturbance and
using profane and obscene language. This had not been the first
time that the pair had cause to complain about the lads; they
had had to do so on a number of previous occasions.

All six boys were cautioned and ordered by the Bench to pay
2s.6d. each. Whether peace and respect for the schoolmistress's
authority was fully restored is anyone's guess, but there was
no further boisterous behaviour reported in the press.
Understandably, the petty high-jinks would have proven
somewhat wearisome, and the fact that it necessitated the
intervention of the courts to bring a resolution perhaps proved
bruising to her self-confidence. But these sorts of things were
the daily travails of the schoolmistress, and unless you were
made of the strongest stuff you were likely to sink under the
weight of them.

On 4 July 1896 Thomas George Higdon and Anne Katherine
Schollick were married in Holy Trinity Church, Clifton,
Gloucestershire. The venue was decided upon out of pure
practicality; it was equidistant from Tom's family in Huxham,
and Annie's family in Cheshire. Tom's sister was living close by,
and signed the register along with his brother Frank.

Exactly how Tom and Annie came to meet remains pure
speculation. Tom was desperately looking for labouring work
in 1892, yet when the pair married four years later he wrote on
the marriage certificate that his profession was that of 'teacher'.
Did Tom meet Annie, and through her influence and

69

encouragement enter into teaching as a way of the land? Or did he, when agriculture was beginning to struggle, find his way into teaching and then met Annie?

With the known timeline, and the absence of other facts, there remains the tantalising possibility that Tom undertook his pupil-teacher training during the 1890s, and that he even received his mentoring at East Lydford school. The school was just four miles from Huxham, and Tom was still living in the village. Wherever he was trained and taught, it would have been within a commutable distance (by bike or foot) from Huxham. The assumption has been that, as the pupil-teacher scheme was one of the few means by which intelligent children from the labouring classes could acquire a degree of secondary education, Tom must have done so concurrent with his statutory minimum provision. Yet if that was so, he found no teaching job afterwards and continued to work as a labourer into his twenties.

Possibly Tom did enter into teaching at the East Pennard School, or another school within the vicinity, and through inter-school competition, religious service, community event or a professional forum, his life and that of his future wife began to mix. There is probably a higher likelihood of this than for Tom 'the labourer', as the life of such rarely afforded much time and any distance away from the farm and cottage.

The last years of the century were a precipice of change for everyone. Rural trade unionism had retreated back into a full and deep slumber, but without the past twenty-odd years of struggle the labourers' position would scarcely have been any better today than it was in 1872. The union had won better pay, the franchise, improved cottages and larger allotments, and in doing so had sown the seed its own demise. Of the great men who had made the biggest sacrifices for the common interest, most had now retreated into retirement or the grave. In December 1897 they were joined by the seventy-five-year-old Samuel Schollick, who died while staying with his son Alfred Smith Schollick in Toxeth Park, Lancashire.

The youngest Higdon children had both left the land, and Frank was soon to marry Sarah Jane McIlhagga and shortly thereafter move to 8 Vestry Road, Street, Wells. Mary Anne, who left Huxham, had now returned and was working as a self-employed needle woman, and the Reverend Charles Tucker Eland had made a geographical side step by taking up an appointment as the Vicar of Felsted, Essex in July 1899.

Within a few days of Eland's official notification, Mr and Mrs Higdon were on the move. From July 1899, the Higdons decamped to London, where Tom became an assistant master at St James's and St Peter's School, a Church of England school in the poor quarter of Soho. They both loved the natural world and immersing themselves in the small beauties that lay in the morning chorus of birdsong, or changing seasonal leaf colouration. It would have been a wrench to leave, but their passion for education and social justice was a missionary pursuit for them, and now it had taken them to apply themselves in a crucible of urban destitution.

One thing the move guaranteed was that the Higdons were now living together, though in lodgings rather than in a home of their own. Their address at 15 Berners Road, Wood Green, Middlesex was not too far from brother James Heaton Schollick, who had in the late 1890s moved on to a railways clerk's post there. The Higdons' landlady, Constance Tanner, was a thirty-nine-year-old widow and pianoforte teacher. Annie's own proficiency on the organ would be a tribute to the additional evening tutorage given by Mrs Tanner. Although only thirty-five years old herself, Annie Higdon already had nigh on twenty years of continuous teaching experience, and did not idle her time away but worked as an elementary teacher at a yet unidentified school.

Three schools had merged to form the modern St James School: St Anne's, founded in 1699, St James's in 1827 and St Peter's in 1872. The school's location in Great Windmill Street originated from 1872, when it was St Peter's (as carved on the outside walls). Each of the three schools had originated as charitable foundations dependent on voluntary giving, and the new St. James School provided regular medical and dental checks, and school meals; something the parents of the surrounding slumland children could ill afford but desperately needed.

The responsibility for the St James School lay with the clergy of the various churches who chaired or sat on the committee of managers. The Higdons' time passed without much lasting legacy, but thankfully also without any apparent disputes or court cases, which was to become a rarity in the life of a Schollick-Higdon. Tom applied himself diligently to his work, and without any tensions developing with the Anglican school authorities. On 26 July 1901, the testimonial provided by the Rector of St. James's Piccadilly was commending:

Mr. Thomas G. Higdon has been working as an Assistant Master in the above School for nearly two years with great Satisfaction to the Managers.

The Government and Diocesan Reports during that period have been "Excellent" and the Headmaster confirms me in my opinion that Mr. Higdon's share in those results has been all that could be desired.

Shortly afterwards, in August, the Headmaster was to give his own testimonial:

Mr. Higdon has worked in the above school to my satisfaction during the past two years and you will find him an energetic and conscientious teacher.

He has taken the First and Second Standards comprising 60

boys and has loyally carried out any suggestion which I have offered him.

I can only add that I shall be sorry to lose him.

I am, Yours Truly, W.H.Atkinson

Good work had been done, and Tom had surely benefited from the challenge of teaching up to sixty children from an urban cesspit of destitution. But perhaps enough was enough, and with the incessant yearning for the countryside that never leaves those raised within it, the search for a new and joint appointment had already been triggered.

# Chapter 7

# Welcome to the Boot Club

### 1902–06

The meeting of the Sancreed School Board on 13 February 1902 had two pressing issues for discussion: the level of attendance of some pupils, and the appointment of a locum tenens owing to the illness of the present master. Those children who were the most irregular were to be brought before the board. In some cases the excuse for the irregular attendance was measles, but in others it was stated that the children were old offenders and was decided to take the necessary steps to enforce attendance—they would move to fine the parents.

Moving down the agenda, the board had received a number of applications for the temporary position from interested parties: H. Bretton, Harlow, at £2; E.W. Edwards, Burnington, £2 per week; G. Parker, London, £90 per annum; George Crookall, Penzance, £95 per annum; John Bryant, London, £2.2s. per week; W.E. Culling, Muddleton, £1.10s.; W. Daphne, Winchester, £10 per month; J.E. Boaden, St. Austall, £100 per annum, J. Warren, Newton Abbot, £30 for the three months; J. Samuel Keightley, Pembroke, £70 per annum; and T.G. Higdon, London, £2. After some discussion it was decided to appoint Mr Crockall—the Higdons would not be heading to Cornwall after all.

Rather, it would be Wood Dalling, the village and parish situated some nineteen miles northwest of Norwich and twelve miles east of Fakenham, that would accept the appointment of the Higdons in the joint role of Headmistress and Assistant Master. Without full certification, Tom was never to go beyond the level of an assistant. Not that he seemed to care; the couple were heading back to the countryside.

The Higdons' arrival in Norfolk coincided with a new Education Act that was intended to increase the provision of secondary schooling by substituting the old school boards with local borough or county councils, Local Education Authorities (LEAs). The Act was also to end the divide between voluntary schools, which were largely administered by the Church of England, and schools provided and run by elected school boards.

The 1870 Education Act had been popular with radicals as they were elected by ratepayers in each district thus enabling Nonconformists and Socialists to obtain influence over local schools. The new Act, also known as the Balfour Act, provided funds for denominational religious instruction in voluntary elementary schools owned primarily by the CoE and Roman Catholics; 'Nonconformists considered it an unfairness that they should pay for a religious education with which they disagree with.'[1]

Nonconformists and supporters of the Liberal and Labour parties campaigned against the 1902 Education Act. The self-educated Baptist leader John Clifford formed the National Passive Resistance Committee to fight the Act, and by 1906 more than 170 men had gone to prison for refusing to pay their school taxes. The Act became a major political issue and was one of the main reasons for the Liberal Party victory in the 1906 General Election. In Norfolk, 'though very few labourers were involved, for the simple reason that few paid rates, small tradesmen and farmers often were, including a few who were to emerge, after 1906, as local figures in the union movement'.[2]

The Higdons found the state of Wood Dalling Council School to be of such disrepair that it was quite unsanitary. The Education Act had resulted in a national school-building programme, but thirty years on many of them were barely fit for purpose. At Wood Dalling, a long backlog of works had accrued, largely as a result of the school managers' lack of willingness (and perhaps personal competence) to invest. In

1901 the then master, Mr Pearson, had noted in the logbook that 'there being no quorum [at school managers' meeting] nothing could be definitely settled about painting the school premises'. No fresh paint was to find its way onto the walls of the school prior to the Higdons' appointment.

Certainly, the basis of some of the friction to come between the Higdons and the school managers was evident long before Annie began her unrelenting efforts to attain improvements. For a number of years, Master Pearson had also been recording his own concerns over how irregular attendance was making the work of teaching difficult. He was to do his best to improve matters, both writing to the parents of the worst offenders and requesting the attendance officer to instruct caution. If the attendance officer was lacklustre in the application of his purpose, the maintenance of attendance, the School Board itself was not exactly constructive. In 1901, the board decided to use the school for the School Board election, but did so without giving any prior intimation to Pearson that it was to be used for the purpose of polling.

In rural areas, the attitude among most farmers towards the merit of educating labourers' children had not matured since the 1870s; it was still widely felt that 'this filled them with unhealthy ambitions about their future employment and made them reluctant to take up land work in later life'.[3] Putting children to work at an early age meant that they would grow into efficient adult labourers. The Wood Dalling School Board was constituted almost exclusively of local farmers. The Higdons, though, could not have seen things more differently.

Closing the school for elections was one matter; the logbook records several entries of its closure when the Hounds or Harriers hunt visited the village, 'in accordance with the Board's resolution'.[4] Cruelty to animals was one thing neither of the Higdons would tolerate, although there was no dewy-eyed sentimentality; killing animals for 'sport' was something they considered neither decent nor sporting. Tom was even remembered telling the children not to chop up worms when gardening, and one future pupil in Burston, Violet Potter, recalled how Annie 'would buy dog biscuits and feed any dogs she thought looked a bit hungry. She would even give her own lunch to a dog.'[5] The new vegetarian schoolmistress was never going to look kindly on the children's education being disrupted by the local hunt.

On 14 April 1902 the Higdons commenced their work in the school. Immediately, Mrs Higdon began recording her complaints of the illegal employment of boys by the local farmers during term time. '16 April 1902: Visited by the attendance officer to whom reported the case of George Grimes, aged nine, absent from school, 'crow scaring' for Mr Gray'. On the 17th George Grimes returned to school after three days of 'crow keeping'; '9 May: Albert Cottrell absent on 7th cattle driving'.[6]

The illegal employment of children during school hours was widespread practice and was to prove all too soon the source of irritation that would ignite Tom Higdon's indignation. The farmers of Wood Dalling were used to employing children as casual labour and they had no intention to stop. '1 July: Yesterday Albert Cottrell was employed by Mr Gamble haymaking in the field opposite the school room. A note was sent to Mr Gamble asking him for the return of the boy to school and stating that he was under age and had no labour certificate. No reply was received to note and the boy continued his employment.'[7] The following day the case was reported to the attendance officer, who did nothing.

The Higdons were gradually settling into their new home and roles. It would be another four years before the labourers themselves would give rise to the creation of a 'Second National' Agricultural Labourers' Union, and Tom would really start to become irksome in the eyes of the local farmers. Although, it would be incredible if he paid no attention to the conditions in which the local labourers lived, and contrasted that with his own experience. It would have been impossible to miss; the farm workers' in this part of Norfolk were in receipt of no better pay, or housing, than in the East Somerset of his childhood.

Wood Dalling had both a Wesleyan and Primitive Methodist chapel, which Tom attended and would sometimes preach in. Annie, though completely comfortable in the chapel, seems to have continued to attend the local church. Perhaps the new schoolmistress felt it only right that she should be seen there by Reverend R. Vicars; who also happened to be Chairman of the School Board.

Initially, at least, the two had a cordial relationship, and Annie as the headmistress left a number of appreciative references during the first years of their tenure. The reverend would often step in and take a class for reading, or an occasional harmonium lesson; and being a qualified doctor, he would attend to dress any scrapes that the children would suffer, including setting broken bones. Tom Barnes, a pupil at the time, left an affectionate portrait of a peculiar English character:

> The Reverend Vicars was a funny man. He kept about twenty cats [other accounts say forty–fifty]. When his wife died he shut himself up, he locked his gate and wouldn't let anybody enter the house. Even the postman and the man who brought the fish had to arrange a time when to call, and he would meet them at the gate . . .
>
> He wore big, hob-nailed boots even when he was taking the service in the church. He did not mix with the congregation. He didn't speak to his parishioners at the door when they came in, like other vicars do, and after the service he would disappear out of a side door of the chancel.

He also rode a 'boneshaker' type of bike, where the wheels were the same size but the pedals were on the front axle; but as Tom Barnes (there were fourteen children named Barnes who lived in Wood Dalling at the time the Higdons were in charge) continued to recall, 'he was good to the children. He used to wait at the school gate at dinnertime, with a football and he would let the boys kick it about in a field until he came for it again. He would come back in time so that they wouldn't be late for the afternoon school'.[8]

Later, he would stop calling altogether.

The school year ended on 30 June. Though the Higdons had only been in place for less than three months, the official government report for the year ending noted the positive changes: 'Mixed school. There has been a complete change of staff. At the second visit the new teachers had only commenced their duties and a creditable start has been made'.[9] But the longer term understaffing could not fail to be noted: 'The present staff, however, is quite inadequate and another qualified teacher must be at once engaged . . . Infant Class. The infants are creditably taught but do not receive sufficient attention owing to the multifarious duties of the mistress . . . The Board of Education trust that the Staff will be made good without more delay . . .'.[10] The new school year was to begin with an additional qualified teacher; Alice Maria Pask from Hackford Board School commenced work 24 September.

The Headmistress's persistent petitioning of the school managers was also to produce dividends. In time, better porches were put up for the children's clothes, the lavatories improved, new flooring put in, and the building repainted—by the time of the couple's departure, Mrs. Higdon would effectively bring about a compete rebuild.

But those days were ahead. Firstly, and most immediately, there was the job of teaching, and the lifting of the educational standard for all. In the pursuit of this, the Higdons soon acquired a reputation for generosity. Just like her uncle Edward, Annie was generous to the poor families in the village and out of her own pocket she would provide whatever was required so a child would not miss school. Very often, this would be clothing and new boots, which along with disease was the biggest reason for non-attendance at school.

Perhaps also, the invisible hand of uncle and doctor Thomas James Schollick was at work in her actions over the general welfare and health of the children. As a precaution, if any child in a family had an infectious disease like measles or whooping cough, she would send the other children in the family home, and 'when it rained she would feel the children's clothes to see if they were wet. Some children had two miles to walk to school. If they were wet she would take them into the Schoolhouse and dry their clothes. Sometimes she would give the boys Tom's clothes to wear while their own were drying.'[11] Furthermore, she liked to keep the schoolroom well ventilated.

After the register was taken, each day would open with prayers, the singing of hymns and the recitation of times tables. Lessons were delivered according to age groups. To help matters, an additional teacher had been recruited; first Alice Pask, and then Mrs Seely (who remained at the school for several years of the Higdon tenure) taught the infants. The headmistress would teach the oldest children, and Tom those in between. In many schools at the time, the space used for teaching was little more than a single room; and with mixed age groups, the need to maintain discipline was vital.

Tom Higdon would be warmly remembered by his former pupils, but he was not reserved in his use of the cane. On one occasion, 'Jim Bussens' boy was playing about his watch one morning in class and Mr. Higdon told him to stop and he went on doing it so he was caned. Mr. and Mrs. Bussens were very upset and they took their children away from the school.'[12] In 1907, Mr J.J. Bussens would be elected chairman of the school managers.

But some of the older boys were known to be difficult to control. The previous master, Pearson, had resorted to the cane frequently, but that had caused him trouble with the bigger boys when one day some of them set on him. It was after that incident that Pearson went away to Holt, Norfolk creating the vacancy for the Higdons. As the head, Annie would sometimes stop Tom from beating the boys. 'She would come into the classroom and say, "Don't do that, Tom." Sometimes when they had a difference she would go red in the face and walk out.' But generally, she was not hesitant to pick up her assistant in front of the children if she felt it necessary. On occasion, 'Tom wouldn't come into school and it was known that there had been a bit of a tiff; but it was obvious that they thought the world of each other'.[13]

Tom wanted the children to learn as he wanted the labourers as a class to rise out of their abject conditions. And he would get very infuriated by those bodies or individuals that interfered with it. In November 1902 things would come to a head with one farmer who persisted in employing children during school hours. On 10 November, the head recorded in her logbook that Tom was an absentee from the school for most of the day while attending court at Reepham for an assault on Mr Gamble, local farmer. The *Norwich Mercury*, 16 November, carried the details of the case:

A stranger case of assault than that investigated at Reepham Petty Sessions on Monday rarely comes before a bench of Norfolk Magistrates. Thomas Higdon, schoolmaster, of Wood Dalling, was summoned for assaulting Henry Gamble, a farmer, of the same place, on the 22 October. Mr. G.C.Chittock appeared for the prosecution and stated that amongst others employed by Mr Gamble was a school boy named Cotterill. On the day in question defendant came into the field where Mr Gamble was and asked why he had been poaching boys from his school. If parents sent their children to school he must let them come. After a few words more defendant hit complainant with his fist and knocked him down, and then hit him when on the ground. Mr Gamble had suffered a lot from the effect of the blows. His eye was blackened, his face cut, and he had also several bruises on his head and back. Evidence was given by prosecutor, Frederick Leatherswick, and Alfred Clarke. Defendant, in defence, said the prosecutor was employing the boy illegally during school hours, and the same thing had occurred three times during the last six months. On one occasion he sent to prosecutor, and asked him to allow the boy to come to school; but no notice was taken of it. He then sent a polite note but prosecutor took no notice of that either. On the day of the assault the lad came to school and had his dinner on the school premises, and Mr Gamble sent for him to go and lead the drill horse in the afternoon. The field where the boy was working was directly opposite the playground, and the other children could see him at work. The magistrates considered it one of the most extraordinary assault cases that ever came under their notice. They could not understand the defendant giving away to such a fit of violent temper and committing such an unprovoked assault. He would have to pay a fine of 40s and 12s and 6d costs.

'The magistrates' surprise at Higdon's behaviour shows how accepted the custom of employing schoolchildren was';[14] and though the fight was the talk of the village, it did little to stop the practice. One of the worst offenders during the first half of 1903 was Mr Bussens, who repeatedly engaged children to work on his bowling green. Bussens, as well as being a farmer, butcher and landlord of the Jolly Farmers, was also captain of the Heydon cricket team; an all-round sportsman, who happened to be 'not a very good sport' when he lost.[15] He had also been chairman of the old School Board in April 1902, when the Higdon's were appointed—a decision that he would come to rue.

The regular attendance of the children was no less important to Mrs Higdon than it was for the assistant master. Another local farmer, and the County Manager, Mr Williams, was served with a warning from the attendance officer because she had reported him for repeated offences. On the day of its issue, Williams would come down to the school house and taunt the mistress as 'Lady Higdon' and the master as 'Tom' in the presence of the assembled children—it may have surprised many that he did not end up with a black eye and a cut face.

Annie, who would become referred to as 'Jinny' for an unknown reason, was soon taken into the children's affection. There was nothing that she would not do for her children; no shortage of boots and clothing were gifted, and 'she was very strict over the girls' hair. If a girl's hair was dirty she would take her into the Schoolhouse and wash it'.[16] Tom was popular too, but he wielded 'the stick', and she was 'determined to educate her children, not as fodder for the farm or as slaves for domestic service, but as individuals who could build new futures'. She would not favour any child over another.

Mrs Higdon did like her children to be on top. 'The Wood Dalling children won the schools singing competition several times. The judges used to go from School to School, hearing the children sing and giving marks.'[17] As she could play the violin, harmonium and organ, she would give the children lessons and organise evening socials outside of school hours. She would not turn away from anyone in need, and was known to 'give any old tramp a good meal. There was one man who tramped the local countryside with a barrel organ and she would get him to play the organ while the children sang.'[18]

The boys and girls were kept separate in the playground, but all were encouraged to see the world beyond the limited confines of the village. In 1903, Mademoiselle Blanche, a friend from France, came to stay, and she was instructed to teach the children a little French. They were taught the hymn 'Forever With The Lord' and then sang it in the Salvation Army hut. As a French speaker herself, Mrs Higdon went so far as to petition the Norfolk Education Committee to make the teaching of French official, but they refused.

The world beyond was rapidly changing and she didn't want them to be left behind. Tom Barnes would fondly recall when she told the children about the Wright Brothers getting their 'flying machine' off the ground, when it was still 'news'. The Higdons would also share their own interests (and home) with the children, as the school logbook repeatedly testifies: '27 January, 1903: Mistress took first class for a winter ramble, leaving the school room at 11.15am and returning at 12.40. The ramble was very greatly enjoyed, the children taking a keen interest in all the objects seen and discussed and returning to school laden with evergreens, mosses, ferns, and stones.'[19]

The attendance issue continued to be a major point of dissatisfaction for the Higdons during the first half of 1903. Mr J.J. Bussens, chairman of the school managers (then in place temporarily, although he was to return to the role), was repeatedly reported as a frequent offender. While Mr Blades, the attendance officer who happened to double up as Clerk to the School Managers, seemed less than committed in his efforts to bring the particular offender to book—although he had recently up his game in his pursuit of the labourers' parents.

The relationship was to deteriorate from there. On one of his rare visits to the school in his capacity as attendance officer, he was to make a complaint about the registers. Possibly Mrs Higdon had marked one child present who was not. Whatever the minor error, Tom Higdon did not consider it worthy of making an issue out of and a blazing row erupted in front of the children. It all ended abruptly when the assistant master instructed Mr Blades to 'go and preach another sermon in the Chapel'.[20]

Tension between all parties rose during the summer over the much more serious concern of a whooping cough epidemic. Initially, the concern was all Mrs Higdon's. On 3 July, she had drawn the attention of Chairman Bussens to the absence of a number of children and he, not unreasonably, had deferred to Dr. Perry. Perry, a friend and contemporary of Rev. Vicars at medical college, was inclined to think the coughs were not whooping cough, and the school remained opened. Over the next two weeks the school was repeatedly opened and closed as cases were confirmed, as Annie had originally reported to the board. She had, as per her usual precaution, immediately sent home any children from families she suspected might be infected. After a full month of indecisiveness from the board, the school was declared closed until further notice. It remained closed until 28 September, but attendance on the day of the re-opening was only fifteen because it was unknown to the parents, and the headmistress only being acquainted with the fact by the arrival of the Chairman's children at 9 A.M.

Few buttercups were blooming in May of 1904 in Norfolk; by that spring a permanent frost had settled over the relationship between the Higdons and the school managers—but some heat was soon to rise.

Shortly before the end of April, Tom sent in his resignation to the Norfolk Education Committee. He had not tired of teaching but he had tired of the inadequacies of the school managers. Despite the managers' intransigence, and the long closure due to the epidemic, the Higdons had been officially noted by government inspectors as turning around the situation in the school. Personally, Tom was not intimidated by any of the managers, but was he really running away from the fight as he did?

Throughout their lives together the Higdons were a solid partnership built on a deep mutual love and admiration. Tom adored his wife to the point that, at one public meeting, he threatened to stick a man's head up the chimney if the individual continued to talk about her in a way that he disliked. Before the action was taken husband and wife, Headmistress and Assistant Master, clearly would have discussed the situation, and the decision was a joint one. Resigning in the long run would have only hurt them both. So why threaten to do so?

On the horizon in early May were elections to the School Board. Tom had until 20 May to withdraw his resignation and no decision was to be made by the Education Authority until after that date. After two years at Wood Dalling, the Higdons' opinion of the managers was so low as not to be measurable. Tom's resignation was a means, perhaps the only way they could see, of putting further pressure on the existing managers, and facilitating some degree of change.

It was more than coincidentally that on 2 May, Mr Blades, acting in his capacity as Clerk to the School Managers, wrote to the Education Committee to explain that 'both Teachers ignore the Managers altogether and are scarcely on speaking terms, with one exception, which is the late Chairman. There is a feeling that a change in both cases is desirable'. The managers were moving to seize their own change, although at the time this remained hidden from the Higdons.

The threat of resignation, if the intention had been to initiate some kind of favourable change in management, failed. On 4 May 1904, Mr T. Williams and Mr Gamble both became school managers. The current situation was discussed at the first meeting of the school managers, soon after the new members joined the board, and was recorded in the minutes:

17 May, 1904: The question of change of school staff was considered and a letter read from the Education Committee to the effect that Mr. Higdon had withdrawn his resignation as second teacher, which if he had not done so would have necessitated the withdrawal of the head teacher, after consideration it was agreed that the clerk write the committee to the effect that the teachers remain only on condition that Mr. and Mrs. Higdon acknowledge the office of the managers

and that in the future all communications to the head office be made through them and the committee be asked to write them a letter to this effect . . . It was thought desirable that the managers should often pay visits to the school. Check registers etc. and they were asked to do so.

Present: Rev.G.R. Vicars, Ward, Gamble, Williams, Cotterell, Jarvis.[21]

Whether the Higdons stayed or went was ultimately down to the Higdons, or post 1902 Education Act the Norfolk Education Authority, on the basis of any submissions from the managers.

Despite tensions, life went on. Farmer Bussens continued to employ children on his bowling green and to drill the fields opposite the school. Mr Blades was to inform the mistress that he had popped in to ask whether Mr Bussens had been illegally employing children, but he was out at the time, and as he couldn't ask, there was no case to answer. In June, Mr A. Williams did receive a 'warning' by the attendance officer but Tom's frustrations were so great that he was bursting to be recommended for the job of attendance officer. The Rev. Vicars was to even provide a recommendation:

Mr.T.G.Higdon has shown much interest and zeal in the attendance of the children at Wood Dalling School, and as he is a good cyclist, and has much knowledge of school work, I have great pleasure in recommending him for the post of Attendance Officer for the Flegg District. G. Raleigh Vicars, Rural District Councillor, Chairman of Wood Dalling School Managers & Parish Council.[22]

It was a near gift to the managers, who would have seen Tom leave the job as the second teacher had he been successful. As it turned out, both Higdons would remain teaching at the school for a further six-and-a-half years; a fact welcomed by both children and (most) parents alike.

The end-of-year (the teaching year) Government Inspector's annual reports were rather more restorative than a job change:

14 September, 1904: Attendance is excellent and the children are under good discipline. The teachers work with industry and energy. The progress of the work has been very much impeded this year by sickness in the village, and the consequent closure of the school from July to October. Arithmetic and Spelling will require much attention. Geography deserves praise. The Mistress had conducted a cookery class in her own house, and though no grant can be recommended, she is to be commended for her effort to give the older girls some instruction in this most useful subject. It is hoped that arrangements may be made for these girls to attend a cookery centre at Hackford. The floor of the school is an extremely bad condition and requires immediate attention. Infants. The Infants are taught in a sensible manner.[23]

The headmistress was to take the visits from the inspectors very seriously and she would prime the children so they were to be seen and not heard when they came visiting. But the teachers were doing a good job by all measures, and constantly going above and beyond their professional requirements. The only criticisms in the reports stemmed from the systemic failings of the School Board, and that left little room for manoeuvre for the managers, who were by now almost to the man personally opposed to the Higdons.

But little room for manoeuvre was not the same as no room for manoeuvre. Gamble and Williams were constantly looking to make life as awkward as possible for the teachers. Without being overwhelmed by the irony, the pair would regularly check over the registers for irregularities. They then moved to ensure that all materials for sewing work were procured through the Education Committee, as per a provided list. No word of thanks was given to Mrs Higdon for providing the school with her own Singer sewing machine for use by the older girls.

In December 1905, the managers then appointed Miss Kate Ward in the office of school cleaner. There were just two problems with the appointment; Miss Ward was the daughter of Mr W.H. Ward, the school manager, and she couldn't clean.

Her father, Mr 'Billy' Ward, was also the local blacksmith and was well known locally as a 'rough sort of bloke'. He was fairly well educated, and a member of the Wesleyan Reformed Church, but he was known to be cruel to the horses if he got upset. Around the village there were high expectations among many that any potential Ward–Higdon fisticuffs would prove to be quite the knockabout.

As it happened, both managed to restrain themselves from any physical bout, but the mistress began to record the inefficiencies of Miss Ward in her logbook: 'sweeping and dusting having to be finished by the children and teachers, fires inadequately made; daddy tried to wade in on his daughters defence.'[24] Eventually, this lead Tom to address a school managers' meeting, where he reminded them all that they were supposed to meet in the interests of the school, and not one particular manager. The private interference of the clerk (Mr Blades), as a friend of Mr Ward's, in the matter of the school cleaning was also protested against. Tom, at least, got to enjoy the quiet satisfaction of having the opportunity to refer to the attendance officer's own neglect of duty as he had visited the school only once in the past year.

Thereafter, there is frequent mention of visits made by the attendance officer and of his attention to specific cases in the school logbook—and the name of Mr W.H. Ward vanishes from all minutes of future managers' meetings, as the committee dismissed him for calling Mrs Higdon a liar at another meeting.

The unfortunate consequence of the affair was that December was not to prove an opportune time to have the managers consider plans for alternations of the school buildings. 'After considering them they formed an opinion that for the great outlay of between four and five hundred pounds the advantage and improvements would be inadequate as very little was to be done to the house, which is not at all satisfactory, this opinion the secretary was ask to forward to the E.C.'[25]

After the building inspector visited in September, the Headmistress had wanted to raise the issue of the much needed repairs in the school house at the managers' October meeting but had been given no notice of the meeting by the clerk. The chairman claimed that he had not been instructed by the clerk to do so, but the following day Mr Blades claimed it was no part of his duty to do so. The Higdons were not ones to let a snub go unpunished, and if the managers were not prepared to manage the school in the best interests of the children, then the Higdons would, as much as possible, just bypass the lot of them.

In the early weeks of 1906 the labourers across Norfolk were to assert their own increased spirit of independence. The campaign of resistance against the Education Bill had ushered in a 'period of intense political activity by Liberals and Nonconformists in the Norfolk countryside',[26] and with it a massive political awakening. Local factors, like wages, were to mix with the national factor—a decisive general election. The result was a landslide for the Liberals. In Norfolk every seat returned a Liberal, and in the two-member constituency of Norwich, the traditional balance was forever overthrown when a typographer from Chedgrave, G.H. Roberts of the Independent Labour Party, was voted in. Roberts had been a pioneering Socialist candidate, one of the first twenty-nine Labour members to be voted in. In 1894 the Norwich branch of the ILP had been formed, of which he was a founding member. He had also been president of the Norwich TUC and a School Board manager. Although he was elected to an urban seat, his rural village background made him a natural spokesman for the labourers in Parliament.

Across the county it had been a labourers' victory. But once the cheering had stopped life was not to be made easy; the farmers were after revenge. Men suspected of voting Liberal were sacked and blacklisted, with many losing their homes along with their jobs. The wave of general victimisation fused with the raised expectations created by the general election, to create the strongest need for a trade union since 1872. And it was to George Edwards that the labourers turned. Former members of Arch's union like Josiah Sage, began to write to him in increasing numbers, urging him to restart the union. At the age of fifty-six, he felt that the task was now well beyond his own powers, and he was not confident that the labourers would stick to the union—yet the letters kept streaming in.

'If you make the effort, I will make the sacrifice,'[27] Charlotte Edwards had told her husband as he mulled over the situation. It was enough to encourage George to take up the challenge. The founding conference of the new union was held on 6 June at the Angel Hotel, North Walsham, Norfolk. 'Upstairs in the "assembly rooms" on that Friday gathered a mixed bag of Liberal grandees and farm workers.'[28] Despite the success at the elections, the Liberals had no permanent organisation in the countryside to anchor themselves to, and the grandees in Norfolk and elsewhere supported the new union. Edwards made direct appeals for money from several prominent Liberals, including George Nicholls MP, Richard Winfrey MP and Herbert Day to pay for the event—they sent money and offered a commitment to attend. Many others present, like Josiah Sage, William Codling and Edwards himself, were survivors of the earlier unions.

The chair was taken by George Nicholls MP, and the resolution before the founding meeting was clear (and strongly reflected the Liberal Party influence):

> That this conference composed of delegates representing the agricultural labourers of the Eastern Counties take definite steps to form a union, the object of which shall be to enable the labourers to secure proper representation on all local bodies and the Imperial Parliament, protection from political persecution, and better conditions of living; and that a central fund be raised for organising purposes.[29]

Its general secretary was to be George Edwards, the president George Nicholls, vice president W.B. Harris, and the treasurer was Richard Winfrey MP. Other executive members included J. Binder, J. Sage, W.G. Codling, J. Bly, C. Holman, J. Stibbins and Herbert Day. The first branch of the new union was founded at Kenninghall by Josiah Sage. Both 'Comrade Joe' and Codling were soon dismissed from their work for being union men.

The time for debate was now over; a new union for the agricultural labourers had formed, and for the Eastern Counties Agricultural Labourers' and Small Holders' Union it was time to get organising.

# Chapter 8

# The Clatter and Clumper

## 1907–11

George Edwards was a little humpety-backed man, his body bent by childhood malnutrition and adult farm work. He kept his chin clean shaven and his moustache was a bit boyish, 'though his original and interesting face bore many and deep traces of the hardships that he had undergone all his life'.[1] He had started working on the land at the age of six as a 'crow-scarer', and was the man in Norfolk that the labourers had turned to in their need. Old George may have lacked unrestrained charisma and oratorical fire, yet he maintained an ability to induce an attentive audience, and an uncanny knack of getting people to undertake the necessary duties.

The new union had been moving forward with optimistic strides since the end of that year's harvest. By then, George had become a paid organiser and he would leave home early each Monday morning and head out into the villages. In all weathers he would trudge on, a 'spare figure bent over the handlebars of his bike'.[2] If only one measure was used to track the union's advance, it would be how far George could cycle in a day. If the first National Union had been built out of the chapels, then the new union was being organised from the saddle.

In the first quarter of 1907, a meeting was called at The Plough, Wood Dalling. The village had only two pubs, and Mr J.J. Bussens' Jolly Farmers was no place for union agitations. Tom Higdon arrived in good order but not early enough to get to talk to George Edwards beforehand. Some men were at the bar, but not Edwards, who, as a teetotal Primitive Methodist lay preacher, was not particularly comfortable holding meetings where alcohol was served.

In Tom Higdon's own account, after he had sat down, Edwards 'eyed' him a 'time or two'. No doubt, the tall, broad-shouldered school teacher cut a different figure to that of the local labourers. Before long Edwards went over to the door that led to the bar room and called out for the boys to come along.

Higdon commented:

Sure enough, the boys all came trooping in with clatter and clumper and filled the room. I shall never forget the faces of some of those men as they sat there, typical bearded Norfolk labourers. Their faces were so sad—some of them with families to provide for on twelve shillings a week . . .

There was no chairman . . . a chairman would have broken in too harshly upon Edwards' own quaint personality at that meeting . . . He spoke quietly and deliberately, warming up at times at the end of his argument. His address was simple and clear and spicy all through with quaint 'Norfolk'. His appeal to join the union seemed irresistible, and the men remained to join. I joined along with the rest, and felt I was doing what I had longed to do all my life, and I was pleased to see so many men joining.

The question of secretary arose. There was no volunteer, and by and by somebody suggested "the skulemaster". Edwards cast a steady, benevolent eye upon me at the same time and I responded heartily forthwith. He very kindly and circumspectly welcomed me and handed me the new branch books and put me into the way of keeping them.[3]

Within a short time, Tom would be heading out on his own bike to set up branches across South Norfolk. He would never take any payment for the work; money was no motivator for an ex-labourer serving the cause of the labourer.

The Wood Dalling branch of the Eastern Counties Agricultural Labourers and Small Holders' Union had barely been established, and the farmers were taking control of the one local body that could intervene with the employment (and home) of the Higdons.

On 16 May 1907, before Tom really had a chance to irritate the local farmers with his new union work, Mr J.J. Bussens was elected chairman of the school managers. Reverend Vicars' tenure as chairman had only been for an interim period, and the new chair was guaranteed to be a farmer, as all other members of the managers were farmers. Bussens was the natural choice to be chair, as he was, by 1907, one of only two managers that dared to venture into the school to see the Higdons.

The real problem with the farmers is that they practised class solidarity. The young Tom Barnes would grow up to be a farm horseman in the district and understood all too well how they operated. 'They always stuck together. You could hear them talking together at the markets. You'd hear one say, "How much are you paying your men for harvest?", "Six pounds ten.", "I'm only paying mine six pounds five. You ought to do the same. You're making it difficult for all of us. You're letting everybody down.'[4]

The existing divisions between the Higdons and the school managers were crystallising into a microcosm of historical farmer–labourer antagonisms—and the two sides were digging in.

The managers' meeting of the 16th was a planned regular affair; it was only to become noted because of the future events that would later transpire. After the appointment of a new chair, it was back to the usual agenda—dealing with Mrs. Higdon petitioning for improvements to the infrastructure of the school:

Repairs. Mrs. Higdon wrote calling attention to several things needing attention, which were considered and it was agreed that gravel be procured to level school yard, and that the clerk see Mr.Howard respecting the cleaning of gutters, repairing or altering chimney, etc., and the Messrs. Williams, Gamble and Manthorpe meet Mr.Howard to see what is needed to be done but any extensive alternations be referred to the E.C. who are expected to make alternations during the summer. This was proposed by Mr.Williams, seconded by Mr.Manthorpe.

The Clerk was asked to write to the E.C. calling attention to the defective construction of the chimney in the Infants' Room and asking that the Committee Inspector give this his attention.[5]

The minutes record, as only minutes can, a quite positive and engaged set of managers happy to get things resolved. But the decisions on any major expenditure were to be deterred to the Education Committee, though they had enough funds. And, along with the issue of the defective chimney, there had been a long-standing problem with the fire grates that had resulted in the rooms being inadequately heated over the winter. There is no evidence that the clerk ever wrote to the E.C. on the matter.

The day after the meeting, the mistress was again writing a letter to the managers in order to draw their attention to the 'bad state of the Girls' Playground, the Infants' door step, the smoky chimney in the Infants' Room, the smell from the drain outside the Boys' Playground door and several other matters urgently requiring attention for many years'.[6] Perhaps the Higdons were under the impression that a change in Chairman may have been a catalyst for action, or perhaps they just wanted to lay on further pressure—whatever the motivation, two weeks on and no reply had been received regarding the letter of 17 May.

Worst of all—or possibly not—there were to be no more managers' meetings between 16 May 1907 and 23 June 1908.

The Higdons were often accused of being totally incapable of accepting advice or guidance, and though they were both strong-willed individuals who sought to do what they thought best by the children, the accusation is not entirely fair or accurate. If the managers of the school were to go missing in action for over a year, then what could the headmistress do but run things as she saw fit? Many issues relating to the condition and running of the school had been consistently presented to the managers (including before the Higdons' arrival) and had not been acted upon. In light of that, what could a conscientious mistress do but to keep raising them? A logbook entry for 25 November 1908 reveals Mrs Higdon's openness to informed advice:

H.M. Inspector having advised freer exercises, such as dancing and games in lieu of certain 'drill' lessons, the mistress has immediately adopted this pleasant form of exercise for the Infants and a first display passed off very delightfully, the little arms and legs responding most successfully to the happy dancing of the 'The Keel Row.'[7]

Any accusation that the Higdons did not suffer fools in positions of power who served themselves and not the wider interests of those on whose behalf they were in said position to act, would certainly be a charge harder to refute. But there was one thing that even their fiercest opponents could not credibly claim, and that was that the Higdons were poor teachers. The 1907 end-of-year Inspectors' report was further independent evidence against such a suggestion.

Unfortunately, Mr J.J. Bussens was not a man to let another good government inspectors' report, or for that matter his own poor performance, get in the way of a personal vendetta. One year on, and the list of inadequacies that could be levelled at the Chairman of the School Managers had grown considerably, as had the head teacher's 'trouble and annoyance in the matter of obtaining the Chairman's signature for closing School for the regulation holidays, half-holidays, etc., and by his refusal to close when advised by mistress for Diphtheria ... refusal to sign Salaries Bill, failure to hold Managers' Meetings and neglect of matters of School Attendance ...'[8]

Tom Higdon even went on to report Mr Bussens to the Education Committee, after he called in at the school and 'used bad language towards him'.[9] A local inquiry was held in November 1908; no action was taken against the Chairman. Shortly afterwards, Mr Bussens made his own official reply by making three charges against Mrs Higdon:

1. Closing School without permission of Managers. (Tom Higdon was to state that permission had been obtained from Mr. Williams, which he was later to deny)

2. Ordering Coal without permission of Managers.
   (T.H: According to precedent of five years)

3. Being absent without permission of Managers.
   (T.H: Not absent at all on the date and time given.
   Total absence in 5 years = 1.1/2 days.).[10]

On 1 December 1908 the first enquiry examining the tensions between the Higdons and the school managers at Wood Dalling was conducted by the Norfolk Education Committee. The committee must have seen that the charges were without foundation. 'They said nothing to Mrs. Higdon about these charges after the Inquiry, nor to Mr. Higdon about Mr.Bussens' language . . .'[11] However, the sub-committee did hear 'unmistakable evidence of the way in which the Head Teacher could act and address the Managers' and decided that it was Mrs. Higdon's inability to work harmoniously with her Managers that was at the heart of the trouble. The committee report concluded:

1. The friction between Mr. and Mrs. Higdon and the Managers is so great that some of the Managers will not visit the School as they are afraid of the treatment they will receive.

2. The teachers attribute what they consider the enmity of the Managers towards them to the fact that they have charged some of the Managers with illegally employing children . . .

3. Mr. Higdon charged the Chairman with using abusive language to him and the Chairman denied this and said that it was Mr. Higdon who abused him.

4. The Managers said that the Teachers do not recognize them as Managers . . .'[12]

The committee admonished Mrs Higdon that she must treat her managers courteously and carry out their instructions if she was to remain in service of the committee. 'Another chance' had been granted;[13] the first farce of a Local Inquiry had passed.

The third charge levelled at Mrs Higdon, of being absent without permission of the managers, may not have been true on the date and time given but it was correct on another occasion. The Higdons had recently started to bring parties of London schoolchildren to the village for a fortnight's summer holiday. It was all arranged by them through a charity, and 'there would be two lots in a year, one lot would have their fortnight's holiday, and then they would go back to London and in a week or two another lot would come'.[14] Mrs Higdon would lodge them around the village, one here, two there, and the families received five shillings a week for each child. Up to fifty would arrive at a time, turning up at Reepham Station, from where they would be transported to Wood Dalling on the back of a horse and cart. On one occasion, Mrs Higdon was required to assist and was absent from the school for one hour without permission.

The Higdons, throughout, continued to arrange additional excursions and treats for their children, at their own cost. A Punch and Judy man would be brought over from Great Yarmouth; Magic Lantern (Annie's own) shows would be held in the evenings; Mr and Mrs Gibbs, friends of the Higdons from Reepham, would come and play piano and sing. Christmas was made particularly special, with visits from Santa, a Christmas tree and a present for everybody.

Much of the winter of 1908–09 was a bleak time for the Higdons, and nothing was to test their resolve as much as the repeated outbreaks of diphtheria that caused the death of three children. Epidemics of children's diseases were all too common, and Mrs Higdon was very particular about getting medical advice for her children and pressing for the closure of the school when she thought it necessary. During the initial outbreak the school was closed until 22 February, and then only reopened with some exclusions as a preventive measure. But one month later, another child died. Dr. Phillips was now the local attending physician, but another child that he was called in to examine on 28 May died the following week. More exclusions and visits by doctors followed, and in July the County Medical Officer attended after a number of sore throats were reported; the verdict was 'no infectious disease'.[15] On 7 July, another case of diphtheria was recorded.

By the end of July—after six wretched months at the school—the friction between the Higdons and the managers was bitingly acrimonious; something the Chairman seemed to be doing his best to accentuate. Mrs Higdon had sent a letter to the Chairman asking for a date of closure of the school for the Harvest Holidays. He did not immediately respond to that, but two days later he visited the school house to tell her that the notification cards for the Flower Show holiday had not been sent to him. Inquiries then made proved that they had been. The local Flower Show Day was an event that the headmistress particularly liked to engage the children with, and now for the first time in years no half-holiday was to be granted.

Next, the attendance officer, in his capacity as clerk—an individual with whom the Higdons had an ice-cold rapport— was sent round to inform the teachers that there would be a meeting in two weeks, at which there would be plenty of time to fix the date of closure for the summer holidays. At the end of July a supply teacher, Miss Lovelace, who had been covering for Mrs Seely (her absence probably related to pregnancy as she and her husband had eight children) left, leaving the school without an infants' teacher for the start of the following week until after harvest.

In light of the intransigence, and with diphtheria still lingering in the village, Mrs Higdon decided to write to the Secretary of the Norfolk Education Committee, asking if an earlier closure might be arranged. That very morning, the Chairman and Mr Williams had 'visited the School, tested the registers, remarked on the bad attendance of several children, and decided that no holiday should be given on Bank Holiday Monday'.[16]

On 20 August, after seven days' notice, the school was finally closed for the Harvest Holidays—such a short notification was not unusual for the time and one suspects that there was relief all round just to have got there.

Tom Higdon's work for the union had not stopped. He had been busy organising the local labourers' when not teaching, and had managed to bring about some small wage increases. In

1909, during the Harvest Holidays, he paid a visit to the veteran Joseph Arch, now eighty-three years of age and living in retirement in his old cottage at Barford. 'The agricultural labourers' movement owed a great deal to the fact that Arch possessed a cottage of his own. Had he rented one, it is possible that he would never have been allowed to do his work.'[17]

Tom's own life was to be eternally tied to the ebb and flow of the agricultural labourers' movement, and his family, like so many labourer families, owed much to Arch. His own contribution to its renaissance was just beginning, whereas Arch was the legendary figure that built it first time around from its infancy. Tom appreciated perfectly well the contribution that Arch had made, and was a true hero in his eyes. One can only imagine his delight and expectation as he travelled to Warwickshire to interview him for the union's new paper.

At the time of their meeting, Arch had married again, this time to the daughter of a Norfolk farmer. For his efforts to raise up the labourers he had repeatedly broken his health, and had been left effectively penniless, dependant on an annuity purchased by Lord Tweedmouth (Mr. Tom Ellis) and other influential Liberals. Now, in his twilight, and left with little to show for his years of endless effort and vilification, he felt abandoned and even a little betrayed by his class.

Biographers of Joseph Arch present the interview in full: a man, and a union leader, looking back on his life's work. Although he was a little embittered, and unfairly reliant on others for his survival, he could still take some satisfaction from the fact that he had improved the labourers' lot to a higher mark than what it had become by 1909. And a little of the old wit still sparkled.

We can only speculate on the informal chit-chat that must have surrounded the printed exchange. Tom had been raised in one NALU stronghold, and had been living in another— Norfolk—for the past seven years. How could the boy from East Somersetshire and Arch not have talked about the magnificent Ham Hill rallies, or perhaps characters like George Mitchell? Although the two men went on to have their own tensions—the most interesting chatter was probably left unwritten.

But because of the events that were to transpire in Burston, and the wider contribution Tom Higdon would play in the history of the second Agricultural Labourers' Union, the meeting captures a movement in transition but also its underlying continuity:

Arch, with old-fashioned peasant hospitality, immediately called to the kitchen for a bottle of beer and set his tobacco jar upon the table, and I should like to record here some of the answers made by Arch to the questions put to him by Mr. Higdon.

"Do you take any part in politics, locally, Mr Arch?"

"Me? No; I'm too old for that now. Besides, Parish Councils cannot do much—neither good nor harm. I have done a little for the village in my time. I can remember when the people in this village had no idea of freedom or liberty. I have taught the villages something of freedom. But my work is still done now, sir. My work is all done," he repeated sadly.

It must have been with a gleam of triumph that the veteran agitator compared the wages received by the farm workers in 1909 with the wages he managed to get for them in the 'seventies'.

"What is this new Labourers' Union they have there now?" he asked suddenly.

"You have heard about it, then?"

"A little; not much," he said rather sarcastically.

"I think its objects are similar to those of your own Union—better conditions and wages. It also takes up the matter of small holding."

"What are the wages in Norfolk now?" he next enquired.

"About 12s. or 13s. a week," was the reply.

"Is that all? Why," he exclaimed, "I got them up to 15s.,16s., and 17s. a week. They got it in Norfolk, they got it all down about here. They got it everywhere."

"The new Union had not done that yet," I said.

"Ah, we did then—in our Union," he said with evident satisfaction at the remembrance of the accomplishment.

"Could these wages have been kept up, Mr Arch?" I asked.

"Kept up? Yes. Why weren't they kept up? Because the Union went down—and the wages went down with it. The Union was wrecked. They broke up their Union and left me without a penny."

"You could do no more for them, then?"

"No; of course I could not. I stood by them to the last. I could do no more. If they had kept up their Union they would have been in a very different position to-day."

"You sympathise with the labourers still?"

"Sympathise with them? Of course I do! I shall always sympathise with them. What do they get for this harvest now?"

"About £6 or £7," I replied.

"We got it up to £8 or £9," said he. "But," he added, "it is a bad system of payment. It stands in the way of a better weekly wage. I always said it was a bad system . . . What strike pay do they give?" he asked.

"Ten shillings a week—lock-out pay. I don't think they believe in striking," said I.

"Oh, we did then," he exclaimed.

"You ordered a strike sometimes, I suppose."

"I don't know about ordering a strike. The men would go on strike themselves in various places—then they would come to me and I always supported them."

"Would you advocate strikes now?"

"Certainly. What else can you do to get wages up?"

Mr Higdon, mentioning old friends by name, was answered by Arch, with a touch of that dramatic fervour which used to set the heather on fire in country districts: "My friends are all dead."

When asked if he knew Gladstone, he replied: "Yes, dined with him lots of times. He was always very kind and friendly towards me. He was a great man—an eloquent man and a good man."

"From what I have heard about you from the labourers in Norfolk, you must have possessed some kind of eloquence yourself, Mr. Arch," I said with a laugh. "Was it that in you which got hold of the labourers so?"

"I don't know about eloquence," he said laughing too. "I used to talk to the farmers a bit, you know, as well as to the labourers," he added with a fascinating twinkle in his eye—which twinkle gave a glimpse of the old time power and personality of Joseph Arch.[18]

'Neither good nor harm'; Tom Higdon could not have disagreed more about the value of parish councils to facilitate change. Whether he challenged Arch over the statement is another matter. As the great man had been a tireless supporter of democratisation in Parliament, and spoke repeatedly in favour of the Parish Council Bill in particular, it must have been a little disappointing to hear that he was now, at best, so neutral about their prospects.

Tom, on the other hand, had been a Parish Councillor for over two years. If there was a problem with the councils it was not in the limits of their existing powers, but in the political composition of those that were predominantly part of them. Arch's real disappointment lay in the failure of the labourers to fully engage with the democratic process and thus take greater control over their destinies. With the next Wood Dalling Parish Council elections just over the horizon in the spring of 1910, Tom Higdon, ILP member, was soon to set to work on that.

For decades, Socialists in Norwich had been making various attempts to gain support in the surrounding villages. William Morris's Socialist League had from the late 1880s held propaganda meetings, and this 'work continued in the 1890's and 1900 with the Social Democratic and ILP holding village meetings'.[19] In 1903 a group of Clarion cyclists headed out to Aylsham to hold a series of meetings and distribute leaflets, and with it 'established a pattern of urban working men, usually artisans, with a sprinkling of labourers,' riding off 'on a Sunday into the villages to spread the gospel of socialism'.[20]

George H. Roberts' first election success provided the Norfolk Labour Movement with a boost in confidence that it could, and needed to, win the rural areas. By August 1908 Bill Holmes was appointed full-time organiser for the ILP in the Eastern Counties. He was to claim that 'the ILP had over

500 members in Norwich and that they were holding twenty meetings a week in "Norwich and District"'.[21]

From 1907–08 onwards, the objective of taking socialism to the rural labourer was a vital and urgent task. If it was not quite a planned strategy, it had certainly become a concerted effort, particularly after a series of articles by Bruce Glasier in the *Labour Leader*, and more significantly for Norfolk, in the months to follow, a series of speaking engagements. After the harvest of 1908, the ILP turned its attention to the labourers with a series of market-town and village meetings. Within the Agricultural Union, the issue of Labour Party affiliation was brought to the fore at the Annual Delegate Conference, and though that attempt failed, by April 1910 things were changing rapidly. It was not an immediate rejection of Liberalism, but an internal political shift was in motion.

With a parish election looming, Tom set to persuading the labourers to vote each other on to the council. What particularly infuriated Councillor Higdon was the council's habit of handing over the rents from some of the council cottages to pay local rates instead of spending the money on necessary improvements and repairs—the only way to reverse the situation was to have more labour(er) representation.

'The local knowledge of the Wood Dalling people, however, enabled them to see matters in a different light to that of the Committee's Local Inquiry,' Tom was later to write, 'and as soon as they had an opportunity of giving their verdict, which was at the Parish Meeting in March, 1910, they gave it in no uncertain manner.'[22] It was just three months on from December's inquiry into the 'friction existing between the Higdons and the School Managers', and the election would prove to be a proxy referendum on the competency of the managers and their class vindictiveness.

The *Norwich Mercury* reported the result on 19 March:

Mr. William Ward presided. There were eleven nominations for seven seats. The voting was as follows: John Cotterell 28, T.G.Higdon 26, Obie Cotterell 25, Mrs.Annie K.Higdon 24, Robert Ransome 21, Alfred Williams 19, Robert

Manthrope 17, Walter Pulfer 17. There was a tie between Messrs. Manthrope and Pulfer, and the Chairman gave his casting vote in favour of the former. These seven were therefore declared elected. Mrs. Higdon, however, thanked the meeting for electing her, and retired, her place being given to Mr.W.Pulfer.

Comrade Higdon's plans had triumphed; labourers had replaced farmers, and Tom himself had replaced Mr J.J. Bussens as Chairman of the Parish Council. 'And there,' as Tom was to write, 'the matter could have rested.'[23]

But nobody would be letting any matter rest. Mr Bussens still remained a school manager, appointed by the County Council. This was not guaranteed to continue, and thinking (though wrongly) that he was still a parish manager, at the last council meeting with its old composition, he attempted to get himself re-elected to the School Board, before the first meeting of the new councillors, who would obviously reject him. Tom resisted the underhand attempt, and after one hour of 'discussion', Bussens retreated blaming 'Mr. Higdon for jumping down his throats.'

That was still not the end of it; next, Bussens and his friend and farmer, Mr Williams, worked every avenue to get him appointed as a County manager, as Williams was himself. This time it was a success. 'Thus Mr.Bussens was reinstalled as a Manager and also as Chairman of Managers, and that in spite of the fact of his only being able to command three votes in the Parish Election. (3 besides his own vote, 4 in all.)'[24]

The move prompted much disapproval in the village as the appointment was considered to have defied the democratic votes of the parish and threatened further mischief. Allies of the Higdons had already picked up on mutterings between the farmer–managers that 'something was going to happen to that school teacher'.[25] The new Parish Council then met on 3 June and its new members were crying out on all hands against Mr Bussens' appointment; a resolution was proposed against it, passed, and sent to the Education Committee. Tom Higdon felt compelled to sign it.

Before June was out a letter was received from the Education Committee stating that a complaint had been made by the school managers that Mrs Higdon had called Mr Bussens, Mr Williams, and Mr Blades 'liars' at a managers' meeting. The complaint dated as far back as 18 March, though this was the first time that it had ever been raised. A distinct odour of finality was beginning to hang in the air; the managers were circling, and looking to strike any way they could.

With gross unfairness, it included the long serving infants' teacher, Mrs Seely. Again, by the end of June (before harvest, when the farmers would be too busy) a complaint was made against Mrs Seely, apparently by a parent, for undue punishment of their six-year-old boy. She had not been informed of the nature or source of the compliant, or in fact of any detail except that a complaint had been made. Unsurprisingly, Mrs Seely immediately asked for details and an inquiry; the managers would not grant one. Mrs Higdon was soon to conclude, 'having made the most searching inquiries and proved that statements complained of to be an absolute invention'.[26] The managers deliberately allowed the issue hang in the air for as long as possible. It would not be until mid-October that Mrs Seely was to receive final communication over the matter, and then told that there were no charges to be answered.

And then there was a dispute over the permission to order coal, and an argument over Bussens' failure to sign a form.

Tom Higdon's work with regard to the Labourers' Union was never directly referenced. But a strike of St. Faith's farm workers had begun in May, and in June, when Bussens and Williams made their complaint against Mrs Higdon, there was clear and considerable ire against labour union leaders going around. Tom was informed that a Mr Elliner, another farmer of Wood Dalling, went up to the Education Committee's office to make a complaint against him (though he did not officially do so), but he firmly believed that: 'he having doubtless had his say while he was up there, or, as someone has suggested, he would not afford the cost of the stamp.'[27] Mr Elliner was also noted to have said 'that "they" would find Mr Higdon a job with more work and less pay.'

On 17 July 1910, because of the 'further friction between the School Managers and Mrs. Higdon a second enquiry was instituted by the Norfolk Education Committee. With some chagrin, she was to note in the logbook on the 21st that; "Headmistress absent one hour this afternoon, it being supposed necessary for her to grant an interview to a representative of the N.U.T.".'[28] It is unlikely that Mrs Higdon considered it a valuable use of her time, but there was no ignoring the situation. Six days later the inquiry was held at the school. As well as the three men of the Education Sub-Committee, six school managers and the attendance officer were also (ironically so) in attendance and, just in the nick of time, her NUT representation made it along too.

The charge against Mrs Higdon was that of calling the chairman of the managers, one other manager, and the attendance officer liars. Tom insisted that she did not call them liars but that in defending herself at the meeting in question had characterised their charges against her as 'lies'. According to his own account, published as *The Burston Rebellion*, Tom was scornful of the whole incident:

> The usual farce of a Local Enquiry, adopted by the Norfolk Education Committee, followed. The NUT lawyer, K.C., arrived a few minutes before the Enquiry commenced, and engaged himself with sending off a telegram about another case. He then spared a few moments to speak with Mrs H. for the first time as to the line of defence to be pursued, which line was to be by way of apology.
>
> 'Apologise for a word I never uttered!' indignantly exclaimed Mrs. H.
>
> 'Whom do you suppose the Committee will believe,' inquired the K.C., 'your Managers or you?'
>
> Mrs. H supposed as the K.C. seemed to suppose.
>
> 'Then don't you think you had better admit that you used the word, and I will explain and apologise for you?' Was the 'kind' advice of the K.C.
>
> 'I did not call the Chairman a liar,' said Mrs. H. looking at the lawyer pretty steadily.
>
> 'David said "All men are liars",' argued the K.C.

'Then I am glad I am not a man,' said Mrs. H., 'and I would not make myself a liar even to make the Committee believe me.'

An Impossible Woman and a Hopeless Case!

For the sake of truth and conscience Mrs H. could not possibly agree with the lawyer, however advantageous to herself it might have been to do so.

Apology being the only thing in the mind of the K.C., Mrs H. had brought witnesses to prove that the statements and accusations of the chairman which she had referred to as 'lies' had been aptly and none too amply described by her as such. The K.C., however, did not call these witnesses, but contented himself with lamely trying to 'smooth matters over', by no means ever hinting that the chairman had, or could, tell lies. The result was that the charge against Mrs H. was returned as 'fully proved'.[29]

As a consequence of the continuing friction, the sub-committee was to 'find it undesirable for the teacher to remain as Mistress of the School',[30] and so on 2 August 1910 Annie Higdon was asked to send in her resignation 'as the most prejudicial form of removal'.[31] It was not for anything but the alleged use of the word 'liar' that Mrs Higdon was being asked to send in her resignation, which she refused to do. She was dismissed and given three months' notice. Tom's own dismissal was to come the following week, when he received a month's notice to terminate his employment.

In an attempt to salvage their jobs, but more importantly their lives, in a community of which they had been a part for eight-and-a-half years, Annie, who was under pressure from all sides to do so, expressed her 'since regret for my lack of discretion in addressing some of the managers of Wood Dalling school in a discourteous manner'.[32] Few words would have been harder for her to write; it was effectively admitting the charge, but the compromise of her principles was a measure of how much they desired to stay in the village.

The managers had no intention of being as forgiving as the headmistress was contrite. Their teaching posts had already been advertised in the press, and at the regular managers' meeting on 15 December, several applications from teachers were presented. Keen to not to end up with a Mrs Higdon mark two, the clerk was directed to write to the Education Committee asking that an all-male team be appointed. On that the E.C. was not listening, and went on to appoint Miss Smeeton as the next mistress. Two more were to follow; perhaps the fact that three mistresses were appointed in quick succession after Mrs Higdon is an indication of the difficulties of the job and the working relationship with the school managers.

The dismissal caused great indignation, but the Higdons were not done yet. All the parents except three (two farmers and Billy Ward, ex-manager and blacksmith) petitioned the Education Committee to reinstate them. The two school managers nominated by the Parish Council protested strongly and wrote to the committee 'resigning their position as Managers as a protest against what they describe as the "scandalous treatment which Mrs. Higdon has received"'.[33]

George Edwards attempted to bring the case up at the County Council, but it was ruled out of order by the Conservative-Farmer Chairman, Sir William Folkes. Letters of protest from the Parish Council and from the local branch of the Agricultural Labourers' Union were sent, but to no avail. Tom was particularly contemptuous of Mr Ager's, the NUT's co-opted member on the Education Committee, weakness to fight on his wife's behalf.

'All these efforts, however, have not been entirely without success,' Tom was able to write; first he 'was to be offered another appointment; then, after a time, Mrs. Higdon was to be offered one as well; and then they were to be both offered an appointment together in the same School at the same salaries as they had been receiving at Wood Dalling.'[34] In the confidential Education Committee report there was to be no mention of the protests made, simply that 'in light of Mrs. Higdon's apology' the Education Committee decided on 17 December to endeavour to transfer the Higdons to Burston.

# Chapter 9

## Two Pedestrian Strangers

Shortly before dusk on 31 January 1911, Tom and Annie Higdon walked into the village of Burston, coming from the direction of Diss. They had done the four or five-mile tramp from Diss Railway Station, as the train from Norwich had taken them through Burston Station without stopping, as was often its habit. 'Pretty as the village is,' Tom would write, 'with its windmill, its bridge over the stream, its pink-washed cottages, its slopes, patches of green and plantation, and with, of course, its less beautiful spots of housing dilapidation and its church without a tower,'[1] they took little notice of the scenery at the time.

They were carrying just one case, and they were to commence work in the morning. The rest of their 'goods' had not yet arrived. The NUT had offered payment for their removal but the Higdons felt unable to accept the assistance over the union's failure to adequately defend them against the Wood Dalling managers. Yet, 'it was not for want of money, however, that the said "goods" had not been packed and despatched in a business-like respectable fashion and the inhabitants of Burston duly impressed by their arrival, but rather for lack of real heartiness of interest in this new appointment on the part of this pair'.[2]

As they walked past 'the sweet bit of common which the land-grabbers of bygone days had unwittingly left',[3] they were to come across the village postman, Harry Ellis. He was then lodging at his brother's cottage, and when he got home later that evening, he was to inform his eleven-year-old niece, Violet Potter, that her new teachers, 'the Kingdoms', had arrived.

Tom's own reminiscences of the couple's arrival, written five years later and two years into the school strike, are not infused with retrospective joylessness for propagandist effect, but reflect the genuine bitterness and reluctance the couple felt towards taking up their new posts. Along with the termination of their employment, they had lost their home of eight-and-a-half years. The Norfolk Education Committee had given them no alternative option; and to be fair neither had the Burston School Managers any choice but to accept them as their new teachers, 'as their names had been sent as "recommendation"—which practically amounted to an instruction'.[4] At the foot of his application form, Tom had noted that he did not really want to leave Wood Dalling. Annie had also requested a 'friend in the Wood Dalling district to write to the Burston Managers a report of the troubles with a view to preventing the appointment under any false colours, and thus preventing it altogether'.[5] All to no avail.

On the last day of their given notice, the Higdons had seriously contemplated stopping at the County Education Office in Norwich with a view to getting the arrangements cancelled. 'They had the heart knocked out of them,' Tom was to admit, 'and it was quite a "toss up" . . . whether they would go on to Burston at all or not'.[6] And so it genuinely was.

The labourers' pint mugs may not have been frothing too merrily at the Plough, but equally they were yet to be raised at the Burston Crown Inn. The Higdons were soon to discover that the living conditions were worse than at Wood Dalling. Much of the housing stock was in extremely bad condition; roofs leaked and suffered from damp; large families had to live in two-up, two-down cottages with all the associated grime and lack of privacy. Comrade Higdon could easily identify the root cause: '. . . there were no Labourers' Union Branches anywhere in the district, and, consequently, the wages were lower than in the Wood Dalling district. Landlord, parson, and farmers held sway over the Burston area in many respects more completely than in the district left behind. Parson and farmers ruled the Burston Parish Council'.[7]

Although Burston did not have an existing branch of the Agricultural Union in the village, there were a number of labourers who had belonged to Arch's union. Among them was John Potter, who was to serve the new union both as treasurer to the Diss branch and secretary to the branch at Burston, when it was formed. Other families in the village that included veterans of the NALU included the Garnhams and the Lings, both of whom would become ardent supporters of the Higdons in their struggle to bring about change.

But it was the state of the school that was the new teachers' immediate concern:

> The school premises were ill-lighted, ill-drained, badly heated and wretchedly ventilated. Thus there was much radical wrong, which for very conscience sake, as well as for all practical and healthful reasons, must needs be faced. Indeed on looking round, and looking back, it seems as if to this place Mr. H's had been providentially directed for these very special purposes. Persecutions would again arise, of course. But then—"Blessed are they which are persecuted for righteousness sake, for theirs's is the Kingdom of Heaven." The Kingdom of Heaven–Yea, surely—within, and beyond—beyond. Not at Burston yet awhile.[8]

First, change was soon to arrive at the church—Reverend Charles Tucker Eland was on his way from Felsted, Essex. At the 'Old School' on Wednesday 8 March 1911, his parishioners made their farewell presentations. Over £30 had been raised by the churchwardens and the gifts to the vicar and his wife were generous—for Charles Tucker, a handsome roll-top desk and for Mrs Eland four solid silver candlesticks. After acknowledging their kindness, the school children then presented Mrs Eland with a prayer book and Bible.

Rev. Eland had led the Holy Cross Church for nigh on twelve years, and in many ways it was the right parish for the right clergyman. The parish's sprawling patchwork of small farms was home to a population of over 40 per cent farmers and agricultural workers, but the village had links to Lord Riche, who founded the public school there in 1564. As a centre of education, the village's Old School employed ten schoolmasters, a matron and a domestic servant, all of whom lived-in at the time that Eland was appointed.

As well as the Old School, the parish contained Felsted Preparatory School, with live-in staff and boarders. Its Schoolmaster was a Church of England clergyman. Close by lay Elwyns Boarding House, again with live-in staff and a CoE master. In total, twenty-four live-in schoolmasters, teachers and assistants resided in Felsted.

When the Elands moved into the vicarage the household consisted of Charles Tucker, Mary, six-year-old Arthur, and eighty-one-year-old mother-in-law Martha Collingwood— and two teenage domestics. But Eland's tenure as the parish vicar was nearly cut short when he found himself in a tabloidesque 'hot under the dog collar situation' over an embarrassing court case. In the winter of 1904, Eland was called before Mr Justice Buckley at the King's Bench division, in a case brought against him by a Moorgate Street stock and share dealer to recover £190 5s. 6d., balance of an account of shares sold. The prosecution arose over equity transactions dating from October 1902 that commenced under the so-called cover system for 150 Union Pacifics, and later fifty more. The following year, Eland, the defendant, was put on the Stock Exchange system of account. For Mr Justice Buckley, the only question was whether the transactions amounted to a 'gambling' or an 'ordinary' transaction.

When the mid-June account became due Eland had called the plaintiff–dealer and told him that he was selling other securities in order to pay for the two hundred shares. In the end the reverend failed to pay, and the dealers sold the shares on the market at a loss of £190. Becoming, financially, a little more technical, counsel submitted that when the defendant went on the account system, the transaction was outside a gambling one, and so Eland must pay the loss sustained on the sale of the shares.

When Eland was called to the Bench, he declared that the transaction was a gambling one: that the dealer never suggested his going on the Stock Exchange system of account, that he never contemplated taking up the shares. His Lordship, in giving his judgement, was to state that 'this was a story discreditable, in his opinion, to both sides'. The broker had issued circulars inviting persons to gamble in stocks, and Eland on receiving one had 'fell to it and gambled'.[9] The decision was a question of dates as to whether it was a gambling transaction, or became a real bargain for the sale and purchase of shares. Eland had received notification of the alternation between the parties, and had sent a telegram saying, 'Please place me on the account system', and that fell on a date making the transaction a real transaction and Eland liable, and therefore liable for the loss. Judgement was made for the amount claimed, with costs. Less satisfying was the newspaper coverage in the local *Essex County Chronicle*: 'Vicar of Felsted's Deal in Union Pacifics.— Strong Remarks By Mr. Justice Buckley.'

Aside from the embarrassment, and the repayment of the outstanding balance (which he could quite easily afford), the court case did nothing to prevent the reverend from cementing himself as part of the local village hierarchy. In the run in to the 1906 election, he would act as presiding host to the local Conservative candidate. On 21 April 1906 the *Essex Newsman* was to report that: 'At a meeting of the managers of the Felsted and Rayne Council Schools, the Vicar of Felsted, the Rev. C.T. Eland was elected chairman in the place of the late Mr. E. Brunwin.'[10] In November of the same year, Eland is noted in the Essex press for his contributions as a member of Felsted Parish Council. Though not Chairman, he was a dominant voice in proceedings and is invariably recorded being the proposer of resolutions. The local big issue of that day was the 'Felsted Water Question': where the Local Government Board was proceeding against Dunmow Rural Council to compel them to carry out a water scheme. After a member of the council attended and explained the position of affairs to the Parish Council, Eland proposed the unanimously accepted resolution:

> That in the opinion of this Council, the Dunmow Rural District Council would be acting in the best interests of the parishioners of Felsted by accepting the offer made to them

by a water company to provide a water supply for the village of Felsted, and this Council respectfully urges the Local Government Board to sanction the acceptance by the District Council of such offer.[11]

For the Vicar of Felsted, the interests of his parishioner–constituents was of prime concern. Oddly enough, although he always appeared to be working for his parish dwellers in the snips of press that survive, it did not stop him losing his seat at the next elections, held in March 1907—where he was to finish thirteenth out of fifteen. After eight years as the vicar, the rebuff must have hurt. In the edition of the *Essex County Chronicle* that carried the election results, coincidentally next to the Felsted results, was a report on the court against Dunmow Rural Council taken by the Local Government Board over the village's water supply. The application had come about in consequence of the Rural Councils' refusal to carry out a scheme which would have made all of the parish pay for the provision of a water supply for Felsted only. The King's Bench sided with Dunmow, thus allowing it to continue with its plan to supply water through the agency of a private company, who would recoup themselves by the use of consumption charges. Eland had publicly aligned himself with Dunmow Rural Council, and had picked the winning side in the court's decision, but the issue had been a contentious one and had dragged out the delivery of a water supply by years. Whether that was enough to turn people away from voting for him is unlikely. It is more likely that larger sections of the electorate shifted away because he had not been shy to display his Conservative-supporting credentials in the 1906 General Election, in a rural constituency where many of the labourers swung towards Liberalism. It would not be the last time that Reverend Eland would taste electoral defeat.

The barb of local democratic reform may have stung, but it was not enough to upset the settled and genteel existence of the established rector and his family. He was to take comfort in being elected as a representative member on the Braintree

Secondary Education Committee the following year. And anyway, it would soon be time for the Elands to depart the parish for three weeks to Villars-aur-Ollon-with-Gryon, Switzerland, for a 'summer chaplaincy on the continent'. The annual excursion was arranged through the Colonial and Continental Church Society, and by 1907 it had become a favourite fixture in the family calendar.

In Burston, a new rector, Rev. E.J. Doherty, MA, was inducted on Sunday 22 December 1908 by the rector of neighbouring Dickleburgh. Doherty had previously served the parish of St. John's Plumstead, inhabited by the Royal Arsenal workpeople, where during an incumbency of twenty-five years he raised about £6,000 for a new church and vicarage. After a hymn, the Rector of Dickleburgh said a few words before leading the whole congregation out into the churchyard to witness the induction ceremony. 'The new Rector, after the words of induction, entered the Church alone rang the bell to signify to the parishioners that he was now their Rector.'[12] Just two years later it would be repeated for Rev. C.T. Eland. It would prove unfortunate timing for the Higdons, as Rev. Doherty was to receive the report into the troubles at Wood Dalling, and seemed to be sympathetic to the teachers.

On the Friday of the same week of his induction, Rev. Doherty attended his first engagement at the Burston Council School, where he distributed the attendance prizes presented by the Norfolk Education Committee. After an obligatory short programme of songs and recitations, the thirty-four prizes were distributed; 'the number was fairly good considering that the school year began with diphtheria, and two or three families were absent during the first month or two.'[13] The family names of the prize and certificate recipients were a 'who's who' of village identity: Ling, Moore, Leeder, Garnham, Wilby—though no Potter. Gilt medals, along with prizes, for three years' perfect attendance went to Florrie Wilby, Harold Long and George Durbidge. Young George would become more than peripheral local character—a brute who would die notorious, but also a tender Higdon supporter.

Rev. Doherty barely had time to unpack his travel trunks at the rectory before he was away from Burston to lead a ten-day mission at St. Philip's, Lambeth. The *Diss Express* was happy to relay to his parishioners in Norfolk that 'Large congregations attending the services were visibly impressed with the earnest appeals and spiritual methods of the missioner, who not only moved hearts, but also instructed the minds of his healers'.[14] The mission also included Rev. Canon F.C. Smith, MA, Canon Missioner, Diocese Sierra Leone whose own involvement had been facilitated by the Colonial and Continental Church Society. Doherty's involvement may well have been driven by noble intent and passionate belief, but it was an early indication that his own heart was possibly more into the mission, rather than his parish—and it would not be too long before the intrepid missionary would be away again.

It was far from the case that Rev. Doherty would become an absentee rector, but he was to be away on missions and other preaching engagements an almost eyebrow-raising amount. Still, when he was around, both the reverend and his wife engaged in all the usual aspects of parish life, including activities in the school. On the day of his induction, after prize giving and congratulating the headmistress, Mrs Green, on the children's excellent rendering of their songs and recitations, he offered to provide a prize in each standard for proficiency in Religious Knowledge, although the cheers raised at the end of the August term tea party provided by Mrs Green were genuinely heartier. The expenses for the tea were met from the entertainments of Easter, and the attendance was augmented by some former scholars and London children. The Londoners were personally paid for by Mrs Doherty, and came to the village via the same scheme that the Higdons were involved with in Wood Dalling.

Mrs Green had been the Headmistress of Burston Council School since late 1904, and was warmly appreciated for her teaching and work in general. Her relationship with Doherty was convivial and warm, but it was also to be short-lived. In December 1909 she was obliged to resign her post 'owing to a very serious illness'. The teachers, scholars and friends, 'being anxious to show their appreciation,' the *Diss Express* reported, 'presented her with a handsome marble clock suitably inscribed'. The end of Mrs Green ushered in a series of new head teachers before the Higdons arrived at the school two years later.

Before the close of the first decade of the 1900s, hearty cheers were something that the rector (and school manager) of Felsted still got to experience.

With help of many kind friends and the teachers two monster Christmas trees were provided, adorned with over 200 presents . . . The Chairman of the Managers, the Rev. C.T. Eland, presided, and the annual prizes for attendance and merit granted by the County Council, were presented by Mrs. Eland. Mince pies, oranges, sweets and plum caked were distributed at intervals, and in addition each child received a handsome present. The Vicar expressed the pleasure it had given the audience to see the children so happily entertained, and pointed out the immense amount of work that had been accomplished by Mr. and Mrs. King and the staff.[15]

It was the *Essex Newsman* that would announce the following December that Felsted would be getting Rev. E.J. Doherty as its new vicar. The reasons for Doherty and Eland swapping parishes in an 'exchange in livings' is unknown, but the Essex paper's handsome profile, including portraits, also happened to mention that 'while rector of Burston, Mr. Doherty has been engaged in preaching parochial missions in various parts of the country, and before taking up the work in Felsted is going to Canada to preach a mission in Toronto'[16] Mrs Doherty would naturally be accompanying her husband, to give addresses at meetings for women. It would not be the last time the Dohertys were away from Felsted on a mission.

And so, on 30 March 1911, Rev. Eland was instituted to the rectory and parish church of Burston. By then, Eland was in his mid-fifties, a father of three teenage children, and employer of three domestic servants to cater for them. With the appointment he acquired a large rectory of over twenty rooms and a handsome stipend of £495 a year. 'He also had 54 acres of glebe land [land owned by the church which was part of the parson's living and could be rented out by him], which produced £86 yearly.'[17] It did not take long for the Burston villagers to notice Mary Elizabeth Eland's passion for large hats, but at least they could be afforded.

It was clear that much was going to depend upon the new rector. Shortly after his arrival, the reverend was elected to the Board of School Managers. On his first visit to the school, according to Tom Higdon, he 'peremptorily demanded the Registers, to inspect them. This was the Headmistress's first and only intimation of Eland's appointment as a Manager.'[18] Although he had no cause to complain about the registers, it was still an inauspicious start.

How much the new rector knew about these 'active propagandist Socialist Teachers' is anyone's guess, but without question Tom's reputation as a union agitator had preceded him to Burston. The new headmistress tried to have a productive, if not a congenial, relationship with the new rector, and he was often invited into the school to give religious instruction. Annie would also help out at some of his 'talks' by operating the magic lantern (which was her own) but it was to little avail.

Annie initially attended Reverend Eland's church services, but finding that she obtained little satisfaction from his ministrations, she 'therefore absented herself and went to Chapel—which as mistress of a Council School she had a perfect right to do'.[19]

But their absence from church did not pass unnoticed or uncommented upon: 'The place of the Schoolmistress is at Church, and the children with her,'[20] Eland was reported as asserting to one of his parishioners. At the time, about half the children at the Council School were from Nonconformist families and attended the village chapel. Tom, as a lay preacher, went around preaching in the local chapels, and so:

The parson soon had his grievance—the non-attendance of Mr. and Mrs. H at church. Frequently he reminded them in the course of conversation that they ought to go to church "for the sake of example". He often complained to the teachers, too, of the godlessness of the villagers—the inference being that the teachers should set them the example of attendance at church. He seemed however more inclined to drive people to church than to lead them there, and this driving propensity of his they unmistakably resented. He also raised the burial fees; said the Chapel ought to be shut up; likewise said and did many unpopular things . . .[21]

The rector was far from unusual in his attitude. Though interestingly, a 'curious dispute over a mission hall' in Felsted, which arose in the autumn of 1912, reveals Eland to have had a much more positive relationship with the Nonconformists in his previous parish. A dispute between representatives of Church and Chapel blew up over the right to possess the mission hall. The hall had been built by public subscription, by the former Rev. Stanley, on land given by the Church. Nonconformists had been using the space ever since, and holding non-sectarian services for thirty years. Its ownership had never been clear, but it was widely believed that it was not Church property because it had been paid for by the people. The new parish vicar, Rev. E.J. Doherty, who had held services there, had gone on to demand the key as he wanted to put a Church Army man in procession. It was handed over under protest, because a paper had previously been signed with Rev. C.T. Eland to deliver up the key on demand—a shrewd move, as it was to turn out for the new vicar, but that was most likely unintentional shrewdness. The press coverage detailing the debate over its ownership reveals Eland to have had an open and constructive dialogue with the Nonconformists; he had happily sanctioned the hall's continued use by them rather than shut it up.

Most village parsons expected to play a leading role in school affairs. Eland was no exception, but 'let it be clearly understood,'

Tom Higdon asserted, 'that a Rector or Vicar is not an ex-officio manager of a Council School—yet he may as well be, it seems'. Nevertheless, 'it soon became apparent to the H's that they must proceed cautiously',[22] and they decided to try not to open up a rift. Yet the school was ill-lit, ill-drained, badly heated and badly ventilated, and something had to be done about that.

The Higdons were immediately liked by the rest of the village. Just as at Wood Dalling, the villagers were impressed by their kindness and generosity, and a Burston boot club was soon inaugurated. 'She would send out and buy children boots,' boot recipient Tom Potter would recall, 'and if they came to school and their boots were leaking and this often happened, and she would send out and get them a pair of boots, buy them a pair of boots, I've seen her do it, many times'.[23] And the memories extended well beyond footwear: '. . . on a Thursday, once a fortnight, she used to send out and get ginger biscuits . . . and the whole school would have a treat.'[24] Tom and his brother George were not born until the early days of the school strike in 1914, and were christened Thomas and George in honour of Thomas George Higdon.

Tom's sister, Violet Potter, was eleven in 1911 when the Higdons first came to Burston, and was instantly taken by both of them. Mrs Higdon was a teacher of patience and caring, who:

> . . . was very particular with the poor little children, who had a long way to walk to school, they didn't go in buses then you see, and they'd come to school and their clothes would be wet through. So we're not supposed to have a fire until a certain date and she took it upon herself to have fires lit, I think there was a fire at each end of the school, and dry the children's clothes so that they shouldn't have to go home with wet cloaks . . .[25]

And for such practices, the managers would accuse her of extravagance.

Mrs Higdon's own Oliver typewriter and sewing machine were once again put to use to train the older girls in how to type and sew. Soon, 'she organised a flower show in the school playground . . . for the children to bring, you know, what their fathers could send, turnips and things like that,' Violet vividly remembered; 'we had prizes sometimes and of course the children, when they got a prize . . . went home as happy as could be.'[26] Many extracurricular activities were undertaken outside official school hours, in the schoolhouse.

For the first Christmas in Burston, and though no cook herself, 'she bought a book, and sent eight of the older children, into the Schoolhouse to make plum puddings for Christmas', then on the last day of term, 'she found all the stuff and boiled them in the Council School copper and then the children, they had to bring their own plates and when it was the Christmas holidays they all had this slice of plum pudding'.[27] Annie knew that treats were ill-afforded by many of the parents who were sick or unable to work because they had lost their jobs, and so would pay for them from her own pocket. Such treats were always going to warm the affections of the children, but the official HMI reports, as always, were positive; 11 October 1912:

> The present Mistress has had charge of the School a little over a year and a half, and its condition is now very promising. A good tone prevails; the scholars take pride in their work, and the work done in some of the subjects is very creditable. Mental Arithmetic is well above the average, and the written Arithmetic of the 1st Class is generally praise-worthy. The singing and much of the drawing are good, and needlework is being taught on sensible lines. On the while, the infants and 1st Class children are making more progress than the scholars in the middle section of the School.[28]

Tom was four years' Annie's junior, and although they had much in common from when they first met—both had a love and respect of the natural world and a commitment to social justice driven from an applied overlapping of theological interpretation—he still learned much from his wife (although, apparently, not foreign languages). Although he would go on to make a sizeable contribution in multiple arenas, the difference in their respective employment fortunes, because of the level of formal education acquired when young, remained acute. While it would be harsh to say Tom was always in his wife's shadow as a teacher—partly as Tom was driven more by wider political objectives, while Annie (though sharing the same political outlook) was all about the school and the children—he had only ever held the role of assistant, despite repeated applications. As events would demonstrate, and others soon enough conspire, Tom was forever to be the bridesmaid and never the educationalist bride.

But in the summer of 1912 there would be one more attempt—what would turn out to be his last shot at attaining his own position as a school master. The interest of the application lies not in its failure, or Tom's apparent personal ambition, but in the testimonials given at the time. On 10 June 1912, Clerk to the Managers Mr Frederick Starr wrote of Tom:

> I have much pleasure in testifying to the good character of Thomas George Higdon, whom I have known for the past eighteen months, when he was recommended by the Norfolk Education Committee, by whom he had been employed for more than 8 years, to the Burston School Managers. He is under my frequent observation, & I have found his conduct, & bearing, exemplary in every respect. He is zealous, & industrious, punctual and energetic. He is also tactful & held in esteem by parents. He holds his present appointment with his wife; the discipline and organisation of the School is all that can be desired. I have much confidence in recommending him for the post he seeks.[29]

In June of 1912, even Mr Charles Fisher, school manager and farmer, was approached and happily stated that:

> I think Mr. Higdon most eligible for the post he has applied for, since he had been in Burston, which is about a year and a half, I have known him to be temperate in his habits, very

energetic, and one to be relied upon to do his duty . . .
Parents and children think well of him in this place, as I do,
being a local farmer and School Manager, and am confident
he would serve you well.[30]

References may well have a degree of gloss at the best of
times, but apart from Reverend Eland's irritation at the
Higdons' absence from church, there is nothing to indicate any
strong undercurrent to see rid of Tom from the Council School.
He had continued to be just as active for the Labourers' Union,
and in 1911 became an executive member in the role of trustee.
But his activity, for the most part, was confined to outside of
the parish. It would still be two years before the Burston branch
of the union was founded, and then only after the school strike
had begun. It's not that it all passed unnoticed by the local
farmers—it just had yet to come home.

# Chapter 10

# The Road to Revolution

Had Tom confined himself to teaching and cycling around outside of the parish on behalf of the union, he and Annie might well have been left in peace. 'For two years they steered a clear course—like the wisest of the wise people of the world—except in the matter of their staying away from Church.'[1] But when presented with it, he just couldn't resist the chance to take hold of the local levers of power, even though he knew it was poking a sore bear with sharp stick. In March 1913 came the local Parish Council Election, and the approaching event was arousing some interest among a few labourers and railwaymen in the village. 'They had been talking about the need for some old footpaths restored, bridges repaired, housing improvements, etc.'[2] But the old Council of Farmers had not, and would not, do any of these things, and so one evening Mr Noah Sandy went to the schoolhouse.

Noah Sandy was the only man on the council who was willing to take the matter up. A smallholder, bricklayer and builder, he was the only non-clergyman or farmer who otherwise dominated proceedings—and importantly, his own livelihood was not dependent on their patronage. Noah had come to ask the 'skulemaster' whether he would like to be nominated for the council. He appeared unaware of the details of Tom's involvement on Wood Dalling Parish Council. Tom's thoughts immediately flew back to those days when, 'with the aid of the labourers there, he routed the farmers and set up a Labourers' Parish Council'.[3] He related the event to Noah; he told him how the new council soon stopped the farmers' old game of handing over to the district rate the rents of some parish cottage property, and instead spent it on necessary improvements and long-overdue repairs. Noah—otherwise 'Noar'—blinked his eyes knowingly. 'A rare type of old rustic Radical was "Noar",' Tom thought; he had tumbled involuntarily to the 'new Labour idea' but 'what is more, showed a ready willingness to give the whole revolutionary plan a trial at Burston'.[4]

Thus, Mr T.G. Higdon was once more enthusiastically engaged in Parish Council democratic reform. 'A line of conduct' somewhat opposed to his more recent world-wise inclinations, which were still tinged with the burnt odour of past consequences, but completely in accord with his conscientious principles. This was now no time for discretion—he straightaway set about getting a sufficient number of labourers nominated (along with Noar and himself)—for this perfectly legitimate action; almost certain disastrous results would be brought upon himself and his wife. One can only conclude that, for the headmistress, her own belief that principle should trump self-interest was as resolute as ever.

The schoolroom was unusually packed out at the annual parish meeting, 'much to the surprise, apparently, of the old Council of farmers, who sat ceremoniously at the front, waiting for their re-election, or rather waiting the moment to re-appoint themselves'.[5] Their confidence was to be proven misplaced.

The meeting was opened by Mr Alfred Johnson, Chairman of the old Parish Council, who announced the appointment of a provisional chairman for that meeting as the first business, whereupon it was unanimously agreed that Mr Brown, of Dickleburgh (Clerk), should act in that capacity. There were fifteen nominations to fill the seven places. 'The names of candidates were read out alphabetically', yet Tom was suspicious as 'those of the "Cabinet", so to speak, as represented by B. E. F. J. thus happening to come before the letters of the Labour men, such as the P's, the W's, and the S. Of the Labour Party H. only came before J'. Any alternative course of proceeding was not suggested, but the vagaries of the candidate's surnames added to the unfolding drama. A reporter from the *Diss Express* was seated quietly at the back of the room:

One elector was anxious to proceed with the voting to the minute by the clock, but was told by the Chairman that the meeting was five minutes late in opening, and that the quarter of an hour allowed for receiving nomination papers had yet not expired. The same elector caused some amusement later on by persisting again with his point. Another elector, who turned up none too early with a roll of nomination papers, declared it to be illegal to commence the meeting before eight o'clock. The following names were read out for election: Messrs. A.Johnson,—Ellis, R.Ford, Arthur Boulton, Noah Sandy, Rev. C.T. Eland, John Potter, Ezra J.Potter, Wm, Wilby,—Burdett, Walter Child, B. Prentice, W. Carter, H. Witherley, and T.G.Higdon. Mr B.Prentice, not being present, his nomination was withdrawn, and the Chairman of the meeting ruled Mr. Child disqualified by less than a year's residence in the parish. The names were then taken alphabetically and voted upon by a show of hands, the result being as follows: Messrs. T.G.Higdon 17, W.Wilby 16, John Potter 16, Noah Sandy 15, Ezra J.Potter 15, R. Ford 14, H. Witherley 14, Rev. C.T.Eland 12,—Burdett 11, Arthur Boulton 10, Alfred Johnson 9, W. Carter 9, Harry Ellis 6. The seven standing highest in order on the list were therefore declared elected and, there being no demand for a poll, the electors dispersed.[6]

On the platform, surprise took the form of consternation as it became clear that most of the earlier candidates were failing to reach two figures. 'Surprise and consternation were plunged into the silent rage of anger and despair when the figures leapt up to their zenith at H and sat down again almost to zero at J; J being the initial letter of the Chairman of the old Council.'[7] The game was up for the old 'Government'. Burston had been supplied with a new one, but one not entirely devoid of an 'Opposition'.

Later that evening, the Crown Inn was crowded and the chatter ebullient among the labourers. A great wave of excitement diffused its way around the village, and in the subsequent days the news spread into other villages and Diss newspaper men were despatched to the parish trenches to cover what one paper would call a 'revolution'. The defeated Old Guard gathered to confer with and console one another. The blame for what had happened was generally attributed to Mr Higdon: 'It was the "Skulemaster" who had done this thing',[8] but Tom never thought he would get clean away with his outrageous usurping of the established order—he understood only too well that the clergy and farmers had their own masonic solidarity; 'there was to be constant deep rumblings and vivid forked lightnings in the air until the storm actually burst right over the "Skulemaster's" head—and over the head of his wife'.[9]

Reverend Eland's manner with the Higdons may never have been warm, but it underwent drastic cooling after the election. His own two allies, the churchwardens, 'swore a little more dreadfully than usual and were to be overheard proclaiming that, 'we must get rid of that _____ Socialist'.[10] Eland did not directly aim for Tom, but instead instigated a backroom campaign against Annie as the headmistress of the school. Tom was wanted rid of, and just as at Wood Dalling, as the positions were joint appointments, the dismissal of one would result in the departure of the other.

Eland immediately took up his old grievance of the Higdons (that is, the headmistress's) non-attendance at church. On one Sunday, after the couple had taken in a morning walk, and settled back in at home to read, the rector, 'fresh from the Creed, the Ten Commandments and the Churchwarden's dribble, paid this second after-service visit to the Schoolhouse'.[11] Eland had come to talk long and pertinently upon the importance of churchgoing. Tom considered that he evidently desired to say something more, much more, but was unable to 'to get it all out'. Tom left it to his wife to fully discuss the merits and demerits of churchgoing. Eland left, leaving a rather uncomfortable impression behind him as to what was the real nature of his visit.

But the reverend was soon gifted a golden opportunity. A few weeks after the Parish Council elections, it became necessary for the Norfolk Education Committee to appoint a new Board of School Managers. 'The Education Committee

1. Etching of Aldingham Hall, Lancashire, by J. McGahey (1870).

Council Schools, East Pennard, Somerset.

2. East Pennard Council School (1905).

3. The young farm labourer Tom Higdon, in Huxham (1890s).

4. Anne Katherine Schollick around the time of her marriage (1896), and Thomas George Higdon (1916).

5. Burston Council School before the school strike (1913).

6. George Edwards (seated far left) with George Roberts MP, speaking at a rally in Norfolk.

7. Agricultural rally in Burston with George Roberts MP. The Higdons are seated on the platform to the left (1913).

Burston Vicarage.

109504.

8. The Burston vicarage (1914).

VIOLET POTTER.

9. The leader of the strike: thirteen-year-old Violet Potter.

10. Higdon supporter Harry Ling and his soldier son, before his eviction from the glebe land.

163

April 1st   Only 6 senior children have been
          present morning & afternoon
          & 19 Infants in the morning & 7 in
          the afternoon. The others are on
          strike

April 2nd   The same 6 senior children present
          There are no Infants this morning
          Ernest Hasler, Infant, came in at
          10 o'clock

April 3rd   Only 8 children present.
          School closed this afternoon for
          Att. Holiday.

April 6th   Still only 8 chs. present.

April 8th   School closes today at noon
          for Easter holiday & reopens
          April 20th

  ..       Only 8 children present yesterday
          & today

April 20th  School opened today with
          9 chos
          Miss Barbara Samples,
          uncertificated Jr member of the
          Permanent Supply Staff
          commenced work as Assistant.

11. The school logbook records the beginning of the strike (April
1914).

12. The Higdons and parents outside Diss Magistrates (April 1914).

13. Day Four of the School Strike (April 1914).

14. 'A recitation lesson on the Green' (May 1914).

was authorised to nominate five members, the sixth being the nominee of the Parish Council. The committee consulted the local J.P., Mr. Keppel, and he, in turn, consulted Eland.'[12] Eland suggested himself, his wife, his friend the Rector of Shimpling, the latter's churchwarden and his own glebe tenant. All these were duly elected, and Eland was appointed Chairman. The Parish Council's nominee was Mr Witherley, a farm labourer, but with two parsons and a parson's wife on a body of six school managers, stormy days looked to be ahead for the teachers. It was all too clear to Tom that Eland had brought about a successful counter-coup and 'the line was thus made clear for the carrying-out of this Anti-Socialist, Anti-Labour, Anti-Parish-Council-Election, Anti-Higdon business, and the false, unfounded, lying and hypocritical complaints against Mrs. H. were soon being sent up to the Norfolk Education Committee'.[13]

Soon, but not yet. First, it was time for the Elands to depart the parish to Switzerland for the annual 'summer chaplaincy on the continent' excursion. 'A clergyman's holiday has two good points,' Casey, the fiddle playing Higdon support, was to write in his account of the strike. 'It gives both him and his congregation a well-earned rest.'[14] No truer words may be said, but during Eland's absence to the continent, an epidemic of whooping cough had the audacity to enter the village. The headmistress had to act fast, and she did so in the way that she always had in such circumstances; she moved to close the school. With Eland away, she at once sent over to the other reverend school manager, the Reverend Millard (Rector of Shimpling and vice-chair of the Local Managers Committee), and after consultation, the headmistress decided to close the school for a week. Millard signed the notices and made an entry in the log to that effect. Mrs Higdon's prompt action had helped limit the spread of the disease, but after Eland's return, the Managers Committee informed Mrs Higdon 'that the committee took a very serious view of her having closed the school without permission'.[15] Clearly, Reverend Millard must have kept his head down, his eyes diverted and his tongue still at the meeting where the matter was discussed—but the letter to the headmistress also generously informed her that 'the managers will now let the matter drop'.

Eland appeared to have let matters drop, but only until November when he discovered that Annie was again lighting fires without permission. He saw an opportunity and he pounced. Without discussion with either her, or his fellow managers, he wrote to the Norfolk Education Committee protesting that she complained about too many faults in the school, and she had acted against the school managers' instructions. The Education Committee decided not to act immediately on Eland's recommendations. The building inspector's report did show the school was damp and that substantial alterations were required before the drainage system could even be described as satisfactory. Instead, Mr Ikin, Assistant Secretary to the Norfolk Education Committee, was despatched to give Mrs Higdon an official warning. 'A surprise visit is the most modern form of torture,' Casey was to comment. 'In the olden days they always brought you something. To-day they try to take everything you've got.' His surprise words to Mrs. Higdon were, 'What is wrong between you and the managers?'[16] Mrs. Higdon could only reply that she was not aware that there was anything wrong.

Ikin's visit was the Headmistress's first intimation that something was stirring, and that in light of the complaints made to the Education Committee, the managers had been asking if they would 'kindly remove Mrs Higdon to a sphere more genial'.[17] The visit was followed up by a letter on 29 November which also acted to remind Mrs Higdon:

> ... that this is the second place in which you have come into conflict with the managers ... The Committee have decided that the managers' instructions are to be obeyed, and as they have instructed you that the fire is not to be lit, I am to give you directions to obey these instructions. I trust there will be no further friction.[18]

But the old method of fire lighting still prevailed—Eland had realised that his complaints had been too slight to bring about Mrs Higdon's dismissal and that more friction, not less, was required. At the school there were two Barnardo's children, Ethel Cummings and Gertie Stearness, who were being fostered by the unpopular Mrs Philpot. She 'received a certain sum of money from Barnardo's each week for the upkeep of the children and this was paid out to her by the Rector, who was the Barnardo's local representative'.[19] Mrs Philpot claimed, in part, that her girls had witnessed one boy's 'rude' behaviour in the playground, when he was said to have exposed himself.

On 23 January, the rector then wrote to the Education Committee what Tom Higdon called 'a most remarkable letter, grossly untrue, and absolutely full of unfounded charges':

Dear Sir,

At a meeting of Managers held on the 22nd inst., at which all but one were present, I was requested as Chairman to bring the following particulars before your Committee.

Since the appointment of the Headmistress about three years ago, the Managers have willingly acquiesced in several structural alterations and additions to the School building and teacher's house to meet her wishes and have always treated her courteously, but upon the installation of the new heating apparatus, which efficiently heats the School, they felt bound to refuse to allow the fire to be lighted in the open grate. This was apparently much resented and the Managers' wishes were ignored until they appealed to your Committee and you wrote the Mistress a letter under the date November 29th on the subject. Since receiving that letter the Mistress has been most discourteous to the Managers, both in the School before the children and outside.

On December 10th Mrs. Philpot, the foster-mother of two little girls, aged eight and nine respectively, from Dr. Barnardo's Homes, had occasion to write the Mistress in reference to the rude behaviour of some boys in the School and indecent conduct of one in the playground. These charges the Mistress denied and accused the little girls of lying and being corrupters of the School. The Managers met and requested the presence of the Mistress but she did not appear. They interviewed Mrs. Philpot and the little girls and were satisfied that they spoke the truth, so instructed the clerk to write the Mistress to that effect and that children were to return to the School after the holidays and were to be treated as the other children, and also that should there be any further complaints they would be reported to your Committee. Notwithstanding these instructions, on the re-opening of the School on the 5th inst. The Mistress brought out these girls before the whole School, cross-questioned them and kept them in during playtime, day after day, with the object of making them contradict themselves, wrote letters and telegrams to Barnardo's Homes concerning them and Mrs. Philpot with the view of having the children removed.

The Managers have gone into these charges and find they are without any foundation. Under all these circumstances the Managers feel at loss what to do and ask the Committee to hold an investigation and they consider this constant haranguing the whole School on this unpleasant subject, most tactless and detrimental to its tone and discipline.

Owing to the insubordination and rudeness of the Mistress there is no esprit de corps between her and the Managers and they find it impossible to work with her, so respectfully ask that she may be transferred.

What is most remarkable about the rector's correspondence is not the falsehoods enclosed, but more what it failed to mention—Mrs Philpot had apparently alleged (to the rector) that Mrs Higdon had beaten the girls with a cane—a 'surprising charge to bring against a woman who was widely known to be a pacifist and averse to all forms of violence'.[20]

Mr Higdon reminded the Rev. Eland that the little girl who had made the complaint about rude conduct had only been admitted to the school one day before these tales were started by her. Mr Higdon then reminded the rector that upon the girl being questioned she had said it was in the school she had come from where she had seen these things.

Mr Higdon also reminded the rector of the particularly unreliable and unsatisfactory character of the other girl— the girl with whom this new girl had come to stay. He also gave proof from the registers that the boy complained of was not present at the school when the rude conduct was said to have taken place, while all the school children and teachers knew quite well that the mistress had not punished the girls at all, but that she had only questioned and admonished them upon their false stories about the boy. She had in fact sent for the boy's mother, who came to school and saw and heard her boy completely vindicated by the girls themselves, who turned upon one another, each accusing the other of hatching the story.

Later, 'the girls themselves, when questioned at School freely confessed that the boy had not been rude to them,' according to Tom, 'and that they had not been beaten by the Mistress. They said they were told to tell these stories and that they were afraid their "mother" would beat them if they did not. All the assembled School heard this confession ... They also made this confession to the infants' teacher, Mrs. Ling, when speaking to her alone.'[21]

The confession of the Barnardo children appears to have been very unpalatable to the rector; though neither Eland, nor any representative of the Education Committee, would ever visit the school to hear it. He also instructed the children not to answer any further questions the Mistress may put to them. Irrespective of the substantive truth, Eland was seen to do his best to make them fly—he was seen to visit Mrs Philpot's cottage frequently, and went round to other homes in an attempt to get more parents to back her complaints. Mrs Philpot took to relating the blood-curdling stories of abuse by the headmistress to the mothers of the village. But Mrs Philpot was the one known to beat the children in her 'care'.

In an exercise of attempted rebuttal, the Higdons decided not to let the allegations go free of challenge. The girls were living in no better than insanitary hovels, and they wrote several letters to Dr. Barnardo to recommend that the children should be removed from Mrs Philpot's care. In one letter Tom stated that Ethel Cummings was mentally and morally defective, and a danger to the school. In another, it was suggested that the Philpots were unsuitable hosts for the children because of the foster-father's youthful 'unnatural crime with an animal in a field'. As it was, Barnardo's Homes did not send any representative to investigate the charges or conditions of the children—Instead they sent the Higdon letters on to the rector.

But a rector–chairman of the School Managers must do what a rector–chair must do: 'enquiries'—but no real enquiry, according to Tom Higdon.

> A clear day prior to one of these Managers' Enquiries, at which it was found in Mrs. H's absence—she being absent under doctor's certificate—that there was "good ground" for the complaints of the Barnardo foster-mother, Rev. E. called at the School and, failing to see Mrs H., saw Mr H., to whom with much mock gravity he related the Barnardo foster-mother's story about what he alleged to be the rude conduct . . . and what he described as Mrs H's ill-treatment of these Barnardo girls by severely caning them.[22]

Mrs Higdon felt bound to appeal against the 'untrue and unjust decision of the managerial farce', and the enquiry by the Norfolk Education Committee that was to follow was brought about at her own request. Two afternoons—on Monday 23 and Friday 27 February 1914—were given over to it. Both the Higdons were still members of the NUT (Mrs Higdon's and Mr Higdon's membership numbers were 44,784 and 41,534, respectively. Annie was eventually made a honorary member of the East Dereham Association in 1915.), and accordingly they consulted the union, who asked the committee for an enquiry, but only after warning that it would be held at her own risk. Having previously defended the Higdons at Wood Dalling, the NUT only reluctantly agreed to provide legal assistance.

Initially, the union sent down a representative, Mr Peggram, to persuade the Higdons to come to terms with the employers. As his train moved off from the platform at Burston, he called out to Mrs Higdon that she should 'keep smiling on the Managers'. A letter was then sent back to her, which she was supposed to send on to the Education Committee assuring the committee that she had not punished the Barnardo girls 'excessively'. A frustrated Tom would write:

> She had not punished them at all, and had assured Mr. Peggram so; she therefore, of course, refused to send this letter. She simply could not send such a letter and thus diplomatically admit herself in the wrong, contrary to the facts, in order that she might be forgiven for what she had never done. This kind of thing may do for the NUT; it would not do for Mrs H.[23]

The Norfolk Education Committee sent down three councillors to hold the tribunal: the sub-committee was composed of Sancroft Holmes, Esq., JP (Chairman of Norfolk County Council, landlord, farmer and former Tory Parliamentary candidate for Burston); Mr Jessup. CC, JP (Tory farmer) and Mr Goldsmith, CC (a Liberal farmer). They all lived in the Burston district, and 'in the eyes of these gentlemen, Labourers' Union agitating was bound to be a crime'.[24]

The charges against the headmistress were: 1. Discourtesy to the Managers; 2. Punishment of the two Barnardo's children; 3. Writing letters of complaint against the foster-mother to the Barnardo's Institution; 4. Insubordination, rudeness, and lack of 'esprit de corps' shown by the headmistress towards the Managers. Throughout the inquiry Annie was ill and did not put in an appearance but was represented by the NUT standing counsel, Mr H. Lynn.

Before the enquiry began, Mr Cooper (the NUT Lawyers' clerk) visited Burston to collect evidence. He was said to be delighted with the signed statements obtained and seemed confident of victory; 'A Beautiful case! A beautiful case!' he was said to have exclaimed. And at Monday afternoon's hearing, he showed some spirit and 'did not do at all badly'. Tom thought, 'The Sub-Committee then found that the alleged 'Discourtesy' was 'very slight', but that a 'very serious view' was taken of the caning of the Barnardo children.

> Mr K.C., however, easily cleared Mrs H. of the "Fire Lighting Contrary to Instruction" and of the "Rude Conduct" allegation, and apparently established the view that the alleged "Discourtesy to Managers" was very slight. Had he not asked for an adjournment of the enquiry but finished the job off that afternoon, he might have scored other goals. But the President of the Enquiry, Mr Sancroft Holmes, it seems, could not remain, so the adjournment asked for . . . was granted.[25]

Things appeared to be going quite well, but whether Tom ever believed that the outcome would be favourable is questionable. 'The Committee have made up their minds to dismiss you' Tom was told by Herbert Day (County Councillor, member of the Norfolk Education Committee and then Treasurer of the Agricultural Labourers' Union) in the days ahead of the enquiry. Day, initially was to be no friend of the Higdons' cause. He refused to contemplate that the allegations against Mrs Higdon could possibly be false, and went on to repeat the slanders. What was more, Mr Day deliberately talked as if Mrs H. had gone from school to school in Norfolk quarrelling with the managers at each place. His lack of solidarity extended as far back as the Wood Dalling affair when he had declared that he could see no difference between calling the managers' statement 'lies' and calling the managers' themselves 'liars'. It was then with great satisfaction that on 12 February 1914, Tom Higdon was elected to replace Herbert Day as treasurer of the Union.

Eland, now seeing that the case was not going well for him, called on Norwich solicitor, Mr Reeves, to act for the school managers. On the following Friday, when the sub-committee considered the allegations of Mrs Philpot, the NUT counsel (from Tom Higdon's point of view) badly mishandled the case. Mr K.C. and the managers' lawyer were actually seen chatting merrily in the school playground before entering the enquiry on the Friday. As Tom happened to cross the playground, counsel was on friendly enough terms to introduce the Chairman of the Norfolk County Council and President of the Enquiry to him—the defendant's husband—a handshake of the hangman.

A number of Mrs Higdon's witnesses waited outside the schoolroom all Friday afternoon, ready to give evidence as to who was more likely to have given any weals on the backs of the Barnardo children. The NUT counsel would fail to use any of them. The witnesses were apparently being held back for a future slander case. After the enquiry Tom was quick to state to counsel that: 'I hope you will get the slander action forward as soon as possible'; the reply was a firmly non-committal, 'Oh, I don't know about that yet. I have not yet received instructions from my Committee'. No slander case was to be actioned by the NUT.

Months later, in November 1914, Tom seriously contemplated taking action for slander himself. He went onto pursue the potential for the case with the union solicitor in Norwich (although any action was to be an entirely private matter). The key passages of the solicitor's correspondence were enough to permanently deter the Higdons from embarking on the course of action:

> In dealing with the Slander attributed to the Rev. C.T.Eland we are upon different ground. Mr. Eland occupies a responsible position and could probably be made to pay damages and costs that might be recovered against him and therefore there could be no objection on financial grounds to making him a Defendant. When we come to other grounds we are compelled to recognise the points already alluded to, that there has been a general dispute in the village of which the alleged Slanders are merely a small portion. At the same time we incline to the opinion that Mr. Eland had overstepped the mark . . .

... We feel constrained to add that our sympathies are entirely with Mr. and Mrs. Higdon, but we should be very foolish if we were to allow our sympathy to run away with our judgement. Experience proves that when there is quarrelling going on between two individuals or among a number of individuals Juries are not disposed to attach any importance to defamatory statements made in the course of the quarrel, although if those defamatory statements have been made under more peaceful circumstances the same Jury might have been willing to award damages.

If Mr. Higdon were a man of means we should then not advise him to commence proceedings. If he should be possessed of small savings we should be still less inclined to advise him to take action ...

The rector barely had witnesses himself; 'two old women, one of whom was the mother of several illegitimate children—seven they say. The other was the Churchwarden's washerwoman who had felt herself bound to attend the Enquiry when told to do so.'[26] Though completely superfluous to the case, knowing absolutely nothing whatever about it, and seemingly unconcerned in any way, it was the best the school managers could muster. But Mrs Philpot, having lost heart after the Monday session, was heard on the final day of the inquiry shouting, 'I'm not dead yet! I'm not dead yet!' After, 'lamenting the fact that she had been forced by the Rector, against her will, to go on with this business',[27] she had clearly enjoyed an uplift in spirits; the contributing factor was not obvious to anyone observing the hearing.

As the Higdons expected, the case went against them: 'That two respectable teachers should be hounded out of house and home simply upon the testimony of a poor Barnardo waif,' Casey would comment, 'who privately denied what she publicly confessed, excusing herself by saying "she would have been thrashed by her foster-mother if she had not said so"—seems beyond belief.'[28] The Higdons had been condemned unheard, Tom equally with his wife, over statements made by him in a letter to Barnardo's. Yet, prior to the enquiry he had been given to understand that there was no complaint whatever against him, and that he was not required even to attend. Trivialities and farce oft lead to tragedies and injustice; the sub-committee concluded:

1. That the Head Teacher had been discourteous to the Managers.

2. (a) That in view of the direct conflict of evidence with respect to the caning of the Barnardo children, they are not able to give a decision on this matter; but they are strongly of opinion that there is no evidence at all that the girl (E.C) is mentally and morally deficient, or a danger to the School, as stated in the letters of the Head Teacher and her husband.

   (b) That, in their opinion, these children are well treated and cared for by their foster-mother, and that the children are not afraid of being beaten by her.

   (c) That, in their opinion, the communications sent by the Head Teacher and her husband to Dr. Barnardo's Institution were not warranted by the facts of the case.

The Sub-Committee, after most carefully reviewing the whole of the evidence, advise: That it is to the interest of elementary education in the village that the Head Teacher should seek other employment with as little delay as possible. That no punishment book having been kept in this School by the Head Teacher prior to this occurrence, she be directed faithfully to keep such a book.

As the main charge, the 'caning' of the Barnardo children, had effectively collapsed, the sub-committee had made what they could of the other minor allegations. That was despite, on the Monday afternoon session, it being agreed that the 'discourtesy' to the managers was slight. 'The letters written by the Higdons to Dr. Barnardo's Homes, asking that body to investigate the conditions in which their children were fostered in Burston, were inadmissible evidence.'[29] They were forwarded on to Reverend Eland, 'who was the organisation's official paymaster to the foster-parents of Burston',[30] and Eland had produced them at the enquiry without warning and the Higdons had not been allowed to substantiate them. The letters were irrelevant and should not have been introduced. There is no reference in the findings to the 'Fire-Lighting Contrary to Instruction' charge, or the excessive 'fault-finding' of Mrs Higdon that had previously provided sufficient justification for an application for her removal. It was Mrs Higdon's alleged acts of discourtesy, as at Wood Dalling, that were the prime reason for her dismissal. 'It appears that Mrs. H did not bow to Miss E., the Rector's daughter, as she whizzed past her on a bicycle one day during the Christmas holidays,' Tom was to list; that Mrs. H. had given Mrs. E. a 'cold reception' one afternoon when the latter visited the school in her capacity as manager, and that Mrs H. did not reply to Rev. E. when he passed her in the road one day and said, 'Good day.'[30] (Mrs Higdon was at the time buying vegetables from an itinerant greengrocer and had her back to the roadside as he passed.) To be added, was the accusation that when called to a managers' meeting, she had entered the room without knocking and sat down without greeting them.

It was all over, as far as the sub-committee was concerned, and that it should be stated in their findings 'that the Head Teacher should seek other employment with as little delay as possible' was assumed to be enough to be construed as an irrefutable request. The Higdon's did not respond.

A month on from the last session of the enquiry and the annual parish meeting was held in the Council Schoolroom. The atmosphere was somewhat terse, and among the parishioners and electors present were the Rev. Eland and his two churchwardens. First on the agenda was the Charity Accounts (Eland was Chairman of the Burston Charity Commission), which he was there to present. Immediately after his statement, Tom began a forensic line of questioning on who exactly the Charity Commission men were and how they were appointed, and for how long. Three of the five turned out to be Eland and his two churchwardens, and the rector had to admit that he thought they were appointed for life. In response, Tom said that other people of the present generation would not have much chance then! Finally, after asking if there was any written constitution of the committee, and nobody being able to provide clarity, it was proposed that the Charity Commission should be written to for information.

If Eland was made uncomfortable over the scrutiny of the charity, the second, and only other, item on the agenda, was to send him into silence. Next up was a discussion on the proposed dismissal of the school's teachers. Some of the rector's supporters present objected on grounds of illegality, but this was overruled by the chair, Mr Noah Sandy.

Before the discussion was entered into, John Sutton, Primitive Methodist lay preacher at the chapel, read a long statement on behalf of the school teachers, yet the press failed to report one word of it. Speaker after speaker condemned the situation as outrageous and unjust. Tom allowed his supporters do the talking. Mr W. Wilby proposed, and Mr G. Durbidge seconded the resolution:

That this annual parish meeting of the electors of Burston here assembled, having heard the complaints which have been made with a view to obtaining the removal of Mr. and Mrs. Higdon from the School, believe the said complaints to be false, unfounded and untrue, and such being the case we protest strongly against the proposals for the removal of these teachers, which have during the past three years given us, and all the parents of the children attending the School from the two parishes of Burston and Shimpling, the fullest and greatest satisfaction in the conduct of the School and in the education and general treatment of the children; and we, the electors, parents, and residents of Burston, earnestly appeal to the Norfolk Education Committee not to accede to the request contained in the letter of Rev.C.T. Eland on January 23rd.

The rector, chairman of the school managers and named target, remained passive throughout.

The resolution was considered at a meeting of the Norfolk Education Committee a few days later. At the full meeting, the communication from the Burston Parish clerk was read out, on the request of Mr J. Sancroft Holmes, and a point of order was made. The suggestion made was that the matter might be better dealt with in the first instance by the Staff Committee, because being a very important matter, to 'thrash it out in public would be an unwise thing'. The general opinion was that the sub-committee had already gone into the matter much more fully than the Parish Council meeting had done. Interestingly, it was already noted that the decision of the sub-committee (chaired by Sancroft Holmes) had caused a great amount of unrest in the village, and that the only thing that could come of furthering the discussion was more unrest. It was thought better to stop that rather than prolong it. Holmes felt compelled to state that he was very sorry that the case had to be brought up, 'for he had never dealt with a more unpleasant one'. The meeting then resolved itself in the committee (staff), and the matter was discussed at some length, in private. They were to be unable to find any grass long enough—more unrest was not far away.

A few days after the receipt of what Tom referred to as this 'Seek Other Employment' document, and two days after the parish meeting, the Higdons received two days' notice to leave the school on 31 March.

With the teachers' official dismissal becoming widely known, a general outcry among the villagers began. The first public signs took place on Burston Green the same evening. During the day a printed bill in large type had appeared around the village calling for the meeting, 'To consider the School question and the steps which shall be taken'. The man behind the so-called 'midnight meeting'—and its chair—was George Durbidge. Young George had been a top-grade pupil of Mrs Green and he had grown into a large man; quite charming when in good temper, but a heavy drinker prone to fits of violence and pub brawling. Despite his antics, which included poaching and selling his ill-gotten gains in Diss market, he had done well as a fish hawker and was an

THE ROAD TO REVOLUTION

avowed Conservative; but it did not alter his sense of loyalty to the Higdons.

The father of six children considered himself to be a natural leader of the other parents, and under his direction he gathered them around his fish stall. The clouds swept by overhead, driven by the last keen night wind of the month. The common was lit by two of his large flare lamps, and the *Norwich Mercury* was on the scene to report:

> The Chairman proposed the following resolution: 'That we, the people and ratepayers of Burston, and the parents of the children attending Burston School, do most empathically protest against the high-handed action of the Education Authority in terminating the services of Mr and Mrs Higdon at the Burston School. Under the unjust circumstances, we protest against the introduction of new teachers to the School, and we urgently request the County Education Authorities to reconsider the whole matter with a view to our retention of the teachers whose services are so generally appreciated amongst us. That owing to the mischievous interference with the conduct of the School in regard to the Barnardo children, we protest against their attendance at the School, and their presence in the Parish.' The resolution, having been seconded by Mr Noah Sandy, was put to the meeting and carried amidst deafening cheers.

The resolution that emerged from the mist was intended to be sent to the House of Commons. 'Almost the whole village, except for those who were connected with the church or under the influence of the local farmers, came out in a body to show their support. They publicly cheered the Higdons and let out groans and hoots for the Rector.'[31] A number of short but determined speeches were made by men and women who had never spoken publicly before. As the midnight hour approached, George Durbidge stepped up once more to close the meeting with his own short, keen, and jocular advice: 'We can win this thing,' he said, 'if we stick, stick, stick, like bloody shit to a blanket!'

# Chapter 11

# The Village in Revolt

We came on Strike April 1st 1914. We came on strike because our Governess and Master were dismissed from the Council School unjustly. The Parson got two Barnardo children to say that our Governess had caned them and slapped their faces, but we all know she did not. Then our Governess lit a fire one wet morning to dry some of our clothes without asking the Parson. So the head ones said that out Governess and Master had better be got rid of. They had their pay sent and two days' notice to leave the school. Governess did not know we were going on strike. She bought us all some Easter eggs and oranges the last day we were at the Council School.

From 'Our School Strike' By Emily Wilby

When Mr Ikin, Assistant Secretary to the Norfolk Education Committee, appeared at the Burston schoolhouse early on the morning of 1 April 1914, he came armed with cheques for salary in lieu of notice. After the Higdons refused them, he left them on the schoolhouse table. And 'when would it be convenient for Mrs. H. to vacate the School House?' he had also come to enquire. The Higdons could not say. Furthermore, 'Mr. Higdon saw no reason why a cheque in lieu of salary should permit the Committee to retake possession of the Schoolhouse before the completion of the three months' notice'.[1] Ikin did not argue the point.

The Norwich official had arrived on the early train, believing that his business for the day would be over before any children were about. But the youngsters seemed to have been up particularly early that 'First of April Morn', and were soon seen by him and Tom from one of the schoolhouse windows heading to assemble on the green. 'What does that mean?' Ikin inquired with some surprise as he looked on the bright array of children with flying flags and banners. What it meant was that the children of Burston Council School meant business.

What was happening had been well planned, and the young scholars had organised themselves. On the last day of school before the dismissal became effective, the governess had given treats to all the children and wished them the very best. But Violet Potter had brought a paper to school with every pupil listed, and all those that were going on strike had put a cross against their names. One young supporter had actually muttered something about going on strike to the headmistress, but she gave it no credence at the time.

Some other scholars had written in their exercise books before passing them in, 'We're going on strike tomorrow,' and chalked on the blackboard the same striking announcement before finally leaving the school on 31 March. It would not be until the new supply teacher flipped over the board that the message was revealed. A 'similar warning was to be found on a slate hanging in the School porch, whilst the signpost on the village crossroads and several gates in the neighbourhood of the Rectory bore the same ominous augury'.[2] According to Tom, apart from tearing out a couple of the 'offending' pages from the exercise books after the children had gone, the teachers were not in the know of anything. This was only partially true; the Higdons may have been unaware of the fine detail, but as well as the suggestions that something was in the offing on the last school day, at that evening's public meeting (where the Higdons were present), a resolution was passed calling for the children to go on strike the next day.

By the time the supply teachers (Miss Howard, who had previously been headmistress at the school, and Miss Thurlow) arrived and rang the bell for the start of the school day, the green was already a lively scene. The children were being shepherded into a procession by Violet Potter, with the help of some fellow senior scholars and their mothers, all working from her checklist. It was then that the procession moved off, marching behind Violet, who was playing her concertina, and some others who had mouth organs. The smaller children were waving little red or Union Jack flags, with cards and paper trimmings hanging around their necks. Some of the bigger ones carried banners and large cards aloft, 'with the slogans "We Want Our Teachers Back" and "Justice We Want" and at the head of the procession was a banner, loaned by Mrs. Boulton, the proprietress of the Village Shop, inscribed with the one word, "Justice"'.[3] Out of seventy-two children registered, sixty-six had come out on strike. The first morning some mothers sent their infants to the school because they thought that it didn't matter, but it was not to be repeated in the afternoon and only six were to answer the register.

At the school gates, the young strikers had to pass the disapproving glares of Mr Ikin, two school managers (one being Mr Fisher), the supply teachers, Police Inspector James of Diss and Constable Askew. The presence of the police evidently indicated that an inkling that something was going to happen had definitely filtered out to the local authorities from the meeting on the green, of the evening before. Later, the Superintendent of Police from Harleston was to drive up in his tall cart, 'augustly and severely there the Inspector and his two sturdy constables stood their faces alternating between austere authority and smiling confidence',[4] but the children were not to be intimidated and marched on by singing gaily the 'Heart of Oak'. It must have helped to have George Durbidge leading them at that point. The Higdons also appeared on the patch of schoolhouse green proudly waving them on and, it was said, the headmistress shedding more than one tear.

The strikers were following a pre-arranged route that, after passing the school, was to take them around the 'Candlestick', an East Anglian name for a circular walk, round the village. The circuitous route of a distance of a mile-and-a-half was to take them past the cottage of the Barnardo foster-mother Mrs Philpot. After the dismissal of the Higdons became known she had put a card in the window with 'Victory' on it. As the children passed she came out with a dustpan and brush to 'tin' them, but retreated when she saw that the mothers had joined them. Further on, when they reached one of Mrs Philpot's few friends, she jumped up from behind a hedge and did 'tin' the children. The kids easily drowned her out with their collective hoots. When they got back round to Crown Common, Mrs Boulton provided them with lemonade, sweets and nuts. But before enjoying the refreshments waiting for them, the children marched up to the rectory and booed the rector. Reverend Eland had been keeping well clear of events up until that point. At noon the children went home for lunch. But at one o'clock they marched again, and they repeated it on several succeeding days.

'All moonshine!', 'April Fools' and 'Nine Days' Wonder!' were some of the remarks attributed to the rector on first sighting the procession. Some were actually spoken by Eland's ally, the churchwarden, and not all on the first day. Although some of the credit may be misplaced, Eland's own scorn was very much palpable, but the event was already making an impact beyond the district. *The Daily News* and *Leader* were running articles on the strike from 3rd April:

> The children of the Council School of Burston and Shimpling, Norfolk, have gone on strike as a protest against the dismissal of Headmistress, Mrs Higdon, and her husband, who was also on the School staff.
>
> Yesterday only seven scholars met two imported teachers. The other children paraded the district carrying a banner inscribed 'We Want Our Teachers Back'.
>
> The dispute originated in complaints made by the School Managers, of whom the Rev. C.T. Eland, Rector of Burston, is Chairman, that Mrs Higdon had ill-treated children from Dr Barnardo's Homes. The mistress and her husband totally denied the allegation, and asked for an inquiry. The County Committee investigated the matter with the result that Mr and Mrs Higdon were called upon to resign.
>
> The sympathy of the inhabitants is strongly with the deposed teachers, and the opinion is freely expressed that political motives underlie the matter, Mr Higdon's views on politics being opposed to those of the Rector and the majority of the Managers.

Public meetings have protested by large majorities against the dismissal and resolutions have been passed declaring that Mr and Mrs Higdon have been unfairly treated.

Neither Violet Potter, nor any of the other senior scholars involved in the strike, could remember who exactly came up with the idea of taking the action that they had embarked upon. But just as in 1889, 1911–14 witnessed a wave of school strikes which meant that such action was not that uncommon, and some strikes even aroused a good deal of public exposure. Whereas most came to a resolution after a day or two, often failing to achieve their aims, the resistance shown in Burston was in many ways to represent the most subversive achievement of the school strike.

In *Hooligans or Rebels*, the definitive study of working class rebellion in education, Stephen Humphries comments that 'a more subversive explanation for the school strikes wave is, one that is deep-rooted in class conflict'.[5] This was clearly structurally manifest in Burston, where the parent-supported strike action demonstrated 'another way in which pupils and parents sought to assert community control over provided education . . . to support the retention of teachers whose position was threatened by local authority interference'.[6]

Weeks earlier, over the winter of 1914, similar action was seen in Herefordshire when the local authority refused to provide the county teachers, who were among the lowest paid in the country, with a satisfactory salary. In response to the union's strategy of mass resignations, the LEA appointed new teachers, many of them unqualified, and the children's resistance began at the beginning of February, with many refusing to be taught by the new members of staff.

Come 3 February, newspapers across the country, from Aberdeen, Liverpool, Bristol, London and Norfolk, were carrying headlines that eighty schools were closed as part of the action. On what the Birmingham Gazette called a 'Desolate Day', the children at Ashperton School were seen marching up and down the road in battalions, shouting 'We want our old teacher' and 'We won't go back until we get our own teacher'.

A similar state of things took place in Bromyard, where the boys were described as 'very lively'. There, 'led by one precocious boy, they armed themselves with staves and sticks, and declared their intention not to enter the school'.[7] In several cases clergymen were forced to take the place of teachers, but in Brampton Abbots, after a few hours' trial, the clergyman declared that he had had enough and retreated to allow matters to take their natural course.

All across Herefordshire, in Bredwardine, Stoke Lacey, Clifford, Leysters, Yarpole and Ivington, parents held protests meetings, while the children 'took a day's holiday'. Several teachers that had entered into contracts with the authority without the knowledge of the discontent, were beginning to make attempts to get out of them. But the most violent scenes occurred at Ledbury Girls' School, where what was described as an unruly throng developed into a full-blown riot.

On 4 February the *Daily Mirror* described the leader of the riot as thirteen-year-old Vera, 'a handsome, sturdy girl with some Irish blood—and temper—in her'.[8] Unlike Burston, the actions were not planned in advance but developed more spontaneously. Before the registers could be called, the girls broke up, dressed up brooms and wrote on the walls, 'We are going to have our teachers back.' They then played the piano, overturned desks and smashed inkpots on the floor. The new mistress stayed in the school until the scholars left but found a crowd of children waiting for her outside; they then proceeded to surround her and 'hoot' at her along the streets as she made her escape.

After lunch, when the children were due back, about two hundred assembled on the school grounds and after a hurried meeting decided to strike. The efforts of the new mistress to gain entrance to the school were frustrated by the children, who again surrounded her and placed a guard at the doors to prevent anyone entering.

The girls refused to be reasoned with and when several non-striking children effected an entrance unobserved through a window, the strikers stripped them of their hats and jackets and threw their garments out of the window. In the meantime the girls continued to throw around books and inkpots and rip down the blinds. 'One girl then secured a large school bell, and, going to the top window, rang it vigorously.'[9] Throughout, the proceedings were watched by a large crowd, of mostly parents, who were overall very supportive of the actions. At the end of the school day, and after cheers for the teachers on strike followed by more hoots for 'all the blacklegs', and jeering of the new teacher, the girls proceeded back to their homes, declaring they would not return until the old teachers were reinstated.

In the aftermath, all the doors and walls of the school bore a demand written in chalk: 'We want our Governess back again, and we mean to have her.'

At the same time, more lively unrest occurred at the boys' school at Ross Council Schools, where 'much disorder' occurred in the boys' department. The girls and infants had been told not to come in on the Monday; however, when the bell was rung to call the boys together, a general uproar ensued. Eventually all the boys in the upper classes ran from the school and paraded through the streets, shouting and singing. Missiles were thrown at the windows, and though the smaller boys were later marched back into school, the staff provided by the county was nowhere near sufficient to manage over three hundred boys. '"Strike boys, strike", and various other legends were chalked all over the school walls and in the town.'[10]

Under circumstances of mounting dissent and pressure from the Board of Education, the county authority entered into negotiations with the teachers, and the strike was ended. 'Virtually all the teachers involved were reinstated in their old posts.'[11] Without doubt, it had been the children's actions in support of their teachers that had helped bring about a resolution to the dispute.

The Ledbury Girls learned, if no one else dared admit, that on occasion a touch of riotousness can work wonders. It was a lesson that seemed to be taken to heart by many farm workers across the Eastern Counties during the same period. For the union, regardless of the usual tidal flow in fortunes and the strange death of its own Liberal alignment, there was a definite upswing in disputes.

The aftermath of the 1910 St Faiths farm workers' strike helped to initiate considerable changes within the union—a fractious special conference to debate the settlement was marked by internal criticism, a Liberal walkout (Nicholls and Winfrey) and the clear beginnings of a leftward shift. After that uncomfortable day, George Edwards' immediate task was to reverse the decline in membership that the dispute and its outcome had triggered. In that, Edwards was joined by a new young organiser called James Coe, and the pair of them, after much bicycle rubber had been burned, helped put the union back to growth.

Arguably, and not for entirely welcome reasons, the St Faiths dispute was to prove a defining moment in the history of the union and rural trade unionism. At the end of if all, one actual benefit was that it brought the rural union to the attention of urban workers, and 'of more significance was the gradual move by the union towards an identification with both the TUC and the Labour Party'.[12] In other words, the Socialists were beginning to take over.

The union had existing close links with local unions, and especially the Norwich Trades Council, but for the first time on the 1911 May Day platform, George Edwards represented the farm workers. Speaking at what was known as an unequivocally socialist occasion was a clear display of the changing political outlook. After repeated failure to deliver, and grievances over being taken out of industrial activity in the midst of the St Faiths strike to work for Liberal interests in the 1910 elections, Edwards would publicly state that he believed that the 'Labour programme was right for rural workers', and from that year onwards, no Norwich May Day would pass without farm workers' representation.

The main speaker on the day was the popular George Lansbury, who had eventually won election to Parliament for the Bow and Bromley constituency at the December 1910 election. In the summer of 1911, Lansbury was also to address open-air Sunday meetings in West Norfolk. During that time he was one of the founders, and editor, of the *Daily Herald*, which began as a temporary bulletin during the London printers' strike of 1910–11.

By the end of 1912, union membership had grown again, and entirely new sections of the National Agricultural Labourers' and Rural Workers' Union, as it was now called, had been formed in Northampton and Essex. 'In September 1912 the Union applied to the parliamentary committee of the TUC for a grant to aid organising work. This was passed on to member unions and several unions including the dockers and the railwaymen made grants which kept the union going through a difficult year.'[13]

Importantly, the links with the railwaymen were to become more permanent. The NUR was to be founded in the following year (1913) by the mergers of the Amalgamated Society of Railway Servants (founded 1872), the United Pointsmen and Signalmen's Society (founded 1880) and the General Railway Workers' Union (founded 1889). However, links were being built from 1910, and they were proven to be especially important in a farm strike in Lancashire in 1913, when the NUR placed a ban on the movement of farm goods from the strike area. In the same year, in what would become a joint annual demonstration, the NUR and the Agricultural Labourers' Union also came together to rally at Briston, Norfolk, the railway town some twenty miles north west of Norwich.

In the villages, the importance of the railwaymen as builders of the Labour movement cannot be understated, as 'in most rural areas the only unionised workers were the railwaymen'.[14] Being independent of the local farmers for their livelihoods, and generally more secure and better off in their jobs, NUR members could time and again supply considerable material support during struggles. Perhaps, more vitally, the railwaymen acted as conduits taking news of disputes across the country. Once the school strike had started, it was said that: 'If you bought a ticket to Burston at Liverpool Street Station, the porter who let you through on to the platform would look at you and start talking about the Strike and the meetings on the Green.'[15]

In the spring of 1913 the union, helped by the ILP, fought both in County Council elections and some Parish Council elections. Success for their supported candidates was variable, but George Edwards was elected to the County Council for

Freebridge Lynn, and most noticeably, the labourers triumphed in Burston, thus becoming the catalyst for all that was to subsequently happen.

Inside Parliament, George Roberts attempted to get a wages board for agriculture, and was a central figure in drawing up the ILP 'Rural Programme' in September 1913. The bill did not go on to pass, but Roberts had firmly established himself as the 'Labourers' MP'. It was as Roberts who campaigned hard for the rural workers and that, undoubtedly buoyed by the election result, Tom Higdon organised a rally in the parish. Roberts came to speak about his proposal for a board, and land nationalisation. The moment was captured on camera by Tom's brother Frank, who also turned the image into a postcard. Speaking from the back of a hay wagon, Roberts is seen in full flow, with both Tom and Annie sat to his right.

If things were all go on the political front, industrial strikes were fast becoming almost endemic among the farm workers. For many, the Lancashire strike was a testament to how a much more vigorous approach could bring results. Edwards had retired in July, to be replaced with Robert 'General' Walker. Walker was an uncompromising Socialist who had worked as an organiser for the union; but he had been an active ILP member before he joined the organising staff. Under his leadership, the union would sever its links with the Land Nationalisation Society, and later affiliate to the Labour Party.

Eight thousand men would join the National Agricultural Labourers and Rural Workers' Union during 1913. That winter wages had been stable, but in the spring the Executive pushed for an increase of 2s. a week and a half day on Saturday, and with it disputes erupted in the old union heartland of North West Norfolk. Success was to come on the Honingham and Holkham estates, and most famously a campaign on the King's estate at Sandringham, leading to a concession of 16s. a week, a half day Saturday, and six-month tenancies on all tied cottages. Soon the rallying cry was to become a 'King's pay and the King's conditions'; the farmers were not happy.

Victory inevitably lead to victimisation, but the rural union was coming of age. In the middle of the dispute, the union launched the Labourer newspaper, to link the men of Norfolk together and give them news of other strikes which were breaking out in the East, especially in North Essex.

For two years the union had been making inroads into Essex, and by 'February 1914 the Essex Farmers had decided to revert to the tactic of "locking out" and evicting agricultural labourers who had joined the union, no doubt to fight one of the lowest wages in the country at just 13 shillings per week'.[16]

The local leader was Charles Smith of Helions Bumpstead, where a branch was established in October 1913, and where the lockout began. But what started as a defensive struggle for Union recognition would turn into an offence for better conditions. In May, the union wrote to all farmers in the area outlining their demand as 16 shillings per week, and hours of work 6am to 5pm and a half day Saturday. Some eight hundred were supported by the local organisers, but it was James Coe—by now a National Organiser of the National Agricultural & Rural Workers Union of Norfolk—who was in charge of the dispute.

The strike spread quickly to Birdbrook, Ridgwell, Steeple Bumpstead, Strumer, Ashdon (across the border into Whittlesford, Castle Camps, West Wickham, Weston Colville in Cambridgeshire) and even as far as Withersfields, in Suffolk. Regular mass meetings were held, and speakers included George Lansbury, John Scurr (then Chairman of the London District Committee of the Dock, Wharf, Riverside and General Labourers' Union; later MP for Mile End) and Rev Edward Maxted, the 'Socialist' vicar of Tiltly. 'But the largest meeting was to hear Sylvia Pankhurst speak and it was her who led a procession through the village of Helions Bumpstead at which over 2,000 were present on Sunday 26th July 1914.'[17] It was only the impending outbreak of World War One that forced the protagonists to reach a settlement on 3 August 1914, just one day before the war was declared. The men returned to work on 5 August at a rate of fifteen shillings a week and £8 for harvest.

As fortune would have it, April 1914 turned out to be one of the finest springs ever known. The unseasonal warmth helped to keep the school strikers in good heart. The pub never did such good business in ginger beer, and the village shop's trade in sweets and chocolate skyrocketed. The Higdons, unsurprisingly, had a lot to consider, and because of it, at least as the stated public reasoning, no new domicile arrangements had been made by them.

From 1 April, the children continued to stay away from school, and every day they continued to march past with their banners and bunting. It was a challenge that the Norfolk Education Committee could not overlook. Within a few days the committee had summoned eighteen of the parents for failing to send their children to school. 'The proceedings,' reported the *East Anglian Times*, 'aroused a great deal of interest in the town and there was a large gathering in the vicinity of the Court Room to watch the arrival of the strikers and their parents.'[18]

On the morning that they went to court all the older children dressed up and assembled at the Crossways that lies close to Burston Green. At 9.30am the small but vibrant procession, which numbered about fifty strikers, headed off to march the three miles to the court house; then part of the Corn Hall buildings in Diss. But before they started, Mrs. Boulton was once more on hand with oranges and chocolate. The *East Anglian Times*' extensive account continues:

Preceded by a little girl riding a decorated bicycle, and headed by a red banner bearing the words: "We want Justice," borne by a couple of lads, the strikers, who numbered after nine o'clock and marched the three miles to the court house, which is part of the Corn Hall buildings in Diss. Many of the children carried miniature Union Jacks, whilst most of them had placards, on which were inscribed the words: "We want our old teachers back and justice," and some had even made an attempt to don fancy costume, one lad being conspicuous in a resplendent suit which would have done well at a nigger minstrel entertainment. Several mothers were in the party around with collection boxes, and their appeals for support for the "strike" met with a fair amount of response. The arrival at the Court House did not take place until about quarter to eleven, and the parents and "strikers" had to wait outside whilst the Bench disposed of several other cases.

The defendants were John Aldrich, John Bridges, Joseph Cobb, George Durbidge, Joseph Ford, Walter Garnham, Henry Gotts, Edward Huggins, Harry Ling, John Potter, sen., John Potter, jun., Robert Wilby, William Wilby Burston; George Catchpole, Shimpling; Thomas Mullinger, Robert Sturman, Burston; Alfred Moore, and James Wells, Diss; and they were summoned by Frederick Starr, school attendance officer, of Long Stratton, for each not sending a child to school at Burston on April 7th.

The magistrates felt they were bound to support the prosecution ordered by the Education Committee, but off-record they could argue that they had given the parents a relatively light penalty (fine of 2s.6d. each). In *The Burston Rebellion*, Tom was rather more convinced that they were always bound to support prosecution, whatever. 'Thus the Magistrates appear to have only been too pleased to oblige the Norfolk Education Committee and Rector of Burston'; he was certain because, among the reasons, 'the Chairman of the Bench (now deceased) seems to have been privately approached and influenced. It is known that the Rector of Burston visited the Chairman's house.'[19] Whether Tom would have written such if the Chairman of the Bench had not then been deceased is a different matter.

During the often-comical court proceedings, the children spent their time in a park; only some of the older girls went there later to see what the time was. The procession had been welcomed into town by people lining the streets, with Mrs Wilby bringing along some refreshments. While they were there, a man from *The Sketch* took their pictures for the following week's edition.

When the parents finally emerged from court, the children formed up with them outside the Corn Hall, and to the strains of 'Hearts of Oak' they marched through the town before returning to the marketplace for some bread and ginger beer before starting for home. Their governess also provided them cakes to eat on the way. The children were accompanied by a number of the parents, some of whom made a collection in aid of the 'Fine Fund' along the way.

Emily Wilby warmly recalled that 'when we got half-way home we all sat down and had a rest and ate our cakes'.[20] They finally got to back home about six o'clock. It had been another grand day out for the Burston School Strikers. And, according to Emily, 'it was the next day that the mothers thought that we might begin school on the Common while it was fine weather'.[21]

The parents did appeal to the committee 'by resolution and by petition' but, after the summons and fines failed to bring an end to the boycott, two weeks later the mothers were summoned once more. This time the children did not go to court, but started out for a little way before returning home. Only in the evening did they join their parents in Diss, where they had more ginger beer and their photographs taken by the press. This time thirty-two parents were summoned and the fine was five shillings each.

The summons and fines of the parents just lent additional interest in the growing dispute. On the first Sunday following its outbreak, hundreds of visitors flocked to the village to offer their support—some no doubt out of sheer curiosity. John Sutton, a local farm labourer and Primitive Methodist lay preacher conducted a service on the green. The church services became almost completely ignored except by a few close allies and bonded supporters. The Rev. J.G. Williams, the Free Methodist minister of Diss, would come to officiate at all the 'Strike Funerals'. Rev. Eland would hand over his bill for burial fees all the same, passed on through the sexton. On the first occasion the parents of the deceased child paid, but the next father refused to pay—it was the only issue that Eland did not fall back onto the courts.

But the chapel also saw its own attendance fall, because of the attitude of school manager, farmer, yet prominent chapel-goer, Mr Fisher. As Tom Higdon was to explain, Sutton 'found it necessary to leave the Primitive Methodist Body who, through the influence of Brother Fisher with the Official Heads of the Circuit, condemned his actions of preaching the Gospel of Truth and Righteousness . . . upon the Burston Green'.[22] In total eight members would resign, and Sutton himself would join the Free Methodists, though he would continue his ministrations to the 'Burston Flock in the Strike School, and administers of the Sacrament of Baptism to all Strike Babies'.[23]

Speakers that attended and addressed the large crowds that gathered every Sunday included: Fred Henderson, the noted Norwich Socialist speaker and writer; Comrades W. Smith and Garner, of Wymondham; Segon and Perrement, of the Norwich BSP (British Socialist Party) and Trades Council; Joplin, Anderson and Chapman of Lowestoft Trades Council; the Rev. John Glesson (Congregationalist); and many local Agricultural Labourers' Union and Independent Labour Party officials and members.

On the Sunday after the second summons, the assembled crowd was estimated at between eight hundred and nine hundred persons. They had come to listen to George Edwards who, as a member of Norfolk County Council, had brought forward a resolution with a view to ending the dispute a few days earlier. As was Edwards' style, as a self-declared 'old Methodist local preacher', the proceedings were conducted as a service. Mr. John Sutton assisted in the preliminaries and read the scripture lesson.

To an attentive crowd, Edwards went on to articulate his deep regret that, as he had read in the previous week's paper, law-abiding parents and parishioners had found it necessary to be taken to the Police Courts in order for their protest to be registered. He was not saying whether what they were doing was justified or not, but rather that, as a member of the County Council, being forced into that position was regretful and that if it had heeded his advice the ill feeling that had arisen might have been avoided.

Edwards had moved a resolution at the council calling for a public enquiry; that in the meantime the Higdons should be reinstated, and that whatever the result of the enquiry might be the people would abide by it. The proposal was rejected out of hand. Due to all of the events that had transpired, they had done all they could in relation to the County Council, and their next step was for the parishioners as a body to sign a petition and send it to the Board of Education asking them to hold a public enquiry.

In conclusion, Edwards said that no doubt blame would be cast upon him for the step he had taken that afternoon, but he had a lot of knocking about in his time, and although now an old man he could take a little more—and so could the Higdons and their supporters.

Meetings were now being held thick and fast, but despite the involvement of George Edwards and the Agricultural Labourers' Union in providing public backing to the Higdons—and that included one of their own executive members (Tom had recently come top of the polling in the last AGM)—Burston still did not have its own branch of the union. Tom carried the widespread support of the local agricultural labourers long before the start of the school strike, so it is perhaps an indication of his caution in not wanting to be seen as an agitator on his doorstep that no attempt had been made to form one before. It was six weeks into the strike that, on 13 May 1914, a meeting was held in the Crown Inn to discuss the formation of a local branch. After Tom addressed the assembly of men, it was resolved to finally form a branch in the village—officers were appointed and thirty men joined up on the evening.

On the following Thursday, George Durbidge was back presiding over a well-attended meeting on the green. As chair he called for a public enquiry so the true facts of the case would be brought out, and so then 'justice would be reinstalled in the place which they never ought to have been removed from'. Though recognising that persistence in this course of action would increase their difficulties, he then moved the following resolution, which was seconded by John Sutton and carried unanimously:

That in view of the Educational deadlock, which exists between the Norfolk County Council and ourselves, electors and ratepayers, of Burston and Shimpling, and between the Norfolk Education Committee and is, the parents of children on the registers of the Burston and Shimpling County Council Provided School, which deadlock had been caused by what we believe to be the uncalled for and unjust dismissal of the teachers, Mrs. A.K and Mr. T.G. Higdon, from the school, and in view of the dissatisfaction and uncertainty attending their dismissal, which dissatisfaction and uncertainty have been intensified by recent statements of the Chairman of the Burston and Shimpling School Managers made at an interview and published in the *Daily Chronicle* of Friday, April 24th to the effect that he (the Chairman of School Managers), did not know the reason why the said teachers were dismissed, and that it was preposterous to say that the teachers were dismissed on the grounds of the complaints made by him, notwithstanding an enquiry was held by the Norfolk Education Committee into these complaints, at which enquiry the managers were represented by a lawyer with the Chairman of the managers present, and as a direct result of the findings out of that enquiry the teachers were old to "seek other employment with as little delay as possible." In view of this denial the whole case against the teachers by the said chairman of managers and principle complaint in the matter, fails and we hereby beg to add to our former protests and appeals this our sincere, united and unanimous appeal to the Board of Education to grant us public enquiry into the real facts of the case.

A vote of thanks to the Chairman and cheers for the dismissed teachers brought the meeting to a close.

Throughout it all the NUT, though timid, was not entirely absent from the field of play. Just before the 1916 conference, the NUT Executive Committee Circular 876 concisely summarised their intervention in the case:

It reported that when the result of the Enquiry became known a Conference was held at the London offices of the Union between Mrs. Higdon, her brother (James Heaton Schollick), representatives of the Executive, and the Secretary of the County Sub-Association, and it was then agreed that the County Association should write to the Authority acknowledging the result of the Enquiry, but suggesting that Mrs. Higdon should not be unduly pressed, and should be afforded able time in which to secure a suitable post.

Initially Annie did agree to this course, but subsequently failed to send the letter. Presumably, after time to reflect, she felt it would be conceding to the baseless results of the enquiry, and handing to the school managers what they wanted.

On the day following that meeting, 'the General Secretary wrote to the Education Committee calling attention to the apparent departure from the recommendation of the Authority, and asking that the notice of dismissal might be withheld'. In reply the Secretary to the Authority said that the recommendation 'that the Head Teacher should seek other employment with as little delay as possible' was made, in the first place, with the desire to give the teacher a better opportunity of obtaining a post, but that, as four weeks had elapsed and apparently no steps were being taken to carry out the decision, 'in the interest of Elementary Education in Burston the Sub-Committee moved and the Education Committee unanimously carried the motion to give three months' salary in lieu of notice.'

At Easter, the NUT held its conference in Lowestoft, and supporters of the Higdons had an opportunity to inform the floor of details of the case. At the time, eviction proceedings to recover the schoolhouse were reported to be pending, and that a number of children were not attending the school. In hopes of finding a way out of the difficulty, the Executive received a deputation of teachers in the service of the County Council, and as a result three members of the Executive subsequently went to Norwich to interview the Secretary of the Education Committee. The object of the visit was to secure, if possible, a suitable transfer for Mrs Higdon. This, it was noted, was found to be impossible, but it was arranged that if Mrs Higdon should undertake to vacate the schoolhouse the eviction proceedings would be held over, and that, if the children returned to school and Mrs Higdon refrained from interfering with them, the attendance summonses taken out against the parents would be withdrawn. The union officers decided that Mrs Higdon's best course of action was to give the required promises. A rather ungenerous position was put to her by a member of the Executive, but Annie could not see her way to carrying out the advice tendered.

But because of the way events were moving, it was all largely academic. After the second court case all legal action against the parents was stopped; it was clearly not having any discernible impact, and by now the children were being taught by qualified teachers of their parents' choosing. After three weeks the daily processions had been abandoned in favour of continuing regular school duties to be carried out by the Higdons. At first, though, it was 'in the open air, upon the village green, in the flowery lanes, in coal shed and copper-house, and wherever space could be found'.[24] Books and other materials were forthcoming through donations and, probably, Annie's own funds.

At the same time, negotiations were begun for the hire of a suitable building in which to carry on the school. The search was soon over when blind Ambrose Sandy offered the use of a former 'carpenters shop' that he had on lease situated opposite the green. The villagers mucked in, and it was soon white-washed, and furnished by way of more donations.

On 26 May a crowded meeting was held in the newly acquired 'carpenters shop' Strike School for the purpose of forming a School Committee that would have control of the arrangements of the further development of the dispute and the management of the new educational premises. After discussions, a committee consisting of nine parishioners was elected by a show of hands, five of whom were mothers of the children on strike. The accounts, as they stood at that early point, were read, and a subscription of one guinea that had been generously sent by a gentleman from Brighton was acknowledged with a round of applause. George Durbidge, chairman of the new Strike School Committee, made an appeal to make up any deficiency in funds to meet the 5s. fines imposed by the Diss Magistrates, which had to be paid by Wednesday 27 May.

It was George Durbidge, himself a defendant, who attended the Pretty Sessional Court on Wednesday with the purpose of paying the fines. After producing a medical certificate on behalf of Mary Jackson to the effect that her child was too unwell to attend school on the day specified in the summons, the magistrates agreed to remit the fine in her case. In total £7/5 was then paid to the magistrates' clerk on behalf of seventeen parents who had continued to resist the court's demands to return their children to school.

Further court action was soon to be taken up against Mrs Higdon, who was never going to vacate the schoolhouse before a three-month notice period as a matter of principle. But 'The Committee think a fortnight sufficient time in which to vacate the Schoolhouse'[25] was the ultimatum from the Education Committee to the former headmistress. The ultimatum was ignored. But then the Norfolk Education Committee took up the eviction proceedings. Mr W.E. Keefe argued before the Diss Magistrates that the payment of salary in lieu of notice did not discharge the obligation to allow the usual (and what was a contractual term) three months' notice for vacating the schoolhouse. The case was lost. Later, the solicitor was to state that if funds had been forthcoming he would have liked to have appealed against the decision of the Bench.

On 3 June, the day of the eviction, the Higdons were initially given refuge by the local miller in one of the cottages attached to the mill. The move turned into a carnival of 'men, women, girls, and boys, miller's cart, donkey cart, wheelbarrows, all without fee—joined joyously and sympathetically in the enforced removal of the dismissed and evicted teachers' goods—to coalholes, to larders lacking their proper furniture, to village stores and diverse other places wherever storage room could be found'.[26] At night, when the Higdons went back to the schoolhouse to lock up before going back to their lodgings at the mill, a large number of their supporters joined them on the lawn in the moonlight and remained with them until midnight. —But the Higdons remained bitter over the eviction, and continued to protest that the payment of salary should not prematurely release them from the schoolhouse.

On the Sunday of that week, the *Diss Express* had to report that:

Owing to showery weather the usual outdoor meetings in connection with the school strike did not take place on Burston Common on Sunday afternoon, but the "Strike School"—a disused carpenter's shop—was packed with parents and parishioners. A party of nine members of the Norwich branch of the Independent Labour Party cycled over and two, Mr.R.J.Ingram, a member of Norwich Town Council, and Mr. Aylmer Richardson, took part in the proceedings, which were conducted by Mr. John. Sutton, of Burston, who read the lesson and offered prayer.—Mr. Ingram said he was present to convey the sympathy of the Independent Labour Party with Mr. and Mrs. Higdon. As to the issue of the fight the parents were bound to succeed if they stuck to one another and to the dismissed teachers. A collection was taken in aid of the Parents' Defence Fund.

On Monday Superintendent Bentham and other members of the police force called at the "Strike School" for the keys of the Council School House, vacated last week by Mr. and Mrs.Higdon, the dismissed teachers, and the same were handed over.

What the local press failed to mention, but the *Daily Herald* did, was that Mr Higdon had 'some little altercation' with the superintendent as to the unnecessary strength of his force and equipment, seeing that the key had not previously been applied for, whereupon the majesty of the law replied: 'We are not your servants.'

By early June 1914, the Norfolk Education Committee may have got rid of the Higdons from the Council School and its schoolhouse, but the dispute was escalating, and the first 'Strike School' was now open.

# Chapter 12

# Long Past Moonshine

Next stop, Burston.

By mid-July the London trains now never failed to stop at the village station. As news of the strike spread through Labour journals and papers, like the *Herald* and *Daily Mirror*, the leading lights of the Labour Movement and their followers began to attend the Sunday meetings. Such radical luminaries as George Lansbury, Philip Snowden, Bruce Glasier, John Scurr, Tom Mann, Ben Tillett and more, would arrive on the early morning train to be met by villagers who would march them in a lively procession to the green.

One of the largest to date was on 15 July 1914, when hundreds of railwaymen and curious supporters were brought down on the first special charter to be arranged. Some eighteen trade union banners were arranged around the green; a brass band came from Norwich and another from London. After the usual speeches the children sang songs and did country dances, just as they would perform on every May Day. As on the previous month's 'children's day', held in connection with the open-air services, singing was accompanied by Annie on the organ. Recitations were made by Violet Potter and Emily Wilby; solos were sung and a trio made up of Violet Potter, Marjory Ling and Lilian Bridges also performed—and Casey played his fiddle.

'Casey' was the pseudonym of Walter Hampson, an astonishingly prolific Yorkshire-based-dialect story teller, poet, traveller and fiddle player. Hampson was born on 24 April 1864, and his early education was very brief; a little Dame school teaching in his very early childhood was then followed

by a few months of lessons run by a local master at the age of
eight. An autodidact, he first began writing by submitting
articles to the *Railway Review*. Then, in 1905, he published on
his own account a book of poems entitled 'Songs of the Line'
that brought him to the attention of the publisher W.Nicholson
& Sons.

With his singing partner, Dolly Pickard, the pair would tour
the music halls to raise funds for political causes, and as a
supporter of the Labour Party he would contribute articles to
the *Labour Leader* under the name of Casey. As soon as news of
the rural rebellion reached his desk (which was inside a tent on
his back lawn, as it was apparently the most peaceful place
available to work), he immediately headed down to Norfolk.

Amazingly, Walter worked full time as an engine driver and
managed to find time to get deeply involved in the local Trade
Union movement. He was the Normanton Branch Secretary of
the National Union of Railwaymen, and was responsible for
gaining a three shillings a day rise for his Normanton colleagues.
Sharing both politics and a love of poetry (as well as being a
poet, Walter was an expert on the work of Burns—a particular
favourite of Tom Higdon) Casey was soon putting his full
efforts behind supporting the Higdons. In 1915 his polemical
account, *The Burston School Strike*, was published by the
*National Labour Leader*.

As the Sunday meetings settled into a weekly fixture on the
calendar of many trade unionists and Labour supporters,
George Roberts asked the President of the Board of Education
in the House of Commons if he had received the petition
signed by the parents of the children, and what would be the
nature of his proposed reply? Mr J.A. Pease was well aware of
the situation, but 'the appointment and dismissal of teachers in
a council school', he would declare, 'is a matter for the local
education authority, and I do not think that occasion has arisen
for my intervention'.[1]

Perhaps the president, like the rest of government, had more
pressing matters on his mind. On 4 August 1914 war was
declared on Germany, but initially it had little impact on the
strike except to divert the attention of the press—the *Herald*

still carried reports but the rural rebellion had dropped well short of the front pages. It was only as the conflict escalated and many of the young men in the village volunteered for the army, that the Higdons lost some of their keenest supporters.

Even to a Norfolk farmer, or a churchwarden, the situation had clearly grown beyond a 'nine day wonder'. The Strike School had been formally established, and after the register was taken the daily teaching followed a proper timetable. In the main, Mrs Higdon did the teaching; although Tom was present in the schoolroom he was often engaged in union matters. 'The Strike School ... was visited by County Councillors, by inspectors, by school attendance officers and others: they could find nothing wrong. Indeed, the children were keeping up regular attendances in all weathers, and all were happy under their teachers.'[2] After Mr Everson, Chairman of the Depwade District Council, visited on a very wet, cold day, he was to report back to his council that, '"the room was warm and comfortable, and the children were happy at their lessons . . .", he added that in his opinion, "the parents of Burston were but exercising their right to send their children to whatever School they liked."'[3]

The school managers had seriously underestimated the original turn of events, but they had escaped the scrutiny of a public inquiry. Yet the situation was still a gross embarrassment to them, and they decided to take matters into their own hands and attempt to reach a satisfactory conclusion—although compromise was not to be involved.

In the middle of the summer, with harvest beckoning, the farmers were not prepared to sack the striking labourers, whom they needed. 'Instead they hit upon another place which caused no inconvenience to themselves and broke with an ancient custom that the villagers had come to regard as sacrosanct.'[4] As Rector, Eland had in his gift the distribution of the Church's glebe lands, which were rented out at a peppercorn rent. Many farm labourers, with large families and subsidence wages, could only survive on what they were able to grow themselves on an allotment or a piece of glebe land. The rector and the farmers misguidedly decided that the best way to bring the parents to heel was to threaten to take their glebe land away.

'He took some Glebe land from three poor men,' Emily Wilby would write with a child's simple accuracy; 'One of the men was blind; the Parson took away his Glebe because he lent us his shop . . . He took Mr. Harry Ling's Glebe away because he would not his daughter go to the mock inquiry or go himself to tell a lie. He took Mr Garnham's Glebe away because he attended the Strike School meetings.'[5]

The villagers were appalled at the retaliation. Many families had rented the same land for generations; so they were not going to be evicted without a fight, but blind Ambrose Sandy decided to leave the village before his actual eviction. Sandy had been blinded as a teenager in an accident when larking about with friends and a loaded gun, but despite his disability he had worked in the village all his life. The carpenter's shop he had inherited from his mother and rented out to the Higdons for £3 a year.

Greater upheaval was to follow in the Ling family, although they were already divided by the strike. Both Harry Ling and his brother rented glebe land, at £1 a year for three quarters of an acre. Harry's section was situated right next to the family cottage, where he would grow corn for chickens and straw for pigs. 'Harry was the father of Marjory Ling, Violet Potter's best friend at school [and a key strike leader], and a strong Higdon supporter; his brother, however, was the church sexton and his sister-in-law the infants' teacher at the Council School.'[6] Reverend Eland took Harry's glebe land and gave it to William.

The Rector's actions caused a family rift that became an open sore. Bitter hostilities ensued, with the church sexton ploughing up his brother's corn each time it reached a few inches. And after Harry put his chickens on the land and surrounded them by wire netting, 'someone' came and bashed it all down and removed the hut. 'That's how it went,' Marjory recalled, 'so of course eventually he couldn't cope with it anymore and he gave it all up.'[7]

The brothers would end up not speaking to each other again for fifteen years.

In his attempts to evict Harry Ling and Mr. Garnham (the third glebe tenant), the rector had them summoned three times. The last time they appeared at Eye Court, but the judge awarded the tenants ten shillings damages, and Eland had to give up the lock and chain that had been removed from the entrance to Garnham's glebe.

When the 'Glebe Three' received notice to quit, the Bishop of Norwich was appealed to. 'The *Eastern Daily Press*, July 28th, 1915, which lies on my knee as I write, contains his photo,' Casey wrote in his own polemical account.

He is standing outside the Hospital for the Indigent Blind, in Magdalen Street, Norwich, with the Earl and Countess of Leicester, looking as though he had his meals more regularly than many village folk.

Surely he is interested in the blind of Burston, also? . . . Will he allow his rector to press this injustice? Here is his reply:

The Palace,
Norwich.

Dear Sir,—I directed by the Bishop of Norwich to acknowledge receipt of your letter of the 15th, and to say that if the persons named feel aggrieved they should seek address through the legal tribunals.

Yours faithfully,
J.A. Parsons, Secretary.

E.B. Reeves.

So His lordship, with income of £4,500 per year, palace, etc., advises three poor folk, one of whom is blind, to "seek redress through the legal tribunals." This is certainly His Lordship's grim joke . . .[8]

'Of victimisations and evictions there have been no end,' Tom Higdon further reminisced in *The Burston Rebellion*; 'It is a well-known fact that the Rector wrote the owner of the cottage occupied by Mr. Noah Sandy with a view to getting Mr. Sandy turned out, and that the Rector also asked to be allowed to take over a row of three cottages occupied by Strikers and Strike sympathisers and supporters with a view to turning all these people out.'[9]

In a further move made by the Rector and his committee, was:

> . . . the dismissal, without notice, of two of the Strike parents from their work of scavenging at the Council School, for which work they had been regularly paid fifteen shillings per quarter . . . The School Caretaker was also threatened with dismissal if she did not send her child back to the Council School, while many other intimidations were attempted.[10]

At the parish meeting in March 1915, the dismissal of the Council School scavengers that Tom Higdon references was raised for discussion, and the *Diss Express* reported:

> A meeting of the Parish Council was held at the Council School on Thursday March 18th, Mr.E.J.Potter presiding, the members present being Messrs.J.Potter, sen., W.Wilby, A.Ford, T.G.Higdon, and Noah Sandy (parish school manager). The minutes of the last meeting were read, with acknowledgements from the Local Government Board and Board of Education of resolutions contained therein on the questions of Housing and Education in Burston. There was no discussion on these matters, the clerk (Mr.G.Brown) intimating the advisability of awaiting further developments. A letter was read by the Chairman, dated June 8th 1914, from the Clerk to the School Managers (Mr.F.Starr, Long Stratton), to Mr. Wilby, of Burston, requesting him to cease work as school scavenger, and in reply to questions from members of the Parish Council, Mr. Noah Sandy (parish school manager), said that he did not know by whose authority this letter had been sent to Mr. Wilby. The matter had not been mentioned at any meeting of the Council School Managers, and the managers as a body knew nothing of its being sent. He had asked Mr. Starr about it and Mr. Starr admitted having sent the letter to Wilby, and said he thought this was sufficient notice. He did not say who instructed him to send it. Several members asserted that the work had since been done by another man. The opinion

expressed that Wilby was entitled to a proper notice, and to the statement of some reason why the work was taken away from him . . .

But just as the persecution of strike families failed to weaken their resolve, the rector's interferences grew increasingly desperate and spiteful. After two boys, the next 'strike funeral' to take place during the dispute was that of Sabina Durbidge, the daughter of George Durbidge who died suddenly of meningitis. Sabina, having complained at school in the morning of feeling unwell, was taken home and died later the same day. But Eland and the farmers tried to blame her death on the conditions at the Strike School. Emily Wilby, in *Our School Strike*:

> There was an inquest. A jury of farmers and Parson's men was called together and they tried to make out the child died because she came to the Strike School. They asked the poor mother what time the Strike School fire was lighted, and didn't the children go to meet Governess and Master without any hats, and didn't they have to go across a Common with water on. They called the poor mother into the room three times to worry her with questions. At the inquest the doctor told them why the girl had died. They would not believe him and ordered a post-mortem which is the cruellest thing there was. After the doctor told them the same thing he did at first. The way they treated the poor mother was brutal . . .

Another plot had failed, and it brought nothing but contempt upon its authors.

The strike continued.

Anyone picking up a copy of the *Daily Mirror* on 3 April 1915 could not fail to miss the first anniversary strike coverage—containing a full page of six pictures and commentary; readers would have been left fully aware that the dispute in Norfolk continued. Though on the day there were celebrations, by Burston standards, it passed by in a fairly low-key fashion; Emily Wilby:

On April 1st, 1915, we celebrated our first year. We marched round the village in the morning and in the afternoon we had tea which we all enjoyed. At night our parents had a "social." Mr. Rice, J.P., presented Master with an inkstand and Governess with a clock from us and our parents. Mr. Rice also presented Mr. Sutton with a bookcase because he had taken the service every Sunday when there was not anybody else to take it. After that we had refreshments and dancing. We sang "England Arise", then the Social was broken up; Mr. Potter asked for three cheers for Governess and Master.

The eatables, including many cakes, the *Daily Mirror* would add, were brought in state in a wheelbarrow.

In the same month, to raise money for the Strike School, the *Herald* began to carry advertisements for 'The Labourer' by T.G. Higdon. As with 'To The Departed', Tom's second published work is an extended poem, of thirty-two unpretentious pages. Taking influence from some of Burns's political works, the poem is an account of the life of an unnamed agricultural labourer that follows said labourer through his toils and the hardships of life in a rural idyll. The romance and comfort of his domestic life (although not the housing conditions) are contrasted against the hardships of agricultural labour. The hand to mouth existence of the labourer is set against that of his wealthy master.

With the dispute now entering its second year, all considerations were on how to force the issue to the attention of the general public. The anniversary had reinvigorated coverage but with the war raging it was only going to be a temporary blip. First on the agenda it was proposed to hold a 'great public demonstration' in July, when George Lansbury and others would attend. The *Herald's* editorial was increasingly pushing the point that, 'with a great fight for freedom in Germany, how extraordinary it was that the authorities should allow such a miserably mean dispute to continue here'. It was also now challenging the Right Hon. Arthur Henderson to show what manner a man he was as Minister of Education, and intervene. The paper was certain that it was well in his power, if he had the will, to compel the reactionary education committee to put an end to the unseemly strife.

Whether an opportunity to help provide a spanking to the Education Committee was too good to pass up, or whether pressure from the ranks of the labour movement could no longer be ignored, by the end of June it had been ascertained that Henderson was prepared to act as arbitrator, if the County Council and Mrs Higdon would abide by any decision. Mrs Higdon was strongly advised to agree to the offer. The NUT Executive had reviewed the case, but saw no reason to depart from their position, so third-party arbitration was a welcome means to bring about a final resolution.

A month on and the *Herald* was carrying the same rallying cry as it helped build up the Norwich Labour Party's organised mass demonstration. But its supportive reports were now infused with a sense of urgency; its editorials expressed a graver concern about the vital need to bring more support from the Labour Movement. What were once requests were now reading more like pleas as it asked its readers in all parts of the country to give the matter some more consideration. It now finished all articles with a request to send moral and financial help at once—the first national appeals for funds had begun.

The 4 July demonstration was a noticeable success and further cemented the formation of a Burston national funding campaign:

BURSTON CHILDREN MUST WIN—We Must Help Them Now, £50 Wanted at Once to Smash British Junkerism in Norfolk.

The demonstration in support of the Burston School Strike held on Sunday last, was a great success. Men and women, boys and girls, from the villages and towns assembled in large numbers. At least 1,200 people were present, amongst whom were a goodly number of men in khaki, who listened attentively, and with one or two exceptions were in full sympathy with, and voted for, the resolutions. Men were present from the Herald League and the Clarion Fellowship, the biggest contingent coming from the ILP in Norwich.

Comrade Johnson, of Norwich, presided over the demonstration, which was organised by Comrade E. Reeves, of Norwich, who for months past had given practically all his spare time to the work of obtaining publicity for the strike. Before the demonstration, a procession of children and friends marched around the village singing folk-songs. A great cheer was raised as they passed the Rectory, to show the rector and his friends that nobody was downhearted. On the village green children sang songs, led by Mrs. Higdon, the schoolmistress, and one of them recited Mrs. Hemans's poem, "The Pilgrim Fathers."

E. Reeves told the audience how the village school came into being; how Mrs. Higdon, the head mistress of the village school, together with her husband, who was her assistant, are excellent teachers, having received the very highest commendation from His Majesty's inspectors. No fault whatever has been, or can be, found with their work as educationists. Fifteen months ago, however, a charge that Mrs. Higdon had thrashed one of Dr. Barnardo's children boarded out in the village was brought forward. No inquiry worth the name has been held into the charge, but, as a result of the charge, and almost unheard, Mrs. Higdon and her husband were dismissed. To show what the children thought of their head mistress, they all left the school, and have not been back since. The Education Committee has prosecuted the parents, caused them to be fined time and again, but the villagers have stood firm, and by their own efforts have maintained their own school on the village green; in bad weather it is carried on in the carpenter's shop. Apparently the authorities are at their wits' end how to end the dispute. It has suddenly occurred to the rector that probably he could cut the Gordian knot by exercise of his legal right to harass people whose opinions he happens to disagree with. The carpenter's shop is not on the rector's land, but is built on land rented by the blind carpenter, who has given it for use as a school. This carpenter also hires from the rector two or three acres of glebe land, for which he has paid rent amounting to £7 10s. a year for the past twenty-

15. The 'Carpenters Shop' Strike School (1915).

**LOVE & JUSTICE**

This board is placed to the Honour of
the Scholars, whose names it bears.
Who, on April 1st 1914, when their
Teachers Mr & Mrs Higdon were
arbitrarily dismissed from the
Council Schools of this Parish,
struck in support of them. They
still, April 1st 1917, attend the strike
schools taught by these teachers.

ALDRICH. Charles, Elsie, Winnie, Jack, Edna.
BLOOMFIELD. Cecil, Frank, Gwendoline.
BAILEY. George, Ethel, Lily.
BRIDGES. Lilian.
CATCHPOLE. Elsie.
COBB. Reggie.
DURBRIDGE. Fred, Frank, Honor.
Sabina, Roger, Hettie.
DYE. Eleanor, Gladys.
FORD. Joseph, Richard, Victor.
FINCH. Marjory.
DAY. Johnnie, Harry.
GARNHAM. Willie.
GARNHAM. Charles.
JACKSON. Ivy.
LAST. Eva, Ernest, Cissie.
LING. Marjory.
LEGGET. George, Eddie.
LEEDER. Winnie.
MULLENGER. Jack.
MOORE. George, Bertie.
NORMAN. Amy.
POTTER. Violet, Elsie, Tottie, Annie.
Stanley, Tommy.
POTTER. Reggie.
STURMAN. Gladys, Elsie, Hilda, Arthur.
Minnie.
SPRUNT. Willie.
WILBY. William, Lily, Albert, Dolly, Nancy.
WILBY. Hettie, May, Emily, Percy, Dick.
WOODS. Reggie, Olive, Dorothy.
WELLS. Robert, Charles.

16. The 'honour board' that records the names of the children that went out on strike.

17. The children recreate their march around the 'candlestick' on the first-year anniversary of the strike (1915).

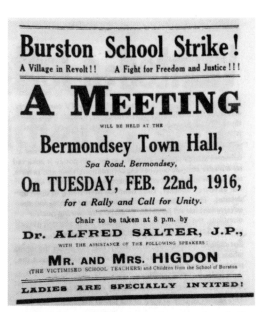

18. Poster advertising one of the campaign meetings in London organised by the NUR (1916).

19. The tablet that caused such division in the Garnham family.

20. Young strikers outside the newly built Strike School (1918).

NATIONAL COMMITTEE
G. LANSBURY, President  R. GREEN, Chairman
C.F. JOHNSON, Vice-Chair, W. CARTER, Treasurer
F.O. ROBERTS, Secretary  W. HOLMES, Asst-Sec

W.R. SMITH. J.P.          R.B. WALKER.
T.C. HIGDON.              E.J. POTTER.
MRS REEVES.              A. APPLETON.
SAM. MARCH.             W. BLACKBURN
J. SUTTON.               J. SCURR.
W. HAMPSON, Crosey       W. SMITH.
B. HIPWOOD               P. SAVAGE.
P. URRELL                W.C. CODLING.
C. EDWARDS, J.P. C.C.    H.C. RUSSELL.
E.T. JONES.              P.A. CUMMINGS.
H.H. LAWRIE.             E.B. REEVES.
H.E. WITTARD J.P         C. MANN.
C.R. PIZZY               H. LING
B.C. MAY                 C. PEDRIMENT.

21. The inscribed stone from the Strike School that records the members of the National Committee.

22. An election meeting for George Edwards at East Rudham, Norfolk. Tom Higdon sits second from left. George Edwards centre, standing.

23. Tom and Annie Higdon shortly before Tom's death (possibly 1938).

24. Tom Higdon's funeral, 22 August 1939 (original image: Eastern Daily Press).

one years. He had never failed to pay his rent, and keeps the land in good order, but, because he had exercised his right to give support to the strikers by giving the use of his shop, the rector, like a good Christian, has stepped in and intends to evict this man on October 10. Not content with this outrage, he has pursued the same tactics against the good friend who had the impudence to act as a Christian, and give shelter to Mr. and Mrs. Higdon in the home which sheltered Joseph Arch thirty years ago. This friend farms a small piece of glebe land, for which he pays 37s. 6d. a year. His fathers before him for nearly one hundred years have held this land. There is no question of rent not being paid, or of improper cultivation; the sole reason for the proposed eviction is that he is in sympathy with the Higdons. Our readers must understand that not a single penny of salary for all the toil and labour of the past fifteen months has been paid Mr. or Mrs. Higdon; the villagers have maintained them by sending them gifts of food. To show how great is the feeling, one poor woman has given the result of a day's charing in order that food may be supplied. The spirit shown all through this dispute has been splendid, for every single power in the village is against the people—farmer, squire, and parson.

In spite of this, however, the workers have captured the parish council, and in the teeth of the village junkers have compelled the County Council to put in hand a housing school which is sorely needed. All this work, and the fact that Mr. Higdon is a member of the Executive Council of the Agricultural Labourers' Union, is the sole reason why the flogging case has been trumped against his wife, and they have been dismissed.

The demonstration last Sunday was unanimous in its condemnation of the present tactics. The Bishop of Norwich, who, as our readers will remember, has been appealed to, has told villagers to go to law. He knows full well that the law is on the side of the rector, as it is always on the side of those that have great possessions, and he knows, too, that no Christian should use the law to oppress and coerce his fellow men. Mrs. Reeves, George Lansbury, W. Smith, and J. Joplin all promised the people that they would do their best to rouse up Trade Unionists and labour people generally in order that this handful of brave men and women should win this fight against oppression. In order to fulfil this promise the *Herald* now appeals to all its readers and friends to come forward and assist in raising the sum of £50, which will see our friends through the coming winter, will enable school equipment to be purchased, and enable the Higdons to live.

Fifty pounds is not much for the *Herald* to raise in normal times. We have often raised much more in a single day. It is more difficult just now, and consequently we would urge our friends to earnestly appeal to everybody who cares for real freedom to help these men and women, poor so far as money goes, but very big indeed and very rich in spirit which is essentially British—that spirit which never knows defeat, but stands erect against all forms of tyranny. The treasurer of the funds is E. Reeves, The Strike School, Burston, Diss, Norfolk, and money sent to him will be gratefully acknowledged. To show how small consideration farmers and others have for the poor in such places it was publicly stated that in a neighbouring village the wife and large family of a man in France fighting for his country are under notice of eviction because the farmer wants the cottage for another man. Consider what this means. Men are urged to volunteer to fight for home and country, and while they are doing so farmers and justices of the peace take care to bring home to their wives and children the fact that they have neither home nor land to fight for. Parliament is killing a deal of time about things and little worth just now. Surely Messrs. Noel Buxton, Soames, and Hemmerde, Members for Norfolk, might find some time in order to put an end to, and also bring some pressure to bear on Mr. Arthur Henderson in order that the Board of Education shall without further delay end the Burston dispute by insisting on the reinstatement of Mrs. Higdon. Money is, as I say, urgently needed, but all of us in Trade Union branches, in the I.L.P, B.S.P., and other Labour organisations, can get resolutions passed urging our own members to move in the matter, and also call upon the Minister of Education to end the dispute, as suggested above. The management committee of the *Herald* have voted £5 to give the fund a start, so roll your postal orders along to Burston.

On 24 July 1915, a conference took place in Norwich between the county teachers and a deputation from the NUT Executive. The offer of arbitration was fully discussed and the conference came to the conclusion that Mrs Higdon would be wise to accept Henderson's offer. Two comrades known to Annie, who had been present at the conference, were despatched to see her; but they now could not persuade her to adopt the course advised. The first offer of arbitration had been rejected because there was no guarantee that she would be reinstated if the case went in her favour. At an evening meeting of villagers on the green, the arbitration offer was openly discussed and unanimously rejected.

The NUT Executive was finding that the situation was dragging on an uncomfortably long time. If it had not been for how the parents and the wider Labour Movement had rallied, the union probably would have completely washed its hands of the matter long back. As it was, that could not happen, but as well as a dearth of enthusiasm, its internal reports were full of exasperation; The NUT Executive Committee's Circular 876: The Case of Mrs. Higdon (Burston):

Throughout the case the Union's task has been made more complex by the fact that Mrs. Higdon was warned and afterwards transferred from her previous school. This transfer was only arranged with great difficultly by the Union through the good offices of the teacher-members . . .

. . . At every stage of the case the best advice which the Executive could tender has been given to Mrs. Higdon, but it has been invariably refused. Under these circumstances the Executive cannot be held responsible for the consequences. Notwithstanding the face that the teacher has been unable to accept the advice offered to her, the Executive have at all times been anxious to bring the unhappy dispute to an end. They have now exhausted every effort to secure a way out, and the deadlock remains, Mrs. Higdon having apparently placed herself entirely in the hands of a committee outside her professional organisation.

But when Henderson further renewed the offer of arbitration, Mrs. Higdon accepted it conditionally. The conditions being:

(1) In the event of arbitration going in her favour, the Norfolk Education Committee must reinstate Mrs. Higdon and her husband in Burston Council School under the old conditions.

(2) In the event of the Norfolk Education Committee refusing to agree to arbitration, the Union to undertake a vigorous campaign against the Authority to secure her reinstatement.

(3) The N.U.U to allow her a free hand as to the choice of legal counsel to represent her before the Arbitration Court.

Now, it was the NUT that would not give satisfactory assurances on the first two conditions and so, consequently, arbitration was refused again.

But the President of the Board of Education did not leave matters there. At a later date he wrote to the Norfolk Education Committee to propose a conference under his guidance. 'To this Mrs. Higdon gave a conditional agreement, but the Local Education Authority could not see their way to take part':[11]

Dear Sir—I have to thank you for your letter of October 21st. I am sorry that you are unable to meet me, because I had hoped that a personal and unofficial exchange of views might have contributed to a settlement of the Burston controversy. As my predecessor explained in the House of Commons, the matter is not one in which the President of the Board can intervene officially. I quite understand, however, your reluctance to take any step in this difficult matter without the knowledge and concurrence of your committee, and I should be much indebted to you, therefore, if you would lay the following statement and suggestion before them at an early date.

Immediately on taking office my attention was called to the circumstances of the Burston controversy, and I acquainted myself fully with the past history as well as the existing state of affairs. While clearly appreciating that the matter was not one for official intervention I thought that I should command the sympathy of all persons interested in the education of children of the county by doing what was in my power personally and unofficially to bring about a termination of the dispute. With this in view I caused an inquiry to be addressed to Mr. and Mrs. Higdon as to whether they, on their part, were willing that the matter should be referred to me personally for consideration and for settlement by way of arbitration if the concurrence of the authority in that course were obtained. After considerable delay, in the course of which I discovered that the dispute had unfortunately been aggravated by the emergence of other topics of controversy Mr. and Mrs. Higdon have accepted a proposal that a conference, consisting of three persons representing the Local Education Authority for Norfolk, and three persons representing themselves, should be held to consider the Burston School difficulty, and they have undertaken that if an agreement is reached between their representative and those of the Local Education Authority they will accept and abide by it. I now ask the Local Education Authority whether they are willing to appoint three representatives to take part in such a conference. I wish it to be understood that my intervention is personal and not official, and that my function would be to assist the two parties in arriving at an agreement, and to formulate the conclusion at which the conference arrives.

I should attend myself if I possibly could, but the authority will understand that the pressure of Ministerial work may make it impossible, and in that event I should appoint a representative to take my place.

While I, of course, recognise fully that it is competent for the Local Education Authority in their discretion to decline to take part in such a conference as I have suggested, I personally should greatly regret such a decision, as I feel that no means should be left untried which might prevent the prolongation of a situation which cannot but be very detrimental to the interests of the children and the parish— Yours very truly, Arthur Henderson.

If the Higdons were placing their commitment anywhere else, it was with their local supporters and with a rising tide of sympathy and material support coming from the wider Labour Movement. According to Tom, 'the last thing heard from the Education Committee was their rejection of Mr. Henderson's proposal for a Conference . . . and the scornful reference to Mr. Towler—a member of the Committee—to that offer as being the result of "the clamour of Labour Organisations."'[12] Tom notes with scorn that Mr Towler was himself at one time, 'when election fever ran high', a member of the Agricultural Labourers' Union.

Towler, though, was not entirely wrong; 1915 was to see two of the biggest and most remarkable public meetings to date. On 10 November a massive joint NUR, ALU and Vehicular Workers Union demonstration was held. It was then repeated on 28 November. At the time Samuel 'Sam' March was the leader of the National Union of Vehicle Workers; his own father was an agricultural labourer victimised for joining Joseph Arch's union in the 1870s.

The *Railway Review*, on 10 December 1915, carried a report on the public meeting of 10 November:

## THE BURSTON DEMONSTRATION
A body of London railwaymen, numbering 150, left Liverpool Street on Sunday last by the 9–10 A.M. en route for Burston, Norfolk, to demonstrate on behalf of Mr. and Mrs.Higdon, the wrongfully discharged schoolmaster and mistress of the Burston Village School, and also to show their disapproval of the action being taken against the glebe tenants of the village.

Bro. W. Carter (organising secretary) was in charge, and practically every London branch was represented by delegates, as well as representatives from Ipswich, Colchester, Bury St. Edmunds, Norwich, Beccles, Diss, etc., and banners from Bethnal Green, Neasden, Leyton No. 1, Southend, Paddington No. 2, Old Oak Common, Chalk Farm, Bermondsey, King's Cross Vehicle Workers, and the Agricultural Labourers' Union, also the Bermondsey Drum and Fife Band. A large number of school children and villagers also joined in the procession.

Arriving at Burston the procession was formed outside the station, and marching by a circling route, halted in front of the vicarage, where eloquent speeches were made by Bro. Carter and Comrade Higdon, cheers being given for our brave comrades for the fight they have put up. The demonstration then reformed and marched to the village green, where a public protest meeting was held, Mr. Higdon presiding.

Mr. Coe (Agricultural Labourers' Union) advocated the linking up of his union with the railwaymen, as our interests are inseparable. A pleasing feature of his speech was the great increase of membership into that society.

Mrs. Higdon spoke of a number of incidents of the strike, and called upon scholars and parents to come on the platform and verify her statements. Several of them gladly accepted. Mrs. Higdon gave some very amusing incidents that had occurred recently with the glebe tenants of the village who have stuck to them.

Bro. Matthews (Old Oak Common) then moved the following resolution: "That this mass meeting of railwaymen, agricultural labourers, and vehicle workers, representing 50,000 workers, protests against the unjust dismissal of Mr. and Mrs. Higdon and the attempted eviction of two glebe tenants by the Rector of Burston, and calls upon the Board of Education and the Norfolk Educational Committee to grant a public inquiry, with a view to the reinstatement of the teachers."

Mr. Appleton (Norwich Branch) seconded, and made several pointed remarks about the tyranny of the Vicar and his clique.

Bros.Butterfield (Southend), Gowing (Chalk Farm), and W.Carter (organising secretary) also supported. Bro. Carter said that the railwaymen had taken up the case of the evicted teachers, and were determined to see the thing through. If they were not reinstated there would be a "jolly row." The demonstration that day testified to the sympathy of the union; but they were also prepared to give financial support. Already they had provided four dozen chairs for the strike school, and he had collected £8 or £9 for other furniture required. With regard to the glebe evictions, he urged that if the tenants were threatened with eviction by the local magistrates the case should be taken to London to be finally settled, and his union would support this course with funds. Further, he was making arrangements for a big meeting to be held in London in connection with this dispute, and promised to secure one of the largest halls, or arrange for an open-air demonstration in Trafalgar Square or Hyde Park, at which Mr. and Mrs.Higdon would be at liberty to relate what had taken place in regard to their dismissal. It might also be possible for the children of the strike school to attend and take part in the demonstration.

The resolution was unanimously carried, and it was decided to send copies to the Prime Minister, Mr.A.Henderson (Minister of Education), Norfolk Educational Committee, Labour Party, Bishop of Norwich, Archbishop of Canterbury, and the National Union of Teachers. The meeting dispersed, and tea served in the strike school and neighbouring cottages, the good dames of Burston doing their best to make everybody comfortable.

After tea there was more speechmaking in the strike school, Mr.Reeves, a local gentleman, telling some very amusing incidents of the strike.

The procession was again formed, with banners rolled, and a march made to the station to the singing of Labour songs, where a grand rally ended by the singing of the "Red Flag."

Arriving back at Liverpool Street after 10, all agreed that a happy day had been spent in a good cause, and determined that if Mr. and Mrs.Higdon are not reinstated in the near future, and another demonstration is required from London, that it will consist of anything from 5,000 to 10,000 Trade Unionists.

Though the eviction of the glebe tenants could not be stopped, the ejection of Harry Ling and Harry Garnham was not brought to completion for some two years after the eviction notices had first been presented. On two previous occasions the matter had been before the court in Diss but adjourned—the first time to allow for a summons to be served on young Edith Moore, who it was alleged had served the notices to quit, and for her attendance to prove the same; and as she had failed to attend there had to be a second adjournment in order that she might be arrested.

'His act in asking for and obtaining a Warrant for the Arrest of the girl, Edith Moore, aged 15, of late in service at the Rectory, in order that she may be locked up and brought to Court to give evidence of Service of Notice on the Tenants speaks for itself.' Tom commented in *The Burston Rebellion.* 'Neither the brave girl nor her noble parents desired to assist the Rector in the eviction of the tenants from their holdings, and were so determined not to assist him that to evade arrest the girl had taken refuge in flight . . .'[13]

Edith was not to be found, the warrant not executed, and the Rev. Eland went on to make the final application for the ejectment orders against Harry Ling and Harry Garnham in January 1916. The case was covered in blow-by-blow detail by the *Diss Express* on 14 January. After a lengthy and detailed examination that included Eland, Harry and William Ling, Garnham, Lavinia Garnham, and Superintendent Bentham entering the witness box, the court was cleared for the magistrates to consult. Upon the re-admission of the public the chairman said they had considered the cases and were unanimously of the opinion that the services of the notices had been proved. An order would be made in each case for possession in twenty-one days.

But the final ejection order did not bring an end to all legal machinations. A month after the actual eviction, Rev. Eland once again took legal action against Harry Ling and Harry Garnham, this time for unpaid rent; £1 in the case of Garnham and £1.7s.6d. against Ling. Both defendants, though, on the nod from the union, countered with a claim for damages. The particulars of both counter-claims was that Eland's servants or agents had broken into and entered the land and removed certain chattels. On the first court day the cases were adjourned. The following week, when they were finally heard in Eye, the arguments of the defendants were rejected and the rent was paid.

'The facts concerning the Burston School Strike are of such character that all Trade Unionists must rally to their cause,' Chairman of West Ham NUR, W.H. Williams wrote in The *Railway Review* after the 28 November demonstration; 'Of all workers in every civilised country in the world the first and most important class in the deepest and truest sense of the word are the actual producers of food—the agricultural labourers.' In Williams' opinion, the great offence of the Higdons, which had damned them in the eyes of the squire and the parson had been their championship of the agricultural labourer.[14] Tom Higdon, the labourers' man, could not have agreed more.

Though planned as a joint demonstration, the second big November rally had been organised by members of London NUR branches in response to an appeal by the Diss branch of the NUR for 'assistance in a big propaganda effort and to publicly declare the sympathy and support of organised Labour with Mr. and Mrs. Higdon and the Burston School Strike'. The railwaymen, who had always been front and centre, were now pressing the matter with even greater effort. Their attendance on the day had been impressive but, more importantly, the demonstration resulted in the formation of a London Committee of Trade Unionists, with the object of bringing the Higdons to London to personally state their case.

Through the offices of Organising Secretary Mr W. Carter, a delegate meeting held on 5 January decided to arrange four meetings in the Northern, Southern, Eastern and Western districts. The first meeting took place at the Kentish Town

Public Baths on 20 February. The next day there was a meeting at the Congregational Hall, Harrow Road, Paddington. On Tuesday, under the chairmanship of Dr. Alfred Salter, JP, there was a meeting at the Bermondsey Town Hall. The location of an intended Stratford meeting was affected by the military that had monopolised all the town halls, and the Conference Hall being refused. However, W.H. Williams was able to secure the Leyton Public Baths, Cathall Road, Leytonstone. As the hall could seat up to 1,100 people, the rallying cry went out to the East London branches to 'back us up!' by sending supporters to fill the hall.

Along with Tom and Annie, some twenty of the striking school children travelled to London for the week. As the ordinary funds of the trade unions were not available to pay for the event, it was decided to issue collecting sheets. Over two hundred collecting sheets were then sent out across the whole of the London Labour movement—trade union branches, trades councils, and the women's organisations were approached and asked to participate. Joining the Higdons and the children on the platforms were George Lansbury, John Scurr, H.B. Walker (Gen. Sec. ALU), Will Godfrey (NUVW), and Casey and his fiddle. During the day deputations were made to the House of Commons and the Labour Party. And the children were given some fun trips to the zoo and a pantomime.

February had been a good month for Tom, in particular. As well as the London excursion, the annual Council of the National Agricultural Labourers and Rural Workers' Union had been held in Fakenham, Norfolk, on Saturday 12 February. The conference was able to cheer the Annual Report, which highlighted an increasing membership and steady financial growth of the funds of the union. Furthermore, according to the *Herald*, 'it is a striking tribute to record the labourers' resentment of injustice in the fact that Mr.T.G. Higdon was elected Treasurer of the Union and also came out at top of the poll for the Executive Committee of the Union.'

Soon, the two-year anniversary came around, and again the children recreated their march around the candlestick. Funds, though, were an ever-pressing matter, and to aid in that effort advertisements for *The Burston Rebellion* by T.G. Higdon began to appear in the left-wing press. Tom, who had always been a keen writer, had been gradually jotting down his version of events over the past year, but the task of revising and editing them into a presentable form was given to Violet Potter, then aged fifteen.

After the London speaking tour, the comrades of the London Committee of Trade Unionists had moved into organising regular fundraising social meetings. Back in Norfolk, with strong support still coming from the parents, Norwich ILP and a variety of trade unions, it was decided that a Burston School Strike and Evicted Glebe Tenants National Committee should be formed to bring together the representation from across the Labour movement. Its officers were to include: President George Lansbury; Chairman Mr Robert Green (National Agricultural Labourers); Vice Chairman Mr. G. F. Johnson (National Union of Teachers, Norwich); Secretary Mr Frederick O. Roberts (Northampton Trades Council); Assistant Secretary Mr W. Holmes (Organiser, National Labour Party); and Financial Secretary and Treasurer Mr W.Carter (National Union of Railwaymen).

In a four-page pamphlet circulated at the time, the reasons why the National Committee had been appointed were made clear:

To appeal for funds for the purpose of maintaining the Strike School in an efficient manner, and to assist the evicted Glebe tenants and parents.

To carry on an agitation through the Trades Unions, Trades' Council and Local Labour Parties.

To attempt to obtain a satisfactory settlement as opportunity presents itself.

The *Herald* immediately started to carry fundraising notices; the target was £5,000 and now the end game was the acquisition of land and the erection of a new school building. 'When victory has come,' the secretary wrote in an 'appeal to all Trades

Councils', 'the building will be handed over to the village in trust as a memorial of a valiant fight.'[15] The committee's secretary, Frederick Owen Roberts, was a compositor from the executive committee of the Typographical Association. At the 1918 general election he was to be elected as Member of Parliament for West Bromwich, but in 1916, as president of Northampton Trades Council, he was an effective writer of appeal notices and an efficient administrator.

By 2 August, Mr W.Carter, the treasurer, was able to report to the London Committee of Trade Unionists that the ongoing fundraising effort had raised £490 to date, and that £190 had been expended on the purchase of land and other expenses. The planned building, when completed, was intended to accommodate 70 children and be suitable to host 100 people for a public meeting. It was hoped that the school would be ready for use by the following October.

In November 1916, the *Herald* was able to state that £859 had been raised towards the cost of the new building. The paper was also to express some frustrations felt towards the LEAs for putting all kinds of obstacles in the way, and especially insisting on 'very up-to-date plans'. But the thing needed above all else was for trade unionists all over the country to continue to send subscriptions so that not merely the building would be paid for, but that it would be endowed with a sufficient sum of money to provide for its upkeep and the salaries of the officers.

The first 'other expense' of the National Committee had in fact been £44 on a wooden pre-fab building. With the eviction from the carpenter's shop, and with fundraising ongoing, the Higdons and the Strike School Committee had been forced into making temporary provision for the pupils. October was little more than six months away and an appropriate piece of land had yet to be purchased—let alone the first sod turned. The new but temporary Strike School was to be situated on the green for the next eighteen months.

Close to the pre-fab, and sandwiched between the green on its western boundary, and the church on its eastern, a small triangular slice of land lay unused. The land in question had been in the ownership of a Mr Middleton, a tobacconist from Bury St Edmunds, since 1905 when he had inherited it from his father. It was useless to him, and one section was purchased in July; but a further 10'6" section adjoining the north boundary was acquired three months later.

Still ongoing in April, the Burston school strike had been brought before a special NUT conference at Buxton. Only by a side-tracking amendment was a full debate averted. A motion against the union's Tenure Committee for its inadequate handling of the Higdon case also fell by 17,814 votes to 47,163. Nevertheless, at a meeting specially convened later in the day, at which 150 delegates were present, a vote of confidence in Mr and Mrs Higdon was passed and subsequently a committee formed to 'place the facts before every local association of the N.U.T.' To do this they published and distributed a pamphlet entitled: The Burston Case—Mr. and Mrs. Higdon—How It Affects N.U.T Members.

By July, ILP and BSP members of the NUT had been working hard to secure justice for the Higdons from their own union. The concerted effort to get resolutions passed at local associations meetings, and have them forwarded to the Executive since the conference, seemed to be working. Still, insiders to that end felt that many associations knew nothing of the struggle long underway, but that it would only require getting the information to them to gain support. Confidence in an internal shift in NUT Executive opinion was high.

By recent measures in Burston, the summer of 1916 passed with relatively little added drama. Even the Diss and Eye County Court had not been graced by a Higdon since March—which was probably a relief to everyone. It was, of course, not to last. With September came new summonses against Harry Ling, Harry Garnham and Thomas Higdon; the actions this time being brought by William Ling, Harry's brother, the new tenant of the glebe and churchwarden. The first action was to recover the sum of £12 (£10 value of wheat and straw, £2 for trespass) from Ling and Higdon. The particulars, as carried by the *Diss Express*, were as follows: 'On or about the 21st or 22nd of August, 1916, the defendants wrongfully entered upon a piece of land in occupation of the plaintiff and cut down and removed a quantity of wheat therefrom, and committed other waste thereon.'

In the other action against Garnham and Higdon, William Ling was seeking to claim redress in respect of a quantity of beans cut and carried away on the 16th or 17th of August, the value of the beans being £6 and the sum of £2 for trespass. None of the defendants were legally represented.

In his opening, the counsel for the prosecution was to helpfully remind the judge that he had been the one to hear the final ejection proceedings in March. And if anyone didn't know, he was also to outline how the situation had been reached. It was then that the defendants started to be called. As far as Ling and Garnham were concerned they had a perfect right to take what they had as they had sowed them. Clearly, there was no reason for the technicalities of the law to get in their way. Tom, being the more articulate defendant, was also the most argumentative, and was in the witness box for longer than the other two defendants combined. For His Honour, the notices to quit were in order, and the defendants were always on a sticky wicket in relation to their justifications of why they had done what they did. All three attempted to widen the discussion over how the notices to quit had come about, but the judge would not allow it.

In the case of William Ling against Harry Ling and T.G. Higdon, His Honour gave judgement for the plaintiff, allowing £4 for the wheat and £2 damages for trespass. In the case of William Ling against Harry Garnham and T.G. Higdon there was also a verdict for the plaintiff with an allowance of £3 for the beans and £2 for the trespass. An injunction was also granted in both cases costs with special allowance for items.

After the judgement had been delivered, Tom asked whether the cases should be adjourned in order that all the defendants might obtain legal assistance. His Honour replied that the application had come too late and refused it.

In December there was still time left in the year for Annie to find herself at the Diss Pretty Sessions Burston, being charged with allowing an ass to stray in the parish. The Aldrich family had been ardent supporters of the Higdons but after a couple of years the family had moved several miles to Rushall for work. Mrs Aldrich still desperately wanted her four children to attend the Strike School, but being such a distance away she turned to Mrs Higdon for advice. The solution was for Annie to buy a donkey and cart for them. Each day, the cart would drive the children the four or five miles to school, and the donkey would be left in the Strike School yard when the children were in class.

Police Constable Askew said he saw the animal repeatedly straying on to the road to Diss, and asked Mrs Higdon to whom it belonged. Annie denied ownership and instead told the constable that it belonged to Mr E.B. Reeves, the solicitor from Norwich. In court she asserted that it had never been in her charge and it was stabled at Harry Ling's.

Mrs Higdon, defending herself, called for Mr Reeves as a witness, but before he could make a statement the Chairman said the case would be dismissed.

An old friend was to re-enter the fray in winter 1917 when, at a special meeting of Norfolk County Council, the Burston dispute was once more brought forward when George Edwards moved the motion, calling: 'That this Council views with regret the unhappy state of affairs at Burston; that we appoint a deputation to hold a public inquiry into the cause, and report the same to the Council, the deputation to be at liberty to hear all available evidence.'

Edwards was to give a lengthy address, and from the outset protested against the false position that the Education Committee had placed him in by issuing a printed statement of their side of the case just before the meeting. The pamphlet that had been produced was, according to the old man, a defence against the charge that had never been made and that he had never intended to make. Furthermore, it went outside the scope of his motion.

He then protested against the Wood Dalling case being introduced into the debate, but then proceeded to comment in detail upon the various statements contained in the pamphlet issued by the Education Committee. Although he believed that the committee did not 'manifest a spirit of political and religious malignity towards these teachers, they had been unconsciously parties to what the general public believed to be an act of political and religious malignity and persecution'.

He then added that three million organised workers now stood behind the Higdons, and nearly £1,000 had been subscribed for their protection. If everything was fair and above board, he did not see why the Education Committee need fear an inquiry.

W.B. Taylor was next to speak, and seconded the motion. But Mr A.G. Copeman from the Education Committee argued that for the council to hold another inquiry could only be seen as a great slur on the Education Committee. 'There had been many inquiries before, and if after every inquiry they were to receive a resolution from the Parish Council that another inquiry be held, where were things to stop!' He would not deny (finally) that Mrs Higdon was a good teacher, but she was clearly a difficult woman to get on with.

Copeman's lackey, Mr F.C. Fisher, moved in straight after to propose a vote full in confidence in the Education Committee and was happy to declare 'that he had great confidence in their judgement'. Lord Kimberley said he had heard more mud chucking in the hour-and-a-half of this debate than he had ever heard before in his life. But Herbert Day, who had formerly been inclined not to believe that the accusations made against Mr Higdon could possibly have been fabricated, did speak in support of Edward's motion.

However, the chairman was perfectly satisfied by the Education Committee, and thought it was absolutely imperative in the interests of local government that the committee should have the power to maintain discipline, but 'Unfortunately they had come in contact with an individual who had proved herself unacceptable and difficult to deal with'. After Edwards replied to that, the chairman put to the meeting Fisher's vote of confidence in the Education Committee; it was carried thirty-seven votes to nine.

The failure of Edwards' attempts to galvanise some fairness and inquiry at the County Council could hardly have been taken as a setback, as the likelihood of success was always going to be marginal at best. But the efforts of Higdon supporters inside the NUT were beginning to bear fruit when Crook and Underdown, the president and vice president of the union, visited Burston on Monday 26 February. The purpose of their visit was to re-hear evidence against the charges, with some score or more witnesses being examined. Their inquiry, held in the Crown, was to last from 11.30am to 3pm, and the subsequent report was to be presented at the NUT Special Conference in London to be held at Easter.

It had been in the Crown Inn the previous week that the National Committee had gathered. With Robert Green presiding over the meeting, the date of the great opening demonstration was fixed for Sunday 13 May.

The NUT Special Meeting was held from 11–13 April. And to the motion 'That the Annual Report of the Executive be adopted, and printed for circulation', an amendment by executive member Mr G.D. Bell, seconded by Mr A.E. Warren (North West London delegate) was moved. Bell and Warren had attempted to get passed a call that:

This meeting is strongly of opinion that both Mr. and Mrs. Higdon should be granted sustentation as from the date their salaries ceased, that the Executive should insist on their reinstatement in Burston Council School, under satisfactory conditions, and that the whole resources of the Union, if necessary, should be utilised to secure their reinstatement.

The vote was lost on a show of hands—for the amendment 23,704 against 37,043—although the proceedings were closed before the result was declared. But like the Higdons themselves, their teacher-supporters in the NUT were too tenacious to simply give up in the face of persistent opposition.

Between the carpenter's shop and waiting for the new Strike School to be declared open, the wooden pre-fab had been a comfortable temporary lodgings for the children. In February 1917, when the plan had been submitted to the Building Committee of Depwade Council for its erection on the green,

Rev. Eland immediately wrote to state his opposition to the application, arguing that it was a gross infringement of the by-laws. In the time the decision had been deferred, the wooden school had been erected and put to use.

The dividing lines in the village were increasingly demarcated; the Parish Council meetings had been shifted from the Council School hall to the temporary Strike School. On the meeting of 3 March there were two main items on the agenda; a resolution was proposed by Tom and seconded by Henry Garnham calling the Bishop and ecclesiastical authorities to the fact that no meeting for an election of parish warden had been held. A resolution was proposed by Mr E.J. Potter and seconded by Noah Sandy stating that:

> The Parish Council regret that they have still occasion to complain of the action of the education authorities in continuing the wasteful expenditure on the upkeep of the Council School, which over the past three years had failed to command the confidence of the majority of the parents and ratepayers of Burston, whose children are still attending the strike school.

And in order to cover their backsides, it was proposed and carried that Mr. Higdon be charged the sum of 10/6 for standing the temporary school upon the playground.

But Eland and his friends were not yet done with the issue. With the District Council failing to order the removal of the Strike School's wooden structure from the Green, the Rector and five other parishioners had hired a solicitor to apply to the Court for an injunction for its removal. In the meantime, though, Tom had moved to give an undertaking to have it removed on or before 12 May, and to 'make good any damage to the Green'. The case was quietly dropped. The use of the wooden Strike School would actually continue into the spring of 1918, but it was all too late; the *Herald* 12 May 1917:

> On Sunday next the new school at Burston will be opened. A procession will start from Burston Station at 1 o'clock and

the meeting will commence at 3 o'clock. Congratulations to the N.U.R, and especially to Comrade Carter, for the great success which had attended their efforts, and congratulations, too, to our colleague John Scurr, who made the first suggestion that the strikers should build a school of their own. This piece of work shows true solidarity; the unions which have put up this money have it up for one purpose only—and that is to preserve the right of teachers to take part in Trade Union and social work generally. Mr. and Mrs. Higdon will now be able to work in the first non-provided school which has been established by the workers. We hope that the school will be linked up with both the Labour colleges—the Central Labour College and Ruskin College—and that the true spirit of comradeship and brotherhood will prevail. The N.U.R special train will leave Liverpool Street Station at 9.10 on Sunday morning and will return at 7 o'clock. As Burston is only a tiny village visitors had better take their own food.

# Chapter 13

# War and Consequences

'The Norfolk Nabobs of the County Education Committee and kindred authorities have been grievously disappointed this week. They are the class of people ever ready to prate about patriotism and British grit on battlefields abroad, but they are shocked when that ingredient appears in the character of the common people at home.'[1] The declaration of war on 4 August 1914 may have diverted the attention of most of the national press, but the *Herald* could still be relied upon to carry a supportive report.

Apart from the rural rebellion dropping off the front pages, the war had little effect on the strike initially. If the rector and his farmer allies had confidently anticipated that the war, and the harvesting operations, would have taken the edge off the determination of the villagers to resist, they were to find that the 'Burston folk are made of different stuff'.[2] But the war remained a potential threat to the long-term viability of the strike—if eyes, minds and funds all became focused on the overseas fight. By November, the *Herald* was having to remind its readers that 'Burston is not heard of nowadays as much as Calais or Ostend, although it is down in Norfolk, and the war in that region is as vehement as ever'.[3]

As the conflict escalated many of the young men in the village volunteered for the army, and the Higdons were to lose some of their keenest supporters. George Durbidge, Arthur Moore, 'who was "walking out" with Violet Potter at this time, and Harry Ling's son . . . were among the band of volunteers who left the village in uniform'.[4] The war was the one issue that the Higdons faced, as was the case with many families and national politics, on which they were divided. Annie remained a firm pacifist throughout, whereas Tom never backed away from what he saw as a just fight. It is not known whether he considered enlisting in some capacity; his brother Frank did join up and became a Major in the Royal Army Medical Corps, but he soon became involved in the war effort. Although even that afforded a local foe an opportunity, when he persuaded a group of soldiers that Tom was in fact a pacifist Socialist anti-war agitator:

> Time and space forbids one to tell of a Recruiting Meeting held at Burston, to which a company of soldiers were invited from Diss by a leading company of Burston Farmers, one of the Churchwardens, and how some score or so of soldiers came armed with clubs to "give that _____ Schoolmaster socks"—as they declared as they passed though the village on their way to the meeting.
>
> A corporal of the company confessed the whole business to Mr. H. a day or two afterwards, and expressed on behalf of his comrades and himself their deep regret for having been misled by their informant, who had, he said "let the Skulemaster down to the lowest," and said that he was opposed to recruiting, etc., etc. Thus they had come to the meeting expecting to find the Schoolmaster as an interrupter, instead of which they found him in the chair; for notwithstanding the presence at the meeting of the Rector of Burston and the Rector of the neighbouring parish of Gissing, the Burston folk assembled would have no one but the "Skulemaster" to preside over the meeting. The principle organiser of the meeting—a well-known Norwich Socialist—had also fixed upon Mr. H. as Chairman of the meeting. Thus the soldiers found no occasion for the use of their clubs. The Churchwarden was not present—for fear of the blows as had hoped to bring down upon other heads than his own.[5]

Tom Higdon was no militarist warmonger, but like many Labour leaders, such as his friend George Edwards, he had come to the conclusion that that there was no other alternative but to enter the war. The war was a struggle for the very existence of the country, and a necessary fight to overcome one of the greatest curses to humanity, namely, militarism. Once the fighting had begun he accepted the need to win the fight, but he did not support forcing people to do the fighting. Tyranny, as Tom was to write in his 1917 New Year address in the *Landworker*, was to be resisted both abroad and on the home front:

The New Year had come and had brought with it the unfortunate legacy of the Old Year—the War—by which sorrow and death have entered, and may yet enter, many homes—homes of labourers. All true union hearts beat in brotherly sympathy with each other under these sad and trying circumstances, as soon we hope to share the joys of peace or victory.

But there can really be no peace or victory for us which does not bring with it freedom for the countryside, liberty and life for the labourer and prosperity and plenty to his home and family. The labourer must henceforth take his place industrially, socially, and politically with the best and foremost of the land. He must do this himself—by force and power of his union. And he can!

Brothers, by the strength of your union during the past year you have accomplished what has never been done during previous wars—kept your wages somewhat apace with increased prices. By a still greater strength of unionism you could have done much more. Much has been lost by your weakness, much gained by your strength; but in the year just begun you must put forth all your strength and consolidate the positions you have won as well as make fresh progress, so that when peace comes and prices are again falling, by holding the ground gained your wages will then indeed be rising—rising—rising! See to it!

You must tackle the land and housing questions yourselves too—and abolish the tied cottage system. You can do it—and only you—through—your union!

Therefore in wishing you all a prosperous New Year can bring, I feel that I can wish you nothing better or more beneficial than a new baptism of the spirit of the Labourers' Union—and I crave the same myself.[6]

But most of the young men that the Higdons knew were still in the fields during the first weeks of the war. The first harvest experienced no shortage of men—the only shortage being that of horses, after thousands were taken into military service. But nationally, by the early months of 1915, 'the available workforce had dropped by 7 per cent', and then the labourers began to flex their muscles.[7] From the middle of 1915 there was not only a labour shortage, but prices were rising, increasing both the profits of farmers and the prices of food for the labourer.

*Poor Labouring Men—Rural Radicalism in Norfolk 1870–1923* by Alun Howkins, comprehensively covers the growing agitation among the labourers in some parts of Norfolk during the war period. But in particular to Tom (working alongside Comrade Joe Smith) he helped establish twenty-three Labourers' Union branches in Norfolk, including at Carleton Rode, Shelfanger, Winfarthing, Gissing, Tivetshall, Kenninghall, Old Buckenham, Tibenham, Billingford, Hoxne, Mulbarton, and Diss.

As an executive member of the National Union of Agricultural Labourers, and having acquired a little fame, T.G. Higdon 'of the Burston Strike School' would also speak at meetings well beyond the Eastern Counties. During the first week of September 1917, the *Western Gazette* reported on a series of meetings in the Poole and Dorchester district addressed by Tom. Meetings were held in Winterbourne, Bere Regis, Milbourne St. Andrews and Tolpuddle. Described as being attended by large numbers of villagers, the result was that branches of the union were formed. At the Tolpuddle meeting, the newspaper was to comment upon the 'large number of women and children attending as well as men, though the latter were to some extent prevented by the harvest operations when the evening was fine'.

Simply, the war was a boom time for organising agricultural labour. As part of a policy to increase home-grown cereal production, a new Food Production Department of the Ministry of Agriculture was created in 1917. A sub-committee of the Reconstruction Committee was subsequently appointed under Lord Selbourne, to consider the methods required to increase production.

The Selbourne Committee did for the labourer what 50 years of trade union agitation had failed to do—it guaranteed a national minimum wage and a fixed working week. The committee recommended a fixed wage as a national minimum to be set by a wages board based on the trades boards of the pre-war era. The board was to consist of representatives of the workers and the farmers.[8]

The Selbourne Committee Report came into being in the Corn Production Act of August 1917. The act 'embodied most of the union's pre-war aspirations—indeed in all but detail it was identical to the proposal put by G.H. Roberts in 1913'.[9] The six representatives elected by the Executive Committee of the National Agricultural Labourers and Rural Workers' Union, were namely: G.E. Hewitt, W. Holmes, R. Smith, R.B. Walker and Mr T.G. Higdon.

Although the Higdons remained childless, they had at the same time the largest family in Burston. Annie Higdon was often described as a 'mother to us all', and she certainly viewed and treated all of her pupils as her children. Some of the older boys, on their arrival in the village, had become old enough to enlist. And some of the parents were young enough to also enlist. By 1916 George Durbidge had found himself in an army camp in Malta, and unable to poach, drink and brawl in quite the same way, he would correspond back home with tenderness:

Dear Mr. Higdon i thank you very much for the nice letter that you sent me and i am Pleased to hear that you and Mrs.H. are in the Pink. Well Tom as i will still call you I was very pleased to hear such good news about the doings of the old strike school. i feel quite proud of you all. you deserve a medal as large as a plate. but I know your old heart is in the right Place. and to stick to the one thing that you have Battled for the last two years. that is justice which is a thing that we seldom get. but at the same time. unity is strength and strength means victory for the Burston Allies. Dear Tom I am very proud of our good and brave companions that have taken such interest in our fight for freedom from the vile and unjust persons that are surrounding us. Please remember me to all at the strike school tell them we will have a good old Beano one day, So I must Conclude with Best Wishes to you all and a good Harvest for them all I Remain Yours Very Truly,

G.W. Durbidge.[10]

From the early days of the war, the Strike School was in full operation, and the school strike just months—not years—old. The pupils were schooled on a daily basis as they had always been, and the Higdons still took some of the children out to Labour meetings. When interviewed in the 1970s, Violet Potter recalled how, when out overnight for one of these meetings:

. . . there were German Zeppelins over . . . some bombs were dropped and we girls, we six girls waked up and of course were terrified. Mrs. H. came into out bedroom and sat by our beds and prayed. Of course everywhere was in Darkness. Groping across the bedroom she tripped over the pot [no bathrooms then] and broke it.[11]

And, though the war was to take away from the people she loved, Annie Higdon was not one to hold any animosity towards the men from the opposite trenches. Violet Potter, musing in a later letter, recalled how 'She could speak German. One evening, during the First World War, she was taking a few of us, me, Marjory Ling, Hetty Wilby, Lily Bridges, and one or two other senior girls, to the Chapel at a neighbouring village. There was to be a talk on "Pilgrim's Progress," with lantern slides, and coffee and biscuits afterwards. That was about two miles from Burston. We passed the grounds of Burston Hall, where some German prisoners-of-war were cutting the hedge.

Mrs. Higdon talked to them in German and told us afterwards that they were quite nice men. One of them, perhaps he was an officer or something, he wasn't working, he was just standing there watching the others, I suppose he was in charge, said he had a wife and children in Germany. He hadn't wanted to fight. He had to do what he was told.'[12]

Yet the Higdons and their supporters were not averse to using the national crisis in aid of their own propaganda campaign. 'At the present time, when our brave soldiers are fighting Junkerism abroad,' begins the 'Prussianism in Norfolk' appeal notice, 'the little village of Burston in Norfolk has been goaded into revolt. Brave-hearted men, women, and children have been evicted from the land of their fathers.' And, if it wasn't already clear, it also helpfully exclaims in capitals: TWO OF THESE MEN HAVE SONS FIGHTING IN THE TRENCHES.

But Harry Ling and Harry Garnham were not the only two fathers with sons in the trenches; Reverend Eland's only son Arthur had enlisted, and Arthur 'Sydney' Steward, Eland's houseboy domestic who had moved with the family from Felsted, was killed by the end of 1914. But even the sharing of loved ones fighting in foreign fields would do nothing to unite the village.

By June 1917 the depth of ill feeling between the parties was such that that a full on melee erupted inside the church. Harry Garnham's son had become a victim of the mass slaughter, and had fallen in the middle of the rector's attempt to evict the glebe tenants. The seeds of the 'tablet brawl' were sown when Garnham's brother-in-law put up a memorial tablet in the church without telling the young man's parents.

A case was subsequently lodged at the Norwich Consistory Court when the Garnham's, supported by Tom Higdon, officially objected to the tablet on the grounds that 'they had not been consulted on the matter; that they regarded the action as an invasion of their rights; and that they proposed placing a suitable memorial tablet to their solider son in Shimpling'.[13]

The defendant's spokesman was to state that the dead nephew and uncle, Mr R. Ford, were on good terms and that he had fair justification for doing what he had done in remembrance. But less than five minutes into his opening statements, the real division that lay at the heart of the matter was exposed when it was suggested that a good deal of friction was due to the Burston school strike. 'The soldier's uncle is a supporter of the rector's party, while his parents range themselves in the side of the strikers . . .'[14]

A short while later it was again back to the strike issue; 'if it had not been for the unfortunate, divisive episode of the Burston school strike there would have been no objection to the very kind act of the uncle in erecting the tablet. Mr Garnham was a "partisan" of the strike while Ford was not.'

When the tablet was erected, Garnham prayed a faculty from the Consistory Court for its removal. Before Ford had made any move he had taken counsel of the rector. When the chancellor asked Mrs Garnham, 'Why should Mr Ford have any spite against you?' again, it was made clear how it was viewed by them: 'Because he holds with the clergy, I am, and my husband went to the services on the green in connexion with the school strike. It is nothing else.'

The judgement of the chancellor of the Consistory Court, Mr F.K. North, was delivered in June, and resulted in what the *Eastern Daily Press* described as 'such an unseemly scene' at the Norwich Consistory Court. The chancellor had decided against the Garnhams; the tablet would not be removed. The dispute, as the paper would note, had given rise to considerable feeling, so after the chancellor had delivered his judgement, 'Mr. Higdon, well-known in connexion with the Burston School Strike, accused the Chancellor of having made unfounded imputations, and having "sucked in a thread of lies," woven by the solicitor . . .'[15] On leaving the court the chancellor was intercepted by Higdon and Garnham. The chancellor declined to continue the conversation in the cathedral, but outside they approached him again and he was 'warmly assailed with renewed accusations of having unjustly determined the case', before following him at some distance. It took the threat of arrest to make Tom fall back.

But the immediate sequel was the determined attack on the tablet, followed by an even more uproarious scene, the following day. One who was present described what happened to a reporter from the *Eastern Daily Press*:

> After the first service the congregation who were not communicating left, "and into the church came Mr. Garnham and his daughter Daisy. They sat quietly during the whole of the administration of the Communion, but they did not partake. Nothing happened until at the close of the service, the rector (Rev. C.T. Eland), the churchwarden (Mr. Johnson), and the parish clerk (Mr. William Ling) were in the vestry. We heard a great smashing of something. I remarked, "Surely, they are breaking the memorial tablet," and we rushed out of the vestry. Mr. Garnham we saw dealing the tablet blows with a heavy hammer. Mr Johnson took hold of him round the waist and pulled him back from the tablet, and Mr. Ling seized the hammer and after some difficultly obtained it. While this was being done Mr. Ling was assaulted by Miss Garnham. She flew at him to prevent him getting the hammer. Afterwards the rector persuaded the Garnhams to leave the church and wait outside. Here Mr. Garnham, demanded his hammer from the clerk, who said he had thrown it away, and excepting that the girl followed us and used strong language, nothing further happened at the time. In the afternoon the churchwarden sent for Police-constable Askew. The constable called on Mr. Ling and went to the church to get possession of the hammer."

Our representative went into the church and examined the tablet, which is affixed to the wall on the south side of the nave. There is a crack extending from the bottom, through the centre and nearly to the top. Numerous bits of the surface of the marble have been knocked off, and some of the lettering has been defaced.

Mr. Garnham and his daughter gave their version of the incident in an interview by the present writer. They make no secret of their determination and that of all the family to get the tablet out of the church by hook or crook. It had been placed there, they say, without any consultation with them for the purpose of annoyance, and is in consequence of a difference of opinion about the Burston School Strike between Mr. Garnham and his brother-in-law, Mr. Ford. "I went to the church with my daughter," said Mr. Garnham, "with the fixed intention of spoiling the tablet, and took a hammer with me. We did not wish to disturb the service, and waited until Communion was over and the rector, the sexton, and the churchwarden were in the vestry. Then I began. I got on to the seat of the pew and struck the tablet three or four heavy blows with the hammer. Then the parson and the others rushed out from the vestry and took the hammer from me, but not until I had altogether hit the tablet some twenty times."

"The tablet," Miss Daisy Garnham said, "is over two pews, that my uncle, Mr. Ford, and the other which belongs to our house, which we will not occupy so long as the present rector is at Burston. Mr. Eland came out of the vestry and pushed me aside roughly, but I pushed him back in self-defence and to keep him from daddy. I told him he was not to touch my father, and that was why I went to the church that morning. Mr. Johnson and Mr. Ling than caught hold of me, and bruised my arm. I fell down in the struggle, and my eye was struck."

"I kept the hammer as long as I could," interposed Mr. Garnham, "and if they had let me alone I would have been using it till now. It is awfully disgraceful to have a riot in a church, but I went there only to wreck that tablet."

Miss Garnham resumed her narrative of the part she played, adding, "It was quite a suffragette's action, but still I don't like it in church. We told the Chancellor after the Consistory Court on Saturday that we would knock the tablet out of the Church. It was put there without our consent and we are all prepared to suffer a great deal to have it out." "Yes, and out it will come," said Mrs. Garnham, "whatever the consequences. We only hope my brother, for his own credit's sake, will take it away. It is all because of the strike meetings on the Green."

Mr. Garnham smiled when asked about what had happened to Mr. Ling on Sunday afternoon. "Mr. Higdon and my son Charles," he said, "met Ling near his home. They said they would just carry him home shoulder high to honour him for the noble part he took in assaulting my daughter in the church that morning. They picked him up and carried him a few yards, and let him down again. That was all."

The commotion led to summonses and counter-summonses that lasted to the end of the year. Harry Garnham was first summoned for wilful and malicious damage to the tablet, and Daisy for violent behaviour in the church and with aiding and abetting her father. Daisy was bound over to keep the peace for a year but her father was sentenced to one month's imprisonment with hard labour for 'wilfully smashing the tablet'. In an attempt to save Garnham from prison, Tom Higdon stated that he was willing to pay £20 or go to prison himself; the Chairman insisted the matter was settled.

Later in October, but originally heard at a July sitting in Diss, a subsequent case was made by Rev. Charles Tucker Eland, Alfred Johnson and Robert Barnes Ford against Harry Garnham, his wife Sarah and daughter Daisy. The plaintiff's (that is, Eland only, in practice) was now claiming:

1. The sum of £11/11, being as to £6/6 costs of erecting the said tablet and as to £5/5 costs of obtaining a faculty for its erection.

2. The sum of £5 for damages for the said trespass.

3. An injunction to restrain the defendants and their servants and agents from in any way damaging or interfering with the said tablet or committing any trespass at the said Parish Church.

4. Such further or other relief as the Court may deem fit.

At the July court, an injunction had been granted against the Garnham family, but it had reserved the question of damage to October pending an appeal made by Harry Garnham at the Norfolk Quarter Sessions against his sentence of a month's imprisonment. His sentence was to be modified to imprisonment only. After a lengthy rerun and examination of the events that had occurred, His Honour announced that he would give judgement for the plaintiff for six guineas towards the cost of the tablet, one guinea the estimated expenses for taking it down, and three guineas towards the fee for the faculty as he saw no grounds for the opposition raised. The prosecutor tried to press for damages for trespass, but the judge declared that 'the defendants have suffered very severely already'. In closing the judge remarked to Mrs Garnham that 'You have not got over that bitter feeling yet'. Mrs Garnham was quick to shoot back: No more than they or they would not have put the tablet there.

The rector, Alfred Johnson, and William Ling were summoned by Daisy Garnham for assault—the case was dismissed. Tom Higdon, Harry Garnham, Anne Marie Garnham and Daisy Garnham were summoned for having used abusive and insulting language to the Rev. C.T. Eland and Mrs Eland on 1 July—they were all fined. In addition, Higdon and Garnham were fined £1 for the 'assault-cum-honouring' on William Ling.[16]

The final case, heard in September but adjourned for the summer so Daisy Garnham could obtain legal assistance, was brought against Eland for assault. The claim was that one evening, when riding through the village on her bicycle, she had to pass the rector and William Ling. As she went by she said she felt a thud arising from the rector who, having a stick, struck her mudguard; near heroically, as described in court, she managed to keep her balance 'although was left very frightened'.

Mr Yorke, the solicitor representing Daisy, asked the Bench to dismiss the question of the Burston school strike and 'other matters brought before them recently as the case was absolutely independent of them'. A bold, brazen effort if ever there was one. The rector, Yorke was happy to argue, should be bound over for a year—just like Daisy had already been.

During what can only be described as a mammoth session discussing which side of the road Daisy Garnham was actually on, the rector alleging that 'she came at full speed at him, just missing his knee, and the bicycle struck his walking stick',[17] the magistrates consulted in private and the chairman announced that the charge against the rector was dismissed.

With the signing of the Armistice with Germany on 11 November 1918, a victory had been gained for the Allies, and an uneasy peace was beginning to settle in Burston. The general election called immediately after the end of the war was to be held on Saturday 14 December—the first election to be held on a single day, although the vote count did not take place until 28 December due to the time needed to transport the votes of serving overseas soldiers.

In preparation for the future election, the July meeting of the Executive Council of the Agricultural Labourers' Union had already considered the question of Labour candidates for Parliament. The recommendation of the Kings Lynn Trades Council that R.B. Walker should stand for the Kings Lynn division was endorsed. The council then proceeded to select four others, providing constituencies could be found for them; the choice fell on George Edwards, George Nicholls (both of whom had severed their connection with the Liberal Party; Edwards finally at the start of 1918), Robert Green and T.G. Higdon.

On 20 November, at a special meeting of the South Norfolk Divisional Labour Party, George Edwards was formally adopted as their candidate of the division. No constituency was to be found for Tom, but he nevertheless threw himself into campaigning for his old friend. South Norfolk was always going to be a tough ask, particularly as a wave of post-war conservatism engulfed the country. Edwards was to lose by a majority of 5,159.

Two years later and further events would prove that the 1918 election defeat had been a temporary one. The winning candidate, Cozens-Hardy (now a Lord) became ill and was not expected to live long, but his elevation to a peerage meant a by-election. Again, the Divisional Labour Party passed a resolution asking the Labourers' Union to find a candidate, for whenever the Divisional election took place. In the end, Edwards, won the resulting by-election in July 1920, with 46 per cent of the votes, with the Liberal vote split between pro- and anti-coalition candidates. George Edwards had become, at the age of seventy, the first Labour MP to represent a genuinely rural constituency.

Tom Higdon was never to be selected to stand for a constituency, either at a national or county election. The Labourers' Union executive would on more than one occasion place him on their shortlist of preferred candidates, but in Divisional Labour Party votes he would poll poorly, if not bottom. He was far from being the only outspoken Socialist on the executive; his 'advanced views' (as less radical executive members would refer to his politics), mixed with his notoriety as the 'strike skulemaster' and that counted against him in some Labour circles.

But whether it was the effect of stirring patriotism, or just that of a lower turnout, mixed with an absence of core supporters at the Parish Council elections in 1919, the former political status quo reasserted itself in Burston. The *Diss Express*, 11th April 1919:

> Some little excitement was caused in this village on Monday in connection with the election of a Parish Council. Polling took place in the Council School, Mr A.E. Scarlett of Long Stratton acting as Returning Officer. The election was mainly on Party lines, and there were fourteen candidates for seven seats. Half of this number were supporters of the Labour Party, who for the last six years have monopolised all the seats on the Council, and they were opposed by seven others who made a strenuous effort to alter the composition of the Council. Indeed, both sides worked hard to achieve success, and tried their utmost to bring up every possible elector to the polling booth.

In the event, Tom Higdon's Labour group received around fifty votes each, and their opponents around seventy. 'Earlier, on a show of hands . . . Tom and his group had received a few over thirty votes, a result similar to that 1913 election, and were declared elected,'[18] but their opponents, once more lead by Rev. Eland, demanded a poll, and succeeded in getting the show-of-hands result reversed. The rector was then elected as Chairman of the Parish Council. A moment of immense satisfaction six years in the making for the clergyman, and one of a few choice words over an ale at the Crown for the Higdon loyalists.

To make things even more niggly, as Chairman Eland now presided over the local housing question, an issue both of passionate importance to Tom, and one on which the labourers swept to power on the back of in 1913. At the parish meeting in December, the best Tom Higdon could do was propose (with Mrs Eland seconding) a motion declaring that there was now a greater need for houses than before the war. The motion was carried unanimously. But the chairman declined to put to the meeting a motion suggesting conscription of houses where the bedroom accommodation was greatly in excess of requirements.

Although the political balance on the parish council may have swung back to something akin to pre-school-strike days, significant numbers of parents were still sending their children to the Strike School and boycotting the established church services. During Eland's tenure as rector, no child of an agricultural labourer was baptised in the church, and only gradually did that readjust after his departure. That came in June 1920 when the Rev. C.T. Eland exchanged livings with the Rev. F.T. Smith, Rector of Sawtry, near Peterborough, and left for parish at the end of the month.

The reasons for Eland moving on at that point are unknown; but perhaps after riding out the stormiest days, and in finally capturing the position that had eluded him, he felt he could walk away on his own terms. His parishioners appear not have gifted the rector anything, yet it was a better ending than George Durbidge was to receive.

'I have shot my father,' Hector MacDonald Durbidge declared to the police after he had run, in his socks, all the way to Diss to hand himself in. Hector, a railway porter at Burston, described in the paper as a 'civil and obliging servant', had shot his father, the 'well-known local character', to death.

Mrs Durbidge had already left her husband and was staying with relatives in London because of threats made by him in the week before. After returning home in what was described at the inquest as a 'very excited condition', he had taken up a gun and threatened to shoot his wife. It was then that she escaped the house and did not return until five the next morning, when she grabbed her youngest child and fled to London. She was not return to Burston until the day after her husband was shot.

George Durbidge always kept a loaded 12-bore double-barrelled gun hanging on the wall, ready for instant poaching. But on the night of Friday 27 February 1920 he had returned home considerably worse for drink. A quarrel followed, and his father challenged his son, aged 19, to a fight. Hector sensibly declined the challenge, but out of fear had loaded his small sporting rifle and, seeing that his father was reaching for his gun, fired. In court he stated that he had only intended to frighten his father, who was felled in front of him. George, aged 51, had been shot through the heart and died instantly.

In only his stockinged feet, and without a jacket, Hector first ran to the Potter house and threw stones at the window, shouting out that he had killed his father. When John Potter appeared, his advice for the boy was for him to go and give himself up, which he immediately did.

Later, when being cautioned by Inspector James, he reportedly said, 'I don't care as long as I have saved my mother.'

John Potter then went to the Durbidge cottage and was said to have seen George through the window sitting in his chair with his gun between his legs. 'He thought he might still be alive so he was afraid to go in. But at that moment the police arrived.'[19] The body was still warm—the discharged rifle was discovered in the garden close by.

The inquest verdict was that George was a quiet, likeable man when not drunk, but he had become increasingly drunk and violent following his return to the village after being demobbed—the medical evidence showed signs of acute alcoholism. When it came to Hector's action, the inquest's opinion was that 'no blame attaches, as our opinion is that the son only intended to disable and not kill his father, and we think the son was justified in trying to disable his father'.[20]

As a boy, George Durbidge had a perfect attendance at school under Mrs Green; he went on to be a successful businessman and a local leader among the villagers. But at Hector's trial at the Norfolk Assizes, the record against the man was that he was said to be a terror to the neighbourhood, had fifty-five convictions, including two for threatening to murder and sixteen for assaults. His wartime experiences had only accentuated his inner brutality.

Hector's defence was a plea of self-defence. The jury returned a verdict of manslaughter under great provocation and sentenced him to six months' imprisonment. A petition signed by his mother was raised, calling for the sentence to be quashed. When one member of the deceased's family was asked if he was sorry that his father was dead he replied, 'Not a bit!'

The family did not stick like shit.

No mention was made of the part George William Durbidge played in the Burston school strike.

# Chapter 14

## Echo of a School Strike

The war was over, but the 1919 Peace Celebration was somewhat marred by an accident during a bicycle race involving E.J. Potter, R. Sturman and Tom Higdon, who were competing in a race around 'The Candlestick'. The celebratory pursuit followed the same mile-and-a-half course made famous by the striking children, but in one part, the sharp corner near Alfred Johnson's farm, the three fast-riding competitors came upon the awkward corner and Tom failed to negotiate it safely. All three were thrown to the ground; Potter and Sturman escaping unhurt, but Tom, [hitting] his head and face on some stones near the side of the road, received a heavy cut over the left eye and some bruising and scratches on the face, and a cut on the elbow and cuts on the knees. Dr Speirs was obtained from Diss and stitched the wounded Tom up.

The year was also not to pass without its quarrels and divisions; yet this time it was to be among old friends. With the Strike School having been completed in 1918, the National Committee had realised its main objective. Although all routes to see the evicted glebe tenants returned to their lands had been exhausted, enough funds had been raised to build the school and to provide a maintenance grant to the Higdons. Through the spring of 1918 the committee still existed, with Frederick O. Roberts as Secretary and W. Carter treasurer, but then it ceased.

Mrs Higdon had quarrelled with some members in its last days; the exact details have not been recorded, but given a case brought at the County Court in Northampton, it's reasonable to deduce it was over funds. When Sol Sandy was interviewed in the 1970s he thought that it might be 'about the funds being used for election expenses', understandable as the case was against Fredrick O. Roberts; it was not that, but rather for £39 and £16.13s.4d. of salaries alleged due to Tom and Violet Potter, who for a time worked as a monitress.

As Treasurer of the Labourers' Union, Tom was a known stickler for accuracy and for not letting funds be used for unintended purposes; or in February 1919, vice-versa. By the time the case came round Roberts had been elected the MP for West Bromwich, but as was made clear in court he was not being sued in a personal capacity but as Secretary of the Burston Strike School Committee. Violet Potter, who was by then working as a bookkeeper in London, was called as a witness. Violet did not attend, and later in life claimed she knew nothing about the case. On the day of the hearing Tom Higdon could not attend; a medical certificate was produced and the case was withdrawn.

Whether there were last minute second thoughts or pressure put on Tom from within Labour circles to withdraw the case is unknown. But it was not quite the end of the matter, as the following week Roberts was the plaintiff and Tom Higdon and Violet Potter (described in the *Northampton Mercury* as a pupil-teacher) the defendants, as his legal representation asked for costs of the sum £10.14s.10d. No defence was made and the bill was quietly paid.

Before the final expiration of the National Committee, the treasurer had reported to the NUT that funds were exhausted, and there were liabilities of £150 owing to the builder. But this was not so, as the balance sheet for the Burston Strike School and Evicted Glebe Tenants' Fund shows a credit balance of £137.7s.2d. on opening. Though possibly a genuine error by W. Carter, it is more likely the reported deficit was part of politicking being used to try to extract funds from the union, whose executive had not made (and did not make) any contribution towards the building of the Strike School, but limited payment to sustentation.

It was a full three years after the outbreak of the strike that the NUT conducted its own enquiry. But despite the lapse of time, the unwillingness for witnesses to attend, and the mass of contradictory statements, after ten meetings the committee concluded:

> ... that the principal witnesses were no longer prepared to accuse Mrs.Higdon of ill-treatment of her pupils. Even the Rector skated round the issue, and, since there was no previous record of the schoolmistress resorting to corporal punishment, the committee ruled that she did not cane the Barnardo children. Moreover, while Ethel Cummings may not have been "mentally or morally deficient" she was, according to the committee, "dull and subject to lapses in memory." But most importantly, the NUT argued that, irrespective of the rights and wrongs of Mrs.H.'s professional behaviour, the manner in which the County Council enquiry was instituted and conducted made their report totally invalid. In the first place Mrs.H. did not attend the proceedings. Secondly, the letters to Dr. Barnardo's Home, copies of which Eland was somehow able to obtain, were inadmissible evidence. Finally, the Rector was too much involved in the case, as he acted both as plaintiff and judge when the managers carried out their preliminary investigation. The Union also admitted that the assistance and advice offered to the Higdons was inadequate and blamed the members of the Law and Tenure Committees, who were jointly responsible for defending the interests of the schoolteachers and yet were unwilling to co-operate efficiently or act decisively.[1]

It was only after these conclusions were reached that the Executive then passed the following resolution with regard to sustentation:

That sustentation up to the limit of the full day's school salary be paid to Mrs. Higdon as from 30 June 1914, to date.

That the Norfolk Education Committee be asked to reinstate Mrs. Higdon in a position of similar value elsewhere in the County.

That sustentation be continued to Mrs. Higdon during the interval of waiting for reinstatement.

That in the event of the Norfolk Education Committee refusing reinstatement, Mrs. Higdon be sustained in the Burston Strike School.

The Norfolk Education Committee declined to reinstate Mrs Higdon, and sustentation grants were not paid in any case for a period exceeding five years. In June 1919, the report of the Higdon Special Committee, a sub-committee of the Tenure Committee, recommended that 'as sustentation had been paid for five years, the time period allowed under its Sustentation By-Laws', payment should stop and the union take no further responsibility for Mrs Higdon's maintenance.

The Strike School had become an institution built and sustained by miners, railwaymen, ILP and various other subscribers from the Labour Movement, but not the teaching union—the NUT was completely adverse to involving itself in the funding of a new form of independent working class education. Each year the Higdons would circulate a new pamphlet and the annual accounts, to stimulate both new pupils and donations to keep the school open. If anyone was unsure what the Strike School was about, the leaflet from 30 May 1919 articulates it clearly:

We thank you for the support we have received in aid of our fight, and for carrying on the work of the strike school. We are herewith sending you our statement of accounts, from which it will appear that funds are still needed, so that comrades and societies wishing to help need not hesitate to do so.

The school strike, which began 1 April 1914, has now been in existence over five years, and has thus seen the war in and out; and still the parents, children, and teachers and their supporters in Burston are solidly united in their protest against injustice and tyranny and in their fight for Freedom.

Many of the scholars who first came out on strike, have, of course, left school and gone to work but forty children are still attending the strike school, and such is the hold of this new democratic, educational and social movement upon the life of the village that most of the infants who come along find their way to the school and take the places of the older children who are constantly leaving. Thus what began as a strike of school children on behalf of their teachers, and was spoken of by the rector, Chairman of the School Managers, as 'all moonshine', 'a nine days wonder' etc., etc., had become a permanent Socialist Educational Cause and Institution [and] 'The first Trades Union School in England.'

The day may come when the Labour movement will officially recognise and finance the strike school, but at present the school depends upon the voluntary contributions of individual sympathisers and the donations of T.U. branches and social societies as seen by the attached balance sheets. Our friends will do us a great service in helping to make our school known in this direction by handing on this circular to other branches or by sending us the names and addresses of Branch secretaries.

This voluntary support has the advantage of leaving the school free and unfettered by officialdom of any kind, provided it is not hampered by lack of funds . . . The fight has ever been sustained, and the work of the school regularly turned out by the constant unity and devotion of the pupils and teachers.

Arrangements are made for boarding scholars, should comrades living at some distance desire to avail themselves of the opportunity of sending their children to the strike school. Burston is a very healthy village. Medical advice for the strike school costs nothing, it is so seldom required. Burston breezes, Burston bread (home-made) and the strike school buildings are all of the best, and it has been remarked that 'the children look the picture of health'. Their playground is the beautiful common, a heritage preserved for them by their forefathers, who fought and died for the common rights of Norfolk.

The new strike school building, besides serving as a free Elementary Day School and for the training of the children in the principles of freedom and socialism, is also used for public meetings on Sundays and week nights in connection with the strike, the Agricultural Labour Union and moral and revolutionary propaganda generally. It is the centre of a new, living movement of educational and social activity which together with the building itself and many inscriptions on its walls will, it is hoped, form the best lasting memorial of the villagers' fight for Freedom and Justice.

It is from the wider national character of our fight, as well as from the local aspects of it, that we feel we can commend our Cause to all sections of the Labour movement.

Although all sections of the Labour Movement continued to rally behind the two dismissed teachers and the Burston families, Tom was disappointed that the strike did not usher in wider national reforms. A great upheaval failed to take shape, as he wished to witness, and for that he was to blame his colleagues in the Labourers' Union for not giving the rank and file a lead in the matter.

But as life settled down, the Strike School stood as a living monument to the struggle against rural tyranny and for democracy. Supporters that the Higdons hadn't fallen out with would still visit and address large audiences on the green in front of the school. The ninth anniversary meeting was noted for Sylvia Pankhurst, naming, at an after meeting, three babies, in lieu of the usual christening. At the 1921 May Day event, Tom Mann got everybody dancing and laughing as the children performed songs to Annie Higdon's accompaniment.

Victor Doomski and Leon Burkanov, two children of members of the Soviet trade delegation, were sent to the Strike School in the 1920s. During the 1926 General Strike six children of miners from Nottingham were sent to be pupils. One boy stayed with the Higdons until he left to join the merchant navy. It was said that Mrs Higdon thought the world of him and wouldn't have a bad word spoken against him.

Mr Higdon sometimes taught the children, but he was more often working on union matters. Tom remained an active executive member of the Agricultural Labourers' Union until shortly before his death. He first became a trustee in 1911, then served as treasurer from 1916 to 1920; he sat on the executive committee from 1914–38, except for a break between

1924 and 1927 that came in the aftermath of 'The Great Strike' of 1923. During that year Tom was on the County Emergency Committee conducting the four-week strike in Norfolk.

As Norfolk County Secretary of the NAUW he continued to organise an annual rally of agricultural labourers in Burston. The last was held on 25 July 1937, where F.A. Broad, MP (Edmonton) and Jack Jones, MP (London), were joined by the President of the Union E.G. Gooch, JP and the Rickinghall Silver Band. In 1938 Tom failed to be re-elected at the annual conference after some delegates held a 'little private meeting' beforehand to persuade a Herbert Coldham to stand on the promise that they would all vote for him, with the result that he was elected. Tom knew nothing of this at the time, and many that knew him said that he went on to die a broken-hearted man because of it.

It was cancer of the bowel that ended the life of Thomas George Higdon on 17 August 1939. In the weeks leading up to his passing, the pair took to sleeping downstairs, in a bed that friends described as '. . . absolutely filthy. The place was full of cats. It looked like a typhoon had hit the place'.[2] Mrs Higdon was never a good housekeeper. She also seemed to be in denial about 'her Tom's' decline. There was to be no doctor called in, just a 'nature man from Yarmouth.' On talk of a possible operation, and fundraising in the village to pay for it, she again resisted.

But unsurprisingly, Annie was heartbroken when Tom died:

> His body was not taken into the church. He was taken into the Strike School. It was crowded to overflowing with personal and trade union friends. Mrs. Higdon knelt down by the coffin and sang beautifully. The coffin was brought to the Strike School on a farm cart, provided by "Fetchum" Potter [Ezra John Potter] . . . Violet Turner [Violet Potter] was there. The Strike School was crowded. Mrs. Higdon sang "O God our Help in Ages Past", and everyone was very moved. Many were in tears.[3]

Tom's sizeable obituary, which ran in the local papers, went on to highlight his considerable local work, serving as he did as a member of the Depwade Rural District Council for Shelfanger from 1931 to the time of his death; the old Board of Guardians for Diss from 1922–25; and as a member of the Management Committee for the Diss Co-operative Society. He may have failed in his ambition to gain a seat on the County Council, but the paper was to mention how, in 1935, George Lansbury paid a glowing tribute to the great work done by both Mr and Mrs Higdon in the cause of Labour and Trade Unions in the House of Commons.

The Strike School prospered for twenty-five years, but by the time Tom Higdon died there were only a handful of pupils left. Annie continued working for a few months after her husband's death, but she was incapable of carrying on alone. Perhaps, if she'd been able to accept the advice of friends and had taken on an assistant, the school could have continued but, characteristically, she would have no such thing. Eventually, the last eleven pupils were transferred to the Council School and the Strike School was closed.

Soon after, Annie began to be found wandering the roads at night in her nightwear. On one occasion, she met the grown-up Violet Potter and asked her politely whether she was 'coming to school.' Win Leeder, another former pupil, felt that in the end her idealism had affected her mind. Annie Katherine Higdon spent her last years in a care home called 'The Vale' in Swainsthorpe, near Norwich, where she survived the Second World War. When there, Win Leeder visited once, but 'She kept looking at me but she did not recognise me. She was very fond of me. The matron said, "There's never a dull moment here. Mrs. Higdon still thinks she is a schoolmistress and she gets the old ladies round the piano and they sing".'[4]

She died on 24 April 1946.

# Postscript

# Inheritance

Both Tom and Annie Higdon died intestate. Tom's estate was assessed at £381.9s.2d.—savings exclusively amassed from his wages as a teacher. Anne Katherine Higdon was declared his lawful widow, and the only person entitled to his estate, but she also died without leaving letters of administration. Although unquestionably generous to all (including animals) her estate's net value amounted to the much more considerable sum of £1,426.4s.3d. As friends and supporters were well aware (although not how it came to be) she did have 'a bit of money of her own', and this allowed her to own several cottages in Burston, including their own home. On 1 August 1947, both estates passed to James Schollick, the lawful nephew (son of Annie's brother James Heaton Schollick); a railway clerk, then living at the Station House, Welwyn Gardens.

The Higdons did accrue a considerable amount of paperwork over the years: letters, logbooks, notes and manuscripts. After the estates were settled, Josiah Sage, the NALU veteran, moved into the Higdons' cottage and went on to burn almost everything, including their love letters. What was not destroyed he passed to Sol Sandy, a former pupil of the Strike School and the last surviving member of the Strike School Committee. Today, the surviving materials are held by the Norfolk Record Office and by the Burston Strike School Trustees.

During World War Two, the Strike School was used for storage, and then afterwards stood empty for a number of years. After Annie's death in 1946, the Strike School was left without a legal owner and so, in 1949, the National Union of Agricultural Workers stepped in and facilitated the establishment of the 'Burston Strike School' Foundation to save the building for posterity and to promote its legacy. On 15 August 1949, the Burston Strike School became an educational charity administered by four trustees. Three new appointees came from the NUAW along with Mr Sol Sandy, who was also a NAUW member.

# Appendix 1

## The Wood Dalling Affair

In mid-January 1911, two weeks before the Higdons took up the Norfolk Education Committee's offer to transfer to Burston Council School, Tom sat down and wrote a fifteen-page version of the events that had transpired. The evidence suggests that this was intended to be sent to the Gladstone League. Whether it ever was is not known, but it is the only extensive personal comment made about the affair.

THE WOOD DALLING PARISH MEETING, PARISH COUNCIL, AND MR.J.J.BUSSENS' REJECTION AND SUBSEQUENT APPOINTMENT BY THE COUNTY COUNCIL AS A SCHOOL MANAGER. HIS ALLEGATIONS AGAINST THE HEAD TEACHER (MRS.HIGDON), ETC.

There were eleven nominations for seven seats; the eight highest polling were as follows: John Cotterell 28, T.G.Higdon 26, Obie Cotterell 25, Mrs.Annie.K.Higdon 24, Robert Ransome 21, Alfred Williams 19, Robert Manthorpe 17, Walter Pulfer 17 . . . (Mr. J.J.Bussens 4.)

Mrs. Higdon retired and the other seven highest on the list were declared elected. It will be seen that Mr.Bussens was quite out of it with only 4 votes, including his own vote. He had been Chairman of the Parish Council during the past three years and some dissatisfaction had been expressed with the management of the Parish Council cottages; also over the neglect of repairs to footpaths. He had also been Chairman of the School Managers, sitting as a Parish Manager, and there is no doubt that the vote was given against him chiefly on the School Management question, it having become well known that the Head Teacher had been put to much trouble and annoyance in the matter of obtaining the Chairman's signature for closing School for the regulation holidays, half-holidays, etc., and by his refusal to close when advised by mistress for Diphtheria, of which 3 children afterwards died, refusal to sign Salaries Bill, failure to hold Managers' Meetings and neglect of matters of School Attendance (one or two cases having become very unpopular). Mr. Bussens also called at the School and used bad language to Mr. Higdon which was reported to the Education Committee and a Local Inquiry held. (This was about November, 1908). Mr. Bussens replied by making three charges against Mrs. Higdon which were as follows:

'Closing School without permission of Managers; (Had obtained permission of Mr. Williams which he now denied.)

'Ordering Coal without permission of Managers; (According to precedent, 5 years.)

'Being absent without permission of Managers. (Not absent at all on date and time given. Total absence in 5 years = 1.1/2 days.)'

All these charges were without foundation, as the Committee must have seen though they did not say so. They said nothing to Mrs. Higdon about these charges after the inquiry, nor to Mr. Higdon about Mr. Bussens' Language, but blamed the teachers for causing 'Friction' and told them that the Committee would give them 'Another Chance.'

(The present case is the sequel to this complete miscarriage of justice.)

The local knowledge of the Wood Dalling people, however, enabled them to see matters in a different light to that of the Committee's Local Inquiry and as soon as they had an opportunity of giving their verdict, which was at the Parish Meeting in March, 1910, they gave it in no uncertain manner. There the matter might well have rested.

But the local electors were astonished a few weeks afterwards to find that Mr.Bussens was still a School Manager appointed by the County Council. He was a Parish Manager before and as such his only chance of remaining a Manager (so he seems to have at first thought) was to get the old Parish Council to appoint him at their last meeting before going out of office. This he tried very hard to do and came to this last meeting armed with a circular from Mr.Cox and declared it to be Mr.Cox's intention to have the Parish Managers appointed at that meeting in March. Upon Mr.Higdon expressing an opposite view, namely that it was for the new Parish Council to appoint these managers at their first meeting in April, Mr.Bussens attempted to silence him by saying, 'Mr.Higdon is a teacher.' (He, Mr.Higdon, was also a Parish Councillor, had been for 3 years.) Mr.Williams held with Mr.Bussens, while Mr.John Cottrell supported Mr.Higdon. Mr.Robert Manthorpe seemed more or less neutral and presently resigned his seat as he said he found he could not please everybody. (Mr.Manthorpe's dissatisfaction seems to have been with the Parish Meeting and he appears to have been particularly anxious that Mr.Bussens should know he did not intend to take his seat on the new Council. He should have resigned at the Parish Meeting, or at the first meeting of the new Council.) In the end, after an hour's discussion, Mr.Higdon suggested the calling of another Parish Meeting, whereupon Mr.Bussens gave in, declaring he would not have cared about appointing the School Managers that night only Mr.Higdon was down his throat in a moment as soon as he mentioned the matter. He had formerly said in the same meeting, 'Mr.Higdon says we can't, now we will.' But this was only to make out he didn't care about it for himself, which was really what he did care about, as he knew very well that if he did not get elected there and then at this last meeting of the old Council, the new Parish Council would not elect him. He left the meeting apparently feeling very bitter against Mr.Higdon for defeating his object. Mr.Williams also remarked to Mr.Higdon, 'You ought to be very well pleased.' He did not mean this approvingly, of course.

Not to be outdone, Bussens' and Williams next move was to get Mr. Bussens appointed a County Manager. As Mr. Williams was a County Manager he was probably able to assist Mr. Bussens very materially in this matter by bringing his name forward before the recommending and appointing authorities, etc. Councillor Wyand at Reepham may know by whom or in what manner he was approached, if it was done through him. Did he know Mr. Bussens' rejection by the Parish? As a County Councillor he must have known of the so-called "Friction" two years previously, a report having been handed to the County Councillors by the Education Committee. He must have known Mr. Bussens well, too. Mr. Wyand has since told Mr. Higdon that he would not have recommended Mr. Bussens but that private letters were sent up from Wood Dalling recommending him. Mr. Vicars says Mr. Williams and Mr. Clark wrote these letters. Under the circumstances special care should have been exercised by the Education Committee in making the appointment. Whereas the Clergyman seems to have been left off quite without his (Rev. Vicars') previous knowledge of what was happening, and Mr. Bussens put on. Mr. Newstead came on, too, and he, with Messrs. Manthorpe and Williams, found no difficulty in making Mr. Bussens Chairman, when they knew very well that Mr. John Cotterell, Parish Manager, could not be present to oppose the appointment, he being absent from home. Thus Mr. Bussens was reinstalled as a Manager and also as Chairman of Managers, and that in spite of the fact of his only being able to command three votes in the Parish. (3 besides his own vote, 4 in all.)

Much comment and disapproval was expressed on all hands at this appointment, which had defied the democratic votes of the Parish and which threatened further mischief. That something was going to happen to Mr. Higdon was heard from more than one quarter. Mr. Higdon was told in a friendly way by someone who had heard a farmer friend of Mr. Bussens say that he (Mr. Bussens' Farmer Friend) could not help hearing things and that Mr. Higdon had better look out. (Mr. Pratt, farmer, said this to George Cottrell.) Another farmer, Mr. Elliner, declared to William Starling that Mr. Higdon was to be found 'another job with more work and less pay.' Etc., etc.. In what manner these omens were to be fulfilled did not yet appear. To show Mr.Higdon did not wish to irritate or oppose Mr.Bussens unnecessarily in any way, it may be pointed out that when the Clerk (Mr.Bussens' Blacksmith) to the Parish Council and assistant Overseer asked, at the first meeting of the new Parish Council, that Messrs, Bussens and Williams may be reappointed as Overseers, Mr.Higdon as Chairman of the Parish Council, did not raise any objection to their appointment; neither did he, when he reported to the newspapers the results of the voting at the Parish Meeting, put Mr.Bussens' 4 votes in the newspapers, but stopped at the last winner, out of pure consideration for Mr.Bussens' feelings. But when the Parish Council met on June 3rd and the people had been crying out on all hands against Mr.Bussens' appointment as a School Manager in defiance of their vote, and it was proposed to pass a Resolution calling the attention of the Norfolk Education Committee to the facts of the case, Mr.Higdon felt it was his duty, as Chairman, to sign the Resolution. This resolution was passed and sent to the committee, who replied that the Resolution had been considered but that no action was taken. That Mr.Bussens soon heard of this Resolution, locally, there is no doubt. 'The Parish Council want to rule the County Council now,' was Mr.Williams' comment upon it at the next meeting of the Parish Council, which followed soon after; and before June was out a letter was received from the Education Committee stating that complaint had been made by the School Managers that Mrs.Higdon had called Mr.Bussens, Mr.Williams, and Mr.Blades 'liars' at a Managers' Meeting as far back as March 18th. Thus more than 3 months had passed between the time of this alleged occurrence and the time of their making the complaint. Still more surprising, this was the first that had been heard about any such thing in Wood Dalling or anywhere else. Not a soul in Wood Dalling appears to have heard about it; neither Mr.Blades nor any single Manager seems to have said a word about it before Mr.Bussens and Mr.Williams went into the Education Committee's offices at

Norwich and made the complaint there 3 months afterwards while they were feeling sore about the Parish Council Resolution. If Mrs.Higdon had called these gentlemen 'liars' at this meeting on March 18th would they not have found themselves hurt then and there at the meeting, and if not in Mrs.Higdon's presence at any rate after she had gone out, whereas not a word of protest appears to have been raised either to her or amongst themselves. On the contrary Mr.Bussens came to the School House after the meeting and handed Mr.Higdon the pen which the clerk had borrowed and thanked him for the loan of it most politely. Mr.Bussens also handed Mr.Higdon the Holiday postcards which he said he had signed for closing School for the Easter Holidays on the Wednesday instead of Thursday before Good Friday according to Mrs. Higdon's request. (He had previously refused to sign these cards for breaking up on Wednesday, Mr.Williams having been very much against it, saying he did not see what the teachers wanted to go away for their Easter Holidays on Thursday for, as he did not go away; and the Managers had at that meeting after an hours' wrangling about it passed a Resolution for breaking up on Thursday evening. It may be explained that the Education Committee have a Regulation for giving the teachers who want to go a distance to their homes or friends a clear day to get there and that Mrs.Higdon was going to Mr.Higdon's home in Somersetshire.) If after all this discussion, Resolution passed against it and everything else, Mrs. Higdon had appeared on the scene and called them 'liars', as they allege, would they have been likely to turn around and alter all this, as they did? Mr.Bussens being so amiable over it, too, immediately afterwards, as well as calling at the School on Wednesday, before breaking up, and wishing Mr. and Mrs.Higdon pleasant Holidays together. This did not look much like making any such complaint to the Education Committee, which they never seem to have thought of doing for more than three months. Why? (The Parish Council Resolution was not vexing them then, nor farmers talking against Mr.Higdon so much.) Mr.Blades was calling at the School nearly every week, too, as Attendance Officer; if Mrs.Higdon had called him 'liar' at the meeting would he not have said something to her, or some one else, about it instead of waiting over three months for instructions from Messrs. Bussens and Williams, and after that excusing himself to Mr. Higdon for doing so on the ground that Mr. Bussens had brought him these instructions to Aylsham from her husband? Plainly he had no such grievance himself before being placed in a position where he was expected to obey the Chairman, Mr. Bussens, and Vice Chairman, Mr. Williams of the Managers (not the body of Managers) as their clerk. The matter was never brought before the body of Managers. This was not a Managers' complaint, though the letter from the Education Committee described it as such. It had never been before the Managers; and if Mr. Bussens and Mr. Williams had been advised when they made the complaint at Norwich to go back and first bring the matter before the Managers, it would have fallen to the ground. Even Manthorpe, the one Manager who has since supported them to a certain extent, told Mr. Higdon that they did not say anything to him about it before complaining to the Education Committee and that he thought these things ought to be settled at home amongst themselves. (Manthorpe is the roadman and his father was working for Mr. Bussens, and it was already known in Wood Dalling that Mr. Bussens had threatened to prosecute a labourer, George Hardingham, if he caught him walking across his field again because the man did not vote for Mr. Bussens at the Parish Meeting.) Manthorpe refused to sign 'Form 9', as did four Managers out of the six, because Mr. Bussens had written 'No' against Mrs. Higdon's Character and Conduct (July 1910) and Mr. Manthorpe probably thinks he had gone far enough in that line against the 'powers' that be.

Not only was nothing heard about any such thing as calling Managers 'liars' at or from the Managers' Meeting in March, but no mention of it appears to have been made at the next meeting a month or so afterwards, when Mr. Bussens was again appointed Chairman. Not a sound of the word 'liar', 'liars', or any such matter, seems to have been heard by anybody in Wood Dalling before the word was sent down from Norwich three months after its alleged utterance, and until notices were sent of an Inquiry. It then caused much surprise, but no one was more astonished and bewildered than Mrs.Higdon herself. When the first hearing of it in a private letter a day or so before receiving the official letter from Mr.Cox she was puzzled to know when or where she could have been supposed to have said it and concluded it must be the result of 'hearsay'. It turned out, however, to be based upon what she said at the Managers' Meeting on March 18th though this was the first she had heard of her having said anything amiss, let alone the word 'liars'. She had used the expression 'Your lies' feeling that this was the only expression which would suit the circumstances. The 'lies' she referred to were as follows:

Mr.Bussens had failed to order School coal, though sent to by Mrs.Higdon two or three times about it. Consequently the School was without coal for four days in winter, snow on the ground, too. Mrs.Higdon herself, however, supplied enough to keep the fires going. She also sent to the coal agent (Bartram, Coller & Co., Reepham) repeatedly, to hear if the coal was coming, only to find that it had not been ordered. Then the coal man called at the School and asked if he should bring it. Mrs. Higdon got 1 cwt. off him, but told him that he had better not bring a load by her ordering; remembering, of course, Mr.Bussens' complaint to the Education Committee at a previous Local Inquiry, that she had ordered coal without permission of the Managers. The coal at length arrived, Mr.Bussens having at length ordered it. But Mr.Blades, at a subsequent visit to the School, told Mrs.Higdon that the coal would have come all right if she had not 'Countermanded the Order.' Mrs.Higdon wrote to Bartram, Coal Agent, to know the meaning of this, and Mr.Bartram replied saying that she had not countermanded the order but that the coal had been delivered the same day as the order was received from Mr. Bussens. This letter she read to the Managers at their meeting of March 18th which proved the excuse of Bussens and Blades to be a lie.

Another letter which she read, in part, at the same meeting was from Miss Loveless, a Supply Teacher who had been at Wood Dalling School in July 1909, and had taken 'Form 9' to

Mr.Bussens, but as Mr.Bussens was not at home she had brought the Form back unsigned. Mr.Vicars and two other Managers signed it, and it was duly despatched without delay. At a Managers' Meeting which followed, Mr.Bussens complained that this Form had not been sent to him, and a letter was received from the clerk asking the reason. The letter from Miss Loveless proved that 'Form 9' had not been sent to Mr.Bussens. 'I well remember taking 'Form 9' to Mr.Bussens, who was not at home,' she wrote. Thus this statement of Mr. Bussens that 'Form 9' had not been sent to him, and that of Mr.Blades that she had Countermanded the order for coal, as well as a statement of Mr.Williams made at the Inquiry, Nov.1908, to the effect that he had not given her his word for closing the School on a certain date, when he had given it, she called 'lies', as lies they were. That this was not turned by them into 'liars' before Mr.Bussens was feeling sore about the Parish Council Resolution, and the farmers were talking about getting Mr.Higdon turned out, speaks for itself. If they felt that this implied that they were liars they should have said so at the time, and not have instructed the clerk to write that she 'called them liars' 3 months afterwards. It is not for anything implied but for the alleged ('Fully Proved') use of the word 'liar' that Mrs.Higdon has been asked to send in her resignation (which she refused to do & was dismissed and Mr.Higdon, too)—a word she did not use, as the circumstances attending their complaint go a long way to prove.

The Committee say that no complaint whatever has been made against Mr.Higdon—Of course not!!!

Again, take the evidence of Mr.Manthorpe, the only man giving evidence who was not a Prosecutor. Asked about the letter from Miss Loveless about taking 'Form 9' to Mr.Bussens, he said he thought it was a letter from Mrs.Higdon's sister-in-law about the holidays. This, notwithstanding the fact that Mrs. Higdon had read with particular clearness and emphasis the portion of the letter referred to, and the name of the writer. If Mr.Manthorpe heard this so badly, how was he so sure about anything, as, for instance, the word 'liar'? The other three denied all knowledge of these letters, all speaking together. It appears they did not wish to remember them; the lies were evidently to be kept dark if possible. Besides, they all gave different verbal accounts of what they wished to convey as having been said by Mrs.Higdon. Mr.Neile, who had been present as the Managers' Meeting in March was not summoned to this Inquiry, he not being reappointed a Manager in April, having left the Parish. He has lately written to the Committee to say that he did not hear Mrs.Higdon use the word 'liar'. The plan of the NUT lawyer was for Mrs.Higdon to apologise, as he pointed out to her just before the Inquiry that she would have four against her and nobody for her, but she said she could not apologise for a word she had never used, though she was ready to apologise for the words she admitted using. This, however, was not accepted, it having been 'Fully Proved' to the satisfaction of the inquirers that she had used the word complained of. (Ten men swearing falsely proves nothing, whereas these could, every one, have been proved liars if the lawyer had cross-examined them on the facts of the case; which facts he entirely ignored, for the reason, one may suppose, that he did not wish to appear to be fighting the Managers, or to offend the Committee. This policy, in this particular case, was a great mistake.)

At a Managers' Meetings held sometime after the Inquiry, Mr.John Cottrell wished to propose a Resolution asking the Education Committee to reconsider the case, but Mr.Bussens, as Chairman of the Managers, said, 'No, I will not allow the resolution to be put.' The Managers, as such, are to have no say in the matter, only the Chairman and Vice Chairman are to count, except in so far as they can get any single Manager to support them in their backstair business with the Committee. Three of the Managers present at the Inquiry were new Managers, neither of whom were present in March when Mrs. Higdon is said to have called the Managers 'liars', and who, therefore, knew nothing about it; so Messrs. Bussens, Williams, and Blades (Attendance Officer and Managers' Clerk), with Manthorpe, had it all their own way. The one other Manager who could have spoken (Neile) not being present—he having ceased to be a Manager not being summoned, as in justice to Mrs. Higdon he ought to have been.

When the people learned that we were to be dismissed they were simply amazed. Nothing could be more unpopular in Wood Dalling and throughout the district for many miles, where Mr. and Mrs.Higdon are well known, and where Mr.Bussens is known too. A petition was got up in the Parish asking for a reversal of this decision, and was signed by the parents of over forty families out of less than fifty having children in the School, but without the desired effect. The two Parish Council School Managers have also written to the Committee resigning their position as Managers as a protest against what they describe as the 'scandalous treatment which Mrs.Higdon has received.' This, also, has met with no more than an acknowledgement by the Committee. Mr.Higdon has also himself placed a statement of the whole case in the hands of the Chairman of the Committee, F.H.Millington, Esq., Thetford. Mr.George Edwards has also brought the case up at the County Council, but had not been able to get a discussion on it, having been ruled out of order by the Chairman, Sir William Folkes. All these efforts, however, have not been entirely without success; first Mr.Higdon was to be offered another appointment; then, after a time, Mrs.Higdon was to be offered one as well; and then they were to be both offered an appointment together in the same School at the same salaries as they had been receiving at Wood Dalling. This last offer is waiting for their acceptance now at Burston, near Diss, and Supply Teachers are at present teaching temporarily in the Wood Dalling School. But Mrs.Higdon feels that she has done nothing to be dismissed for from the School of which she has been in charge 8.3/4 years, which she has always kept in a high state of efficiency (Reports, etc.) and where both parents and children are most grieved to part with her. Mr.Higdon feels it to be equally unjust, especially as this dismissal is really on his account—his wife being only a victim and the excuse—though he does not think the Committee knew this in the first place. Hence the need for a reconsideration of the case and a reversal of this decision and their reinstatement in their former School, as much for the honour of the Education Committee and the re-establishment of common justice as for themselves. Besides,

Mr.Higdon has many friends amongst the Liberals and Labourers (Labourers' Union) in North Norfolk, from whom he would be very sorry to part, and he feels that he is being unjustly and unnecessarily removed from a useful sphere of labour and influence. He feels strongly that he is being removed on account of what may be called political prejudice in connection with his Radicalism and Labour Unionism, and in spite on the part of Mr.Bussens in connection with the Parish Council. John Cottrell had heard Mr.Bussens say, 'Let's get rid of them (Mr. and Mrs.Higdon) altogether.' George Hardingham was heard to say, 'I shall never find you a job because you stand up for Mr. and Mrs.Higdon.' Also 'I'll put your wages down.' He also threatened to prosecute George if he found him walking across his field again, because he (George) did not vote for him on the Parish Council. Also, when Mr.Higdon was billed to speak at Mr.Buxton's (MP) meeting, Bussens (Tory) said to John Cottrell, I wasn't coming up there to hear Higdon talk.' A farmer named Green (friend of Bussens) told Mr.Higdon at Reepham last Christmas twelvemonths, in a Public House, that Jimmy Bussens would knock him a cocked hat, and 'You are making footprints for someone else to walk in, I can tell you that.' (Mr.Bussens was Chairman of School Managers then and had no doubt told Green that he meant to get Higdon out of the School. Bussens declares, however, with much feigned innocence, to anybody who says anything to him about this prejudice, that he has nothing at all against Mr.Higdon, and had nothing against Mrs.Higdon until, according to him, she called him a liar.

With regard to the Labourers' Union, the Strike of St.Faith's began in May, and in June, when Bussens and Williams made their complaint against Mrs.Higdon, there was much talk going around against the labour union leaders, and Mr.Higdon came in for his share.

Mr.Clark, another Wood Dalling farmer, and one whom Mr.Buxton, MP has asked Mr.Higdon to report to the Gladstone league in connection with the dismissal of a man named Breeze, told George Hardingham that Mr.Higdon and George Edwards had all their (the Labourers') money.

Mr.Higdon has never taken a penny from the Labourer's Union. Mr. Elliner, a farmer of Wood Dalling, went up to the Education Committee's office to complain to some thing or to make his complaint in, but it appears he never sent it up, he having doubtless had his say while he was up there, or, as someone has suggested, he would not afford the cost of the stamp. It was he, however, who told Starling that 'they' would find Mr.Higdon a job with more work and less pay.

Mr.Higdon will be glad to answer any questions on the case if there is a case that can be taken up. Also any local Liberals and others in the district may be written to.

Mr.Higdon thinks of refusing the offer of the Burston School, just to hand, and in doing so he thinks that his and his wife's future in regard to Norfolk will depend upon the strength of the law; but the NUT will give him no satisfaction or opinion in regard to this point, as they wish him to accept the Burston School and so end the matter. He does not feel he can do this and would be glad of any advice as soon as possible.

(Has since accepted.)

Thos.G.Higdon, Jan. 18th 1911

# Appendix 2

# Our School Strike

At the time of the first anniversary of the School Strike (April 1915) one of the strike leaders among the children, Emily Wilby, wrote her own short account of their rebellion. The essay was subsequently published by Lusher Bros. of Diss and sold to raise funds for the 'Strike School', at that time being temporarily housed in the old carpenter's shop. The Wilbys were a family of six children and staunch supporters of the Higdons, Emily's father Robert Wilby being a railwayman at Burston Station and a member of the National Union of Railwaymen.

### Our School Strike

*By*

Emily Wilby
(One of the Bairns o' Burston)

---

### Our School Strike

We came on Strike April 1st 1914. We came on strike because our Governess and Master were dismissed from the Council School unjustly. The Parson got two Barnardo children to say that our Governess had caned them and slapped their faces, but we all know she did not. Then our Governess lit a fire one wet morning to dry some of our clothes without asking the Parson. So the head ones said that out Governess and Master had better be got rid of. They had their pay sent and two days' notice to leave the school. Governess did not know we were going on strike. She bought us all some Easter eggs and oranges the last day we were at the Council School.

Violet Potter brought a paper to school with all our names on it, and all who were going on strike had to put a cross against their name. Out of seventy-two children sixty-six came out on strike.

The first morning our mothers sent the infants because they thought they did not matter, but in the afternoon they too stopped away and only six answered the bell.

The next morning the sixty-six children lined up on the Crossways. We all had cards round our necks and paper trimmings. We marched past the Council School and round "The Candlestick". When we got to the foster-mother's house she came out with a dustpan and a brush to "tin" us, but when she saw out mothers she ran in. She put a card in her window with "Victory" on it, but she has not got it yet. Some of our parents gave us cake and drink and many other things. When we got to the Crown Common we had a rest. Mrs. Boulton, the lady at the Post Office, gave us some lemonade and sweets and nuts. She also gave us a large banner and several flags. At twelve o'clock we went home for dinner. At one we marched again. When we got up to one of the foster-mother's friends (who is a foster-mother too) she jumped up from behind a hedge and began to "tin" us. When we hooted her she said she would summons us, but it has not happened yet.

Mr. Starr, the Attendance Officer, sent our mothers a paper saying if they did not send their children to school they would be summoned, but our mothers did not care about the papers; some put them on sticks and waved them. We had our photos taken several times. We marched each day. Two of our mothers asked Governess to come and take prayers on the Common with the children, then she came each morning. Half-a-dozen policemen stood about the road, but there was no need for them.

One day a policeman went round to twenty houses with summonses because we had not been to school. The day we were to appear at Court all the big children dressed up and went to the Crossways. We started for Court about half past nine. As we were going along we sang our old Strike Song. Before we started we had oranges and chocolate.

When we got down to Diss several people were lined up each side of the street. We left our parents at the Court and we went into the Park. Mrs. Robert Wilby brought us some refreshments, ginger beer, etc. Some of the girls went to the Court to see what the time was. There a man took their photos. The fine was half-a-crown each. When our mothers came out of Court we went into the Market Place and had some bread and cheese and some ginger beer. Governess bought us some cakes to eat on the way home. Mrs. Boulton gave us some chocolate. Then we started for home. When we got half-way home we sat down and had a rest and ate our cakes. We got home about six o'clock.

The next day our mothers thought we might begin school on the Common while it was fine weather. We had school on the Common a little while, then we went into the very cottage that the Barnardo children had lived in for a year and a half. Our mothers lent stools, tables, chairs, etc. Mr. Ambrose Sandy said we could have his shop for a Strike School. Sam Sandy came and white-washed it out and mended the windows. He put a ladder up so that we could go upstairs.

Our mothers were soon summoned again. This time the children did not go. They went a little way, then they came back. This time the fine was five shillings each. There were thirty-two of our parents summoned. Our parents did not have to pay a penny of the fine, it was all collected on the Green and in the streets. At night we went to Diss to meet our parents. When we got there we had some ginger beer. A man took our photos for the living pictures. Then we went to see them; they were very good. Mr. Sullings gave us a free performance.

We had meetings every Sunday. We have had some very good speakers. Governess and Master lived at the mill at one time, then they went to Mrs. Woodrow's and now they have a house of their own.

We have had three strike funerals. The first was that of a little boy who got burned to death. Mr. Williams buried him. When the little boy's father paid the sexton for digging the grave, the sexton asked for the parson's fee. The father was full of grief; he paid the parson his fee. The next funeral was that of a little girl who died very suddenly. There was an inquest. A jury of farmers and Parson's men was called together and they tried to make out the child died because she came to the Strike School. They asked the poor mother what time the Strike School fire was lighted, and didn't the children go to meet Governess and Master without any hats, and didn't they have to go across a Common with water on. They called the poor mother into a room three times to worry her with questions. At the inquest the doctor told them why the girl had died. They would not believe him and ordered a post-mortem which is the cruellest thing there was. After that the doctor told them the same thing he did at first. The way they treated the poor mother was brutal. After the funeral Governess told the poor mother to come into school and she made her a cup of tea and told Mr. Durbidge that the poor mother should not be teased by those men any more. So he went and told the jurymen that his wife was not well. The next funeral was that of an old comrade. The sexton would not take off his hat at the funeral. When the funeral was over one of our comrade's sons went to pay the sexton his fee, but the sexton would not take it without the parson's too. The son asked him two or three times but he would not take it. When the people were gone home the sexton said, "This old man lay here and he ain't paid for."

The Inspectors came and looked over the school, but none of them found any fault. Some of the Strike Children were baptised in the Strike School. One Sunday thirteen children were baptised on our Common.

An M.P. came down to speak to us. At some of the meetings there have been over fifteen hundred people. On April 1st, 1915, we celebrated our first year. We marched round the village in the morning and in the afternoon we had a tea which we all enjoyed. At night our parents had a "Social." Mr. Rice, J.P., presented Master with an inkstand and Governess with a clock from us and our parents. Mr. Rice also presented Mr. Sutton with a bookcase because he had taken the service every Sunday when there was not anybody else to take it. After that we had refreshments and dancing. We sang "England Arise," then the Social was broken up; Mr. Potter asked for three cheers for Governess and Master.

We had our photos in "The Sketch". We have had some lovely treats since the Strike began. "Casey" came down to Burston and gave us a very enjoyable evening with his fiddle. We have been to Norwich twice and Ipswich once. We have also been to London; we had some splendid meetings there. We saw all the most important places in London. We all had an enjoyable week in London.

The N.U.R sent us four dozen chairs for our Strike School. A piece of land has been bought for our new School. We are going to beat the Education Committee in one way if we can't another.

Dismissing Mr. and Mrs. Higdon is not the only thing the Parson did. He took some Glebe land from three poor men. One of the men was blind; the Parson took his Glebe away because he lent us his shop for a Strike School. He took Mr. Harry Ling's Glebe away because he would not let his daughter go to the mock inquiry or go himself to tell a lie. He took Mr. Garnham's Glebe away because he attended the Strike School meetings.

Mr. Sandy, the blind man, gave up his land and went away, but the Parson summoned Mr. Ling and Mr. Garnham. They had to go to Court three times. Some of the Parson's men took a lock and chain off Mr. Garnham's Glebe. They also took a fowls' hut off Mr. Ling's Glebe and put it on the side of the road. The hut was taken away at night and the next morning the Churchwarden sent his horse to plough up the land, but Mr. Ling would not let him. The last time they had to go to Eye County Court. The Judge seemed a fair straight man. The Parson had to pay ten shillings damages to each of the Glebe tenants, and had to give up the lock and chain. We strikers are not going to be ruled by a little man like C.T. Eland. This trouble has only been through lies and spite.

Our Master being summoned the other month was only spite. The special constable knew it would please the Parson, so he summoned the Master for riding a bicycle without lights in broad daylight. The Parson could ride eight miles after evening service without lights. Another of the Parson's friends was on the same road at the same time as our Master, in a cart without lights, but the constable did not summons him about his lights. It shows it is only spite, and the Master told the magistrates so. The Master was fined half-a-crown but he would not pay it. Why should he pay? It would be quite different if the others were summoned too. Our Master came away without paying. Since then Inspector James and a policeman have been up to the Governess' house with a distress warrant, saying that the fine and expenses were not four shillings and six pence, and if the Master now paid it, it would be done with, if not they would sell the things in the house, but Governess signed a paper saying that all the things belonged to her. Since then they have heard nothing more.

We had a great meeting on Whit-Sunday. George Allen, the great "Parson Fighter," spoke. It was a good meeting. We all had some Sports on Whit-Monday. Some of our London comrades brought us some prizes. We had some races. The prizes were given away at seven o'clock. We all enjoyed ourselves very much.

On Sunday July 16th, we had a Great Demonstration. About three hundred and fifty railwaymen came from London and other places, and about sixty from Norwich, including a brass band. There were eighteen banners, sixteen from London, one from Norwich, and the Strike School banner. The banners looked lovely when they were all floating in the air beside the green fields and between the hedges and trees. Poor blind Ambrose, one of the evicted Glebe tenants, came into the tent for tea. Governess told him we would get his Glebe back for him. Burston has never seen anything like Sunday. It's a red letter day in our Strike. We children will never forget it. There were fifteen hundred people at the meeting. There were constables to guard us from getting hold of the Parson. The railwaymen went to the cottages to tea. On Monday we had a tea to eat up and bread and butter that was left. We all enjoyed ourselves.

### Are we down=hearted?
### NO!

# Appendix 3

# Court Proceedings

A little over two weeks into the school strike and a number of parents whose children who had gone out on strike were summoned to appear before the magistrates at Diss Petty Sessions. The action, and subsequent fines, did nothing to weaken the resolve of the parents, or prevent the long boycott to come from developing. The Diss Express, And Norfolk and Suffolk Journal (Friday 24 April 1914) provided extensive coverage of the proceedings:

Considerable interest and excitement prevailed on Wednesday when eighteen parents whose children's names are on the list of scholars at Burston and Shimpling School, appeared before the magistrates at Diss Petty Sessions for neglecting to send their children to school. The occasion was taken advantage of to make a demonstration of the youthful strikers, who adorned with various colours, carrying banners and flags, and wearing cards bearing the words 'We want our teachers back', 'We want Justice', etc . . . marched from Burston to Diss. They sang some of their favourite school songs as they covered the distance of three miles separating the two places. The roadway outside the Court was thronged when the children, who were accompanied by a number of parents and friends, arrived. At first they were led into the 'Two Brewers' yard but the police interfered and would not allow them to remain on licensed premises. As other cases had to be disposed of, the defendants, the strikers and their friends had to remain for some time outside the

The defendants were John Aldrich, John Bridges, Joseph Cobb, George Durbidge, Joseph Ford, Walter Garnham, Henry Gotts, Edward Huggins, Harry Ling, John Potter, sen.,

John Potter, jun., Robert Wilby, William Wilby Burston; George Catchpole, Shimpling; Thomas Mullinger, Robert Sturman, Burston; Alfred Moore, and James Wells, Diss; and they were summoned by Frederick Starr, school attendance officer, of Long Stratton, for each not sending a child to school at Burston on April 7th.

The magistrates on the Bench were Mr. Francis Taylor (chairman), Mr. T. Keppel, and Mr. R. A. Bryant.

Mr. H. C. Davis, the Deputy-Clerk to the Norfolk County Council, stated that as each case would have to be dealt with separately, it would be as well that all the defendants should be present in Court from the outset, as the few remarks he should make would apply to them all.

Aldrich was the first defendant to be called forward, and he pleaded not guilty.

Mr. Davis said it was common knowledge, and he thought he might be allowed to refer to the fact, that the cases all arose out of what had been dignified by the name of the Burston School Strike. It was common knowledge that the engagements of the head mistress and assistant master at the school were terminated on the 31st of March. Into the reason for that termination he did not need to go, for two or three very good reasons. The first reason was that it did not affect the charge in the slightest degree, and the second was also a good reason, as he did not know the reason himself. It was only fair to say that the public, through the Press, had only so far heard one side of the case. A public authority by its constitution, was debarred from entering into a newspaper controversy. He believed the dismissal was decided upon at a private enquiry, but it was only fair to say that the benefit of the services of a solicitor and barrister, and therefore it was to be assumed that the case was put before the sub-committee who held the enquiry as fairly and well as the case could be. ("Wrong.")

It has greatly to the credit of the teacher and her husband that they had endeared themselves to the children, but that had nothing to do with the case before the Court. Since the dismissal of the teachers none of the children whose parents were before the Court had attended school, and whether any reasonable cause for non-attendance could be brought forward he could not say. If any case with any pretence at reason was brought forward he should be prepared to meet the objection, but, so far as he could ascertain, there was no reason for non-attendance. Therefore he would ask the Bench to treat the cases as serious ones, because, as would be seen, it was an attempt to undermine the established authority. He would call attention to the fact that the case had been before the Education Committee of the County Council, and asked the Bench to recognise that the position of that authority would be intolerable if one village, or any section of the parents in that village, could dictate as to what staff should be employed in teaching. One the day in question the Burston School was sufficiently staffed and ready to educate the children. Assuming for the frivolous grounds, even then he would as the Bench to say that would be no cause whatever for the parents refusing to send their children to school. He did not like to contemplate the effect on discipline of those particular children owing to their being encouraged to break the law in this way. Unless the authority were assisted by the magistrates in doing their duty in this particular case he was afraid the effect on school discipline and management in the county and throughout England would be very seriously handicapped in the future. Another reason why he asked the magistrates to take a serious view of the cases was because every opportunity had been given the defendants to send their children to school before these proceedings were taken. Mr. Aldrich and the others were written to on the 1st of April by Mr. Starr, the attendance officer, to the following effect: "Take notice that unless your children at once return to school will be taken before the magistrates to enforce the law." Even up to that day if a child had been sent to school he was instructed to ask leave to withdraw the summons against the parents of any children who were at school yesterday morning. Of course there were other children beyond those referred to in the summons who were not at school but in each case the parent was summoned in respect to one child. The chief point he wished to draw attention to was this: This was an attempt to run the education of the school, and the staffing by a few local people, who did not know all the facts and the information on which the committee acted, and who were apparently influenced mainly by what he ventured to say was their private affection and sympathy for the master and mistress. That was not the point of view to be decided. The point he wished to impress was that the County Council were the education authority, and even assuming—he was not able to go into the merits of the case— the dismissal of the teachers was absolutely uncalled for and unjust that was not a matter for the Bench to take into consideration. The point was the parents had disobeyed the bye-laws requiring them to send their children to the school, which was sufficiently staffed and ready to receive children is their parents would send them. That was the case in a nutshell, and he must ask the Bench to support the constituted authority in the exercise of what in that particular instance was a very arduous and unpleasant duty.

Mr Starr, the attendance officer, produced a certificate from the head master of Burston School showing that Winifred Aldrich was absent from school on April 7th. He sent a warning to the parent on the 1st inst.

Aldrich told the Bench that the only reason he had not sent the child to school was because it was unfair to turn the teachers away. There ought to have been an enquiry into the matter. Two "home" children who went to school had caused the trouble, and they wished them to leave before the children were sent back.

The magistrates consulted in private, and when the public were readmitted, the Chairman said the Bench considered the case proved against Aldrich. It was a case which affected a good many persons in Burston besides himself, and also many people outside Burston. The Education Committee had taken a great deal of trouble over the whole question of education in Norfolk, and was composed, he thought he could safely say, of members in whom the county had full confidence. The magistrates felt that they were bound to support the prosecution which had been ordered by the Education Committee, but at the same time they fully recognised the fact that there was strong feeling in Burston of affection and regard for those who had been the mistress and assistant master at the school for some time past, and that the parents and children were distressed at the idea of parting with their old teachers. The Bench were consequently willing to make allowances for what was not an unnatural feeling on the part of the parents and children. The Education Committee, however, had the management of the schools, and they did it to the best of their ability, and did it in a most efficient way as a rule. The Bench felt that it did not become individuals or an individual parish to deal with a case like this in the way Burston had done. Under those circumstances they would make allowances for the feelings or parents, and would not inflict a heavy penalty, but it must be understood that a recurrence of anything of the sort would be dealt with very differently. He supposed there would be no recurrence, but if there was the Bench would have to take into consideration the position of the Education Committee, and would have to inflict a more severe penalty. Defendant would be fined 2s. 6d., and the Bench hoped the leniency would not be misunderstood.

They were fully determined to support the Education Committee, but they had no wish to inflict a fine which could in any way be looked upon as vindictive. They hoped by dealing with the case in that way it might have the effect of smoothing over the feeling which had been aroused in the parish. They hoped parents and children would accept the situation, and that there would be no more trouble with Burston or any other school in the district. Defendant would be fined 2s. 6d., in default of distress, seven days.

John Bridges admitted that his child was not at school, and said he did not agree with the decision of the Education Committee. He should like a public enquiry to see into the matter. He was quite willing and ready for his child to attend school, but wanted a public enquiry so they could know the truth.

The Chairman told him he could easily get advice as to that. He believed he had the power to invoke the aid of the Board of Education. He would be fined 2s. 6d.

Defendant asked for time to pay, which the Bench laughingly declined.

Joseph Cobb pleaded not guilty, and asked for a public inquiry.

The Clerk—You say the same as Mr. Bridges?—Yes.

The Chairman—The penalty will be the same.

Mrs. Catchpole represented her husband, and admitted that her daughter Elsie was not at school on April 7th. She was fined 2s. 6d.

George Durbidge said he could not say if his son Frank was at school or not.

Mr. Starr proved the case.

Defendant—How many times were Dr. Barnardo's children absent?—I cannot say.

Did you go to Dr. Barnardo's children?—No.

Will you tell us how many times they have been absent?—No; we are dealing with this case.

Why are you not instructed to deal with Dr. Barnardo's children?—I cannot say.

Defendant said he had not sent his son because he thought the late teachers had been unfairly treated. Parents who had to clothe and keep their children and pay for their education had an absolute right to know who was in fault and who was not. They were all satisfied with the education and treatment their children were receiving, and he thought it was only right and proper that the parish should know why the teachers were dismissed. All they asked for was justice. If there was a public enquiry, and the parents were in the wrong, the children would be sent to school. He had written to London to the N.U.T., and he had received an answer that his letter would have attention. The Education Committee would not hold a public enquiry. Until the parents were proved to be wrong they would have to take their own course.

Defendant was also fined 2s. 6d.

Joseph Ford said he had sent his son Joseph to school, and pleaded not guilty. He asked why Dr. Barnardo's children could go along the roads.

The Clerk—You must confine yourself to this case.

Defendant—I think it is very unfair; one child can do as he likes and another be punished. He believed the Barnardo children had been trained to do what they had done, and his children were afraid to go to school where they were. He should not send his child to school unless there was a public enquiry.

The Chairman—You say you sent him, and now you say you won't send him. We must deal with you the same as the others.

Henry Gotts was represented by his wife, who admitted that their son had not been to school, although he had been up to the school every day since. Fined 2s 6d.

William Garnham also admitted the offence, and was fined 2s. 6d.

Edward Huggins was quite willing to send his son to school, but asked for a public enquiry.

The Chairman—We cannot order a public enquiry, we can only deal with this case; fined 2s. 6d.

Henry Ling said his daughter Marjorie went off to school at the usual time, and when she got there she joined the strikers. What was he to do? Was he to force the child into school against her will?

The Clerk—What would you do if she did anything else you did not want her to do?

Defendant said he had a conscientious objection to the child going to school. She would sit all alone and fret and pine for the head teacher.

He was fined 2s. 6d.

Alfred Moore admitted his son was not at school, and was fined 2s. 6d.

Thomas Mullinger also admitted that his son Jack was not there.

The Chairman—Any reason to give?

Defendant—No; only he was on strike, and he dare not break the rules. (Laughter.)

The Chairman—We must not break the rule. You will be fined 2s. 6d. (Laughter.)

John Potter, senr., was represented by his wife, who said she should not send her son unless there was a public enquiry, because she though there had been injustice. She did not see why they should be ruled by the parson. (Cheers.)

The Clerk—That has nothing to do with the Bench, and you must confine your remarks to the charge.

He was fined 2s. 6d.

John Potter, junr., said this daughter Mabel was unwell, and he therefor pleaded not guilty.

Mr. Starr stated he had received no medical certificate.

Defendant said the child suffered from asthma, and he sent her to school when she was all right, but since the strike she would not go. He could not make her go, and on the 7th she was ill.

Thirza Moore, called by the defendant, said the child was ill on the 1st April when the children struck, and was ill for several days afterwards.

The Chairman said it was evident the defendant was speaking about the 1st April. The case was with regard to the 7th. He would be fined 2s. 6d.

John Sturman said he sent his daughter Gladys to school. He had seven to work for, and could not afford to lose the time to take her there. Fined 2s. 6d.

William Wilby, who hoped the Bench would use their influence to make peace over the job, was similarly fined.

James Wells and Robert Wilby were also fined 2s. 6d.

# Appendix 4

## Hymns, Songs and Poems

Tom Higdon was as much adored by the children of Wood Dalling School as his wife; yet he could be quite severe with the cane, as the small verse recited at the time recalls:

> Mr Higdon is a very good man
> He tries to teach us all he can,
> Reading, writing and arithmetic,
> But he doesn't forget to give us the stick.

The child strikers of Burston had their own words that they would sing to the tune of 'Tipperary'. In it, Little Willie, as the strikers called him, was Rev. Charles Tucker Eland and Kaiser Bill was Mr Alfred Johnson, the chief churchwarden:

> It's a long way to Burston Station,
> It's a long way to go,
> It's a long way to Burston Station
> To catch the train we know.
> Goodbye Little Willie,
> Farewell Kaiser Bill.
> It's a long way to Burston Station
> But we're all on Strike still.

At the time of the school strike a song went round the village; who penned it is lost from memory but the surviving section was reproduced by Sol Sandy, whose family lived opposite the Higdons' cottage during the time of the strike:

It is but a short time ago
We all remember well
Two meetings in the schoolroom
Held a verdict for to tell
He went all round the village
A few tales he did hear
He put them all together
And a blower he got there.
Then fancy Johnnie Philpot
To show his face up there
For when a boy he went to jail
For riding an old mare
Can you call him a gentleman
Who called his flock a liar
And may the Lord have mercy on him
To save him from Hell fire.
If ever we knew a parson
To Burston ever came
Better than the Higdons
Then I am overcome.

Tom Higdon was a keen amateur poet, and along with his two extended poems published by Jarrod & Sons, he wrote many odes to his love of the countryside and the natural world.

### 'Of the Earth—Earthy'
*By*
Tom Higdon

Oh, I love this old huz of a
    world—I can't help it—I love her!
I love her much better than
    Heaven
Far away and above her.
I love her!—I love what is real:
I am not a dreamer.—She is sinful
I know—not too black

For love to redeem her.
Oh I love the old huzzy I do—So
  wicked and good!
Deceitful, she's honest with me,
I know her old blood.
She is more than a mother to
  me—Than a maiden's her charms;
What tokens and gifts she
  bestows
With her bountiful arms! . . .
. . . She is Mortal—alas! and she
  knows it—When pales her
  complexion;
But my dust she will mingle with
  hers
Till the last resurrection—When I
  fear me the great consummation
Will rend her to pieces—That the
  end of the world will be ending
Both her and my species.

Annie Higdon always stressed Christian values, particularly the need to love and care for each other. Abou Ben Adhem was one of her personal favourite poems which she would ask the children to recite, including at political meetings:

## 'Abou Ben Adhem'
*By*
Leigh Hunt

Abou Ben Adhem (may his tribe increase)
Awoke one night from a deep dream of peace,
And saw—within the moonlight in his room,
Making it rich and like a lily in
  bloom—An angel, writing in a book of gold.
Exceeding peace had made Ben Adhem bold,
And to the presence in the room he said,

'What writest thou?—The vision raised its head,
And with a look made of all sweet accord,
Answered, 'The names of those who love the Lord.'
'And is mine one?' said Adhem. 'Nay, not so,'
Replied the angel. Abou spoke more low,
But cheerily still, and said, 'I pray thee, then,
Write me as one that loves his fellow men.'
The angel wrote and vanished. The next night
It came again with a great wakening light,
And showed the names whom love of God had blessed,
And lo! Bed Adhem's name led all the rest.

The children of Burston learned a number of traditional songs with working-class origins or Socialist standards. These were performed publicly at demonstrations or at May Day rallies in Norwich or Burston. Annie would often accompany them on violin, and on occasion comrades like Tom Mann or 'Casey' were present to play the fiddle.

### 'England Arise'
#### *By*
#### Edward Carpenter

To promote socialist propaganda in Sheffield Carpenter wrote England Arise! A socialist marching song, to rival Connell's Red Flag in the British labour movement.

England, arise! The long, long night is over,
Faint in the East behold the dawn appear,
Out of your evil dream of toil and
    sorrow—Arise, O England, for the day is here!
From your fields and hills,
Hark! The answer swells—Arise, O
    England, for the day is here!
People of England! All your valleys call you,
High in the rising sun the lark sings clear,
Will you dream on, let shameful slumber thrall you?

Will you disown your native land so dear?
Shall it die unheard—That sweet pleading word?
Arise, O England, for the day is here!
Over your face a web of lies is woven,
Laws that are falsehoods pin you to the ground,
Labour is mocked, its just reward is stolen,
On its bent back sits Idleness encrowned.
How long, while you sleep,
Your harvest shall it reap.?
Arise, O England, for the day is here!
Forth, then, ye heroes, patriots and lovers!
Comrades of danger, poverty and scorn!
Mighty in faith of Freedom, thy great Mother!
Giants refreshed in Joy's new rising morn!
Come and swell the song,
Silent now so long;
England is risen, and the day is here!

### 'The Keel Row'

The Keel Row is a traditional Tyneside folk song evoking the
life and work of the keelmen of Newcastle upon Tyne. It was
first published in 1770, but may be considerably older. The
original opening lines of the song set it in Sandgate, that part
of the quayside overlooking the River Tyne to the east of the
city centre where the keelmen lived, and which is still overlooked
by the Keelmen's Hospital.

As I came thro' Sandgate, Thro' Sandgate, thro' Sandgate,
As I came thro' Sandgate, I heard a lassie sing.
O, weel may the keel row, The keel row, the keel row,
O weel may the keel row, That my laddie's in.'
He wears a blue bonnet, Blue bonnet, blue bonnet,
He wears a blue bonnet, A dimple in his chin.
And weel may the keel row, The keel row, the keel row,
And weel may the keel row, That my laddie's in.

The traditional set of words above were later augmented by other versions. Its first two stanzas are now often sung with the traditional ones:

O wha's like my Johnnie, Sae
    leish, sae blithe, sae bonnie?
He's foremost 'mang the mony, Keel lads o' coaly Tyne;
He'll set or row sae tightly, Or, in the dance sae sprightly,
He'll cut and shuffle slightly, 'Tis true, were he nae mine.'

## 'John Brown'
### *By*
### William W. Patton

The song 'John Brown' originated with soldiers of the Massachusetts 12th Regiment and soon spread to become the most popular anthem of Union soldiers during the Civil War. Many versions of the song exist, but Patton's is widely considered the best and is reproduced here.

Old John Brown's body lies moldering in the grave,
While weep the sons of bondage whom he ventured all to
    save;
But tho he lost his life while struggling for the slave,
His soul is marching on.
John Brown was a hero, undaunted, true and brave,
And Kansas knows his valor when he fought her rights to
    save;
Now, tho the grass grows green above his grave,
His soul is marching on.
He captured Harper's Ferry, with his nineteen men so few,
And frightened "Old Virginny" till she trembled thru and
    thru;
They hung him for a traitor, themselves the traitor crew,
But his soul is marching on.
John Brown was John the Baptist of the Christ we are to see,
Christ who of the bondmen shall the Liberator be,

And soon thru'out the Sunny South the slaves shall all be
    free,
For his soul is marching on.
The conflict that he heralded he looks from heaven to view,
On the army of the Union with its flag red, white and blue.
And heaven shall ring with anthems o'er the deed they
    mean to do,
For his soul is marching on.
Ye soldiers of Freedom, then strike, while strike ye may,
The death blow of oppression in a better time and way,
For the dawn of old John Brown has brightened into day,
And his soul is marching on.


### 'Now is the month of Maying'
*By*
Thomas Morley

'Now is the month of Maying' is one of the most famous of the
English ballets. It was written and published in 1595, and is
based on the canzonet 'So ben mi ch'a bon tempo' by Orazio
Vecchi. The song delights in bawdy double-entendre.

Now is the month of maying,
When merry lads are playing,
Fa la la la la la la la la,
Fa la la la la la la la lah.
Each with his bonny lass
Upon the greeny grass.
Fa la la la la la la la la [etc.]
The Spring, clad all in gladness,
Doth laugh at Winter's sadness,
Fa la la, [etc.]
And to the bagpipe's sound
The nymphs tread out their ground.
Fa la la, [etc.]
Fie then! why sit we musing,
Youth's sweet delight refusing?

Fa la la, [etc.]
Say, dainty nymphs, and speak,
Shall we play barley break?
Fa la la [etc.]

## 'Heart of Oak'
### *By*
Words: David Garrick
Music: Dr William Boyce

'Heart of Oak' is the official march of the Royal Navy. David Garrick was a famous actor of the day, and is credited with coining the phrase 'break a leg'.

Come, cheer up, my lads, 'tis to glory we steer,
To add something more to this wonderful year;
To honour we call you, as freemen not slaves,
For who are as free as the sons of the waves?
CHORUS: Hearts of oak are our ships,
Jolly tars are our men, we always are ready;
Steady, boys, steady!
We'll fight and we'll conquer again and again.
We ne'er see our foes but we wish them to stay,
They never see us but they wish us away;
If they run, why we follow, and run them ashore,
And if they won't fight us, we cannot do more.
CHORUS
They swear they'll invade us, these terrible foes,
They frighten our women, our children and beaus,
But should their flat bottoms in darkness get o'er,
Still Britons they'll find to receive them on shore.
CHORUS
We'll still make them fear and we'll still make them flee,
And drub them ashore as we've drubbed them at sea,
Then cheer up, my lads, with our hearts let us sing,
Our soldiers, our sailors, our airmen, our Queen.
CHORUS

## 'Red Flag'
### *By*
### Jim Connell

Connell wrote the song's lyrics in 1889. It is normally sung to the tune of 'Lauriger Horatius', better known as the German carol 'O Tannenbaum' ('O Christmas Tree'), though Connell had wanted it sung to the tune of a pro-Jacobite Robert Burns anthem, 'The White Cockade'.

The people's flag is deepest red,
It shrouded oft our martyred dead,
And ere their limbs grew stiff and cold,
Their hearts' blood dyed its ev'ry fold.
Then raise the scarlet standard high.
Within its shade we'll live and die,
Though cowards flinch and traitors sneer,
We'll keep the red flag flying here.
Look 'round, the Frenchman loves its blaze,
The sturdy German chants its praise,
In Moscow's vaults its hymns are sung
Chicago swells the surging throng.
Then raise the scarlet standard high.
Within its shade we'll live and die,
Though cowards flinch and traitors sneer,
We'll keep the red flag flying here.
It waved above our infant might,
When all ahead seemed dark as night;
It witnessed many a deed and vow,
We must not change its colour now.
Then raise the scarlet standard high.
Within its shade we'll live and die,
Though cowards flinch and traitors sneer,
We'll keep the red flag flying here.
It well recalls the triumphs past,
It gives the hope of peace at last;
The banner bright, the symbol plain,
Of human right and human gain.

Then raise the scarlet standard high.
Within its shade we'll live and die,
Though cowards flinch and traitors sneer,
We'll keep the red flag flying here.
It suits today the weak and base,
Whose minds are fixed on self and place
To cringe before the rich man's frown,
And haul the sacred emblem down.
Then raise the scarlet standard high.
Within its shade we'll live and die,
Though cowards flinch and traitors sneer,
We'll keep the red flag flying here.
With heads uncovered swear we all
To bear it onward till we fall;
Come dungeons dark or gallows grim,
This song shall be our parting hymn.
Then raise the scarlet standard high.
Within its shade we'll live and die,
Though cowards flinch and traitors sneer,
We'll keep the red flag flying here.

### 'The Internationale'

'The Internationale' (French: L'Internationale) is a left-wing anthem—a standard of the Socialist movement since the late 19th century, when the Second International (now the Socialist International) adopted it as its official anthem.

Arise ye workers from your slumbers
Arise ye prisoners of want
For reason in revolt now thunders
And at last ends the age of can't.
Away with all your superstitions
Servile masses arise, arise
We'll change henceforth the old tradition
And spurn the dust to win the prize.
REFRAIN

So comrades, come rally
And the last fight let us face
The Internationale unites the human race.
No more deluded by reaction
On tyrants only we'll make war
The soldiers too will take strike action
They'll break ranks and fight no more
And if those cannibals keep trying
To sacrifice us to their pride
They soon shall hear the bullets flying
We'll shoot the generals on our own side.
No saviour from on high delivers
No faith have we in prince or peer
Our own right hand the chains must shiver
Chains of hatred, greed and fear
E'er the thieves will out with their booty
And give to all a happier lot.
Each at the forge must do their duty
And we'll strike while the iron is hot.

# Acknowledgements

I am grateful to the following individuals and institutions for their assistance, encouragement, and for paving the road travelled: the Burston Strike School Trustees, who for over sixty years have been the guardians of the Strike School and its legacy; the Norfolk Record Office and Norfolk Heritage Centre in Norwich, not least for preserving and providing access to important documents relating to the school strike that are not to be found anywhere else; the same applies to the Somerset Heritage Centre and Mendip County Council; The Country Standard [online], which is such a valuable historical reserve on rural trade unionism. I must thank Picture Norfolk for providing one image courtesy of Norfolk County Council Library and Information. A great deal of gratitude must be paid to the now deceased Bert Edwards, who did so much to popularise the Burston rebellion in the 1970s and 80s, but most importantly was smart enough to track down, interview and correspond with many ex-pupils of the Higdons when he produced his own book. Francis Wheen, to whom I tip my hat on more than one occasion. Simon Haines, for above all making me see that less is sometimes more. Lil Davies, Word Nerd Editing, for her professional and effective scrutiny, polish and opinion. Professor Alun Howkins, for taking the time to provide his generous foreword. Considerable appreciation goes to the brilliant Mark Metcalf, who provided no end of support in bringing about the book's realisation. And finally, my thanks also go to all those who wished me well along the way, but most of all to Tom and Annie Higdon for being uncompromisingly who they were.

# Endnotes

## Introduction: The School of Freedom

The reconstruction of the opening of the Strike School has been made from several primary sources produced by those in attendance. All the accounts were written and published in May 1917, and Violet Potter's reminiscences in the Yesterday's Witness documentary from 1974 are reinforced by the written reports of the time.

1. 'A cottage roof or two, a line of trees in the distance . . .'
   S. Pankhurst's account of the day, 'The Woman's Dreadnought', May 1917. As reproduced in *The Burston Rebellion* by Betka Zamoyska, 1985, p.107.

2. Ibid., p.107.

3. Ibid., p.108.

4. 'He looked a poor soul and one could only feel a great pity . . .'
   J. Scurr, 'How the School was Opened.' *The Herald*, May 19, 1917. p.8.

5. Physical description of the new (and yet to be completed Strike School) comes from the *Diss Express, and Norfolk and Suffolk Journal* coverage, Friday, May 18, 1917. p.?

6. As John Scurr, representing George Lansbury stepped on to the Green. *Diss Express*, Friday, May 18, 1917. p.?

7. Account of Mr W. Carter's speech at the public meeting comes from both the *Diss Express* and J. Scurr's report of the day's event.

8. Violet Potter's own account of the opening of the Strike School speaking in the BBC's *Yesterday's Witness* documentary, 1974. Supported by the press coverage from the *Diss Express* and *The Herald*, May 1917.

9. The poem Robert Green recited for the occasion. J. Scurr, *The Herald*, May 19, 1917. p.8.

10. Departure time of the charter train. *Diss Express*, Friday, May 18, 1917. p.?

## Chapter One: Down the Western Line

The description of labourer households in Somersetshire (1870s) is taken from Francis George Heath's own account and Bob Owen's biography of George Mitchell, both themselves quoting from the government's 1843 and 1870 Royal Commissions. Pam Horn's biography of Joseph Arch, and Bob Owen's account of the life and times of Mitchell are the most definitive accounts available of their respective subjects. The overview of the pre-1872 attempts to build a national union is constructed from Horn, P., Scarth, B., and Groves, R.'s accounts, supplemented by newspaper reports primarily accessed through the British Newspaper Archive (online).

1. 'It has been truly said . . .' *The "Romance" of Peasant Life in the West of England* (1872), p.5.

2. 'wretchedness and squalor are not confined. . .' Ibid., p.10.

3. 'It would be found that in Somersetshire. . .' Ibid., p.9.

4. 'The average wages during the whole year. . .' 'One From the Plough' (2002), p.20.

5. 'Had long believed from my previous knowledge. . .' *The "Romance" of Peasant Life in the West of England* (1872), p.9.

6. 'As far as the eye can reach. . .' Ibid., p.26.

7. 'Even on the hill-sides the pastures extend. . .' Ibid., p.26.

8. 'I stopped and accosted an old labourer. . .' Ibid., p.27.

9. 'John P _____ (the inhabitant of this "cottage"). . .' Ibid., p.29.

10. 'John_____, (a fine young English labourer). . .' Ibid., p.12.

11. 'At the foot of the letter. . .' 'One From the Plough' (2002), p.28.

12. 'He foraged for whatever he could eat. . .' Ibid., p.5.

13. 'When I embarked on this great movement. . .' 'The Farm Labourer Agitation', *The Western Times* (1872), p.2.

14. 'Ignorant as he may be, downtrodden as he has been. . .' Ibid., p.2.

15. 'The wave of agricultural dissatisfaction. . .' 'The Agricultural Labourers', *The Western Times* (1872), p.2.

16. 'The men demand more. . .' Ibid., p.2.

17. 'at first I had laboured under a prejudice. . .' George Mitchell quoted in *The Western Times* (1873).

18. 'A meeting of Agricultural labourers. . .' 'The Agricultural Labourers'. *The Bridport News, And Dorsetshire, Devonshire And Somersetshire Advertiser* (1872), p.?

19. 'The audience consisted chiefly. . .' Ibid., p.?

20. 'It is resolved that this meeting deeply sympathies. . .' Ibid., p.?

## Chapter Two: Rise of the Schollicks

No biography of Edward J. Schollick exists, but Peter Sandbach's article from the Through Mighty Seas website provides any interested party with a valuable overview. The life and times of E.J. Schollick (and John Stonard) has been produced primarily through newspaper reports.

1. 'When she didn't want to answer. . .' Interview with Mr G.C.T. Giles and wife as presented in Edwards, B. (1974) *The Burston School Strike*, p.154.

2. 'She just wouldn't listen. . .' Ibid., p.154.

3. 'She was always very close. . .' Ibid., p.154.

4. 'The bridegroom, instead of following. . .' Report on E.J. Schollick's wedding, *The Westmoreland Gazette and Kendal Advertiser* (1849).

5. 'employing eleven men and three apprentices' Census recording (1851).

6. E.J. Schollick of Aldingham Hall, Ulverston: Begs to intimate to the public. . .' Public notice, *Soulby's Ulverston Advertiser* (1855).

7. 'In the company of Mr * I inspected. . .' Mr R. Rawlison's report, Poulton-cum-Seacombe, *The Liverpool Mercury*, p.?

8. Wallasey Improvements, power was given. . .' Notice, *Chester Chronicle and Cheshire and North Wales Advertiser*, (1957).

## Chapter Three: Sickles and Seaside

If interested in learning about the life of the schoolchild and attaining a valuable overview of the changes in schooling over the Victorian and Edwardian periods, there is no better starting volume than Pamela Horn's 1989 book *The Victorian & Edwardian Schoolchild* (Ed. 2010). Amberley Publishing plc. Again, references previously mentioned in relation to the development of the NALU have provided historical context in this chapter, while the rest has been attained and reconstructed from newspaper articles of the time.

1. 'It was concerns raised over the. . .' *The Victorian & Edwardian Schoolchild*, p.100.

2. 'Employment of any child below the age of eight. . .' Ibid., p.101.

3. 'No child under eight years old might be employed. . .' Ibid., p.104.

4. 'was left to the education legislation of the 1870's. . .' Ibid., p.105.

5. 'Imperative necessity.' Ibid., p.21.

6. 'In order to give every child a school place. . .' Ibid., p.21.

7. 'Thereafter a new rate aided schools. . .' Ibid., p.23.

8. 'The overall principle of design remaining. . .' Ibid., p.38.

9. 'The stratified order to East Pennard village. . .' Conservation Area Appraisal—East Pennard, p.6.

10. 'Throughout the summer of 72 as the N.A.L.U. . .' 'One From the Plough' (2002), p.76.

11. 'Spread the word throughout the farming communities. . .' Ibid., p.76.

12. 'Demand the franchise and decent wages—no surrender!' Ibid., p.77.

13. 'Both in the private yards and Royal yards. . .' *Dockyard Shipwrights*, p.3.

14. 'Some planking intended for the ceiling. . .' *The Liverpool Mercury*, p.?

15. 'He still lies in a precarious condition. . .' Ibid., p.?

16. 'Curious action against. . .' The Observer, p.?

17. 'That the society has to supply the medicines. . .' *The Liverpool Mercury* and *The Observer*, p.?

## Chapter Four: Cometh the Nomads

The brief genealogy narrative of the Eland family of Wesleyan ministers was reconstructed from Census data, 1841–81, and supplemented with personal reflections from the following texts: Eyken, W.V.D. and Turner, B. (1969). *Adventures in Education*. Penguin. Hazell Watson & Viney Ltd; Edwards, B. (1974). *The Burston School Strike*. Lawrence & Wishart, London; and Higdon, T.G. (1916). *The Burston Rebellion*. National Labour Press. Manchester. Reference to the involvement of Nonconformists in education comes from Horn, P. (1989). *The Victorian & Edwardian Schoolchild* (Ed. 2010). Amberley Publishing. Full correspondence of Richard Eland in regard to the issue of the re-baptism of an infant, is carried by the British Newspaper Archive (1853). Re-Baptism of an Infant. *Leicester Journal*. General Methodist history was extracted primarily from Rack, H.D. (2002). *Reasonable Enthusiast: John Wesley and the Rise of Methodism* (Ed. 3, 2002), Epworth. London; and Author: Anonymous (2010). *Infant Baptism*. (Adapted from W.P. 'On Infant Baptism' under the G.N.U free documentation licence, 2010). Global Oneness. Available at: http://www. experiencefestival.com/a/infant_baptism/id/1895554 & Dale, I. (2003). *The Story of Bilston Wesley*. Harold Dale.

1. 'His attitude towards his parishioners. . .' Adventures in Education—*The Burston School Strike*, p.4.

2. 'Little man with big consequences' Letter contained in *The Burston Strike School*.

3. 'Narrow-minded Church bigot and despotic. . .' Tom Higdon quoted in *Adventures in Education—The Burston School Strike*, p.5.

4. 'I am resolved to perform my duties. . .' From letters reproduced in the *Leicester Journal*, p.?

5. 'Trusting that his lordship would. . .' Ibid., p.?

## Chapter Five: Fall and Resurrection.

The history of the Farm Workers' Union during the 1880s is extracted from the same classic texts that also cover its early growth, including: Hasbach, W. (1908). *A History of the English*

*Agricultural Labourer.* Translated by Ruth Kenyon. (1st Ed. English). S. King & Son; Pamela Horn's biography of Joseph Arch and Groves, R. (1949). *Sharpen the Sickle! The History of the Farm Workers' Union.* Merlin Publications. Again, Horn, P. (1989). *The Victorian & Edwardian Schoolchild* (Ed. 2010). Amberley Publishing provides a quality pupil-teacher scheme extrapolation. There are several respected works on the Dock Strike of 1889, the most widely cited being McCarthy, T. (1988). *Great Dock Strike of 1889.* Published by Weidenfeld & Nicolson. The extracts related to the history of Methodism come from Rack, H.D. (2002). *Reasonable Enthusiast: John Wesley and the Rise of Methodism* (Ed. 3, 2002), Epworth. London; and Heitzenrater, R.P. (2005). *Wesley and The People called Methodists.* Nashville: Abingdon Press. All subject areas have been supplemented by newspaper reports from the time.

1. 'The harvest blackened in the fields.' *Sharpen the Sickle,* p.81.

2. 'Between 1871 and 1881, 120,000 labourers. . .' National Census data.

3. 'Up until the year 1877 the "National". . .' *Sharpen the Sickle,* p.83.

4. 'Soon riven with feuds, brought about. . .' Ibid., p.82.

5. 'Who fulfilled certain scholastic, moral. . .' *Pupil-teacher Training,* p.1.

6. From 12,467 to 31,422. . .' Ibid., p. 2.

7. 'To mother, with best love from Tom' *To the Departed,* title page.

8. 'Here I my brother mourn' Ibid., p.3.

9. 'Oh, cruel Death, that this my brother stole' Ibid., p.4.

10. 'And I for him as for a brother mourn' Ibid., p.3.

11. 'In the evening addresses were given by. . .' *The Western Gazette,* p.6.

12. 'A Gospel Temperance Blue Ribbon Meeting. . .' *The Western Gazette,* p.6.

13. 'The chairman in his opening remarks. . .' Ibid., p.6.

14. When from 1885 onwards the trades unions. . .' *A History of the English Agricultural Labourer,* p.297.

15. 'A vital step towards winning for the labourers' *We'll All Be Union Men,* p.25.

16. 'Passing unanimously a resolution. . .' Ibid., p.155.

17. 'All men paying an annual rental of £10. . .' *A History of the English Agricultural Labourer*, p.321.

18. 'Next to the famous year of the start of. . .' *We'll All Be Union Men*, p.155.

19. 'By which the masses of the people. . .' Ibid., p.155.

20. 'In later years attempts to win farm workers. . .' *Sharpen the Sickle*, p.83.

21. 'Zacharias Walker had been conducting. . .' *We'll All Be Union Men*, p. 183.

22. 'The branch delegate had enrolled 56 new. . .' Ibid., p.191.

23. 'That did some organising in Staffordshire. . .' *Sharpen the Sickle*, p.86.

## Chapter Six: Another Grand Time

The changing life and times of the Higdons and Schollicks have been recreated from the following newspaper articles and other documentation. In addition, the changing history of the NALU over the 1890s, and the fortunes of its leaders Joseph Arch and George Mitchell, have been guided by the influential works previously mentioned.

1. 'The rich expanse of embryo corn fields. . .' *The Western Times*, p.3.

2. 'It was a village enchanted into silence. . .' Ibid., p.3.

3. 'It was a picturesque domicile. . .' Ibid., p.3.

4. 'The Dock Agitation' Ibid., p.3.

5. 'Was so poorly paid that. . .' *The Victorian & Edwardian Schoolchild*, p.149.

6. 'Afforded both men and women. . .' Ibid., p.151.

7. 'In the mid–1890's there. . .' Ibid., p.154.

8. 'Bibles, Prayer Books, Church Services. . .' *Epsom High Street West* [online].

9. 'Appointed Agent for the sale of. . .' Ibid.

10. 'Accompanied by his "old and tried friend". . .' *We'll All Be Union Men*, p.191.

11. 'The Dockers' Union was also active. . .' *Sharpen the Sickle*, p.86.

12. 'over Essex, Suffolk and Cambridge. . .' Ibid., p.86.

13. 'Reported that the total Union. . .' Ibid., p.191.

14. 'The agricultural labourers of. . .' *The Western Daily Press*, p.8.

15. 'Increase the wages and. . .' Ibid., p.8.

16. This meeting of agricultural labourers. . .' Ibid., p.8.

17. 'In the winter of 1893–4 most. . .' *A History of the English Agricultural Labourer*, p.302.

18. 'The Bill, which in the main. . .' *We'll All Be Union Men*, p.206.

19. 'Last-ditch bid to preserve. . .' Ibid., p.206.

20. 'She had also played the harmonium. . .' *The Western Gazette*, p.7.

21. 'The parish of East Lydford. . .' *Imperial Gazetteer of England and Wales (1870–72)* [online].

22. 'There are certain female workers. . .' *Supplement to The Cheltenham Chronicle*, p.?

## Chapter Seven: Welcome to the Boot Club

Edwards, B. (1974) *The Burston School Strike.* Lawrence & Wishart, London, provides the most detailed examination of the Higdons' time in Wood Dalling. At the time of writing interviews, and a written correspondence, with many former pupils was possible. In addition, interviews were recorded in the *Yesterday's Witness* documentary from 1974. Tom Higdon fleetingly recalls the events of W.D. within *The Burston Rebellion*, but he left behind an eleven-page account of events that is reproduced in Appendix 1. Various letters and papers are held by the Norfolk Record Office, including the school logbook. The section has also been supplemented by the following books and articles:

British Newspaper Archive (1902). *The Cornishman*—Sancreed School Board, p7. Date accessed: 7 April 2016.

Groves. R. (1949). *Sharpen the Sickle! The History of the Farm Workers' Union.* Merlin Publications.

Howkins, A. (1985). *Poor Labouring Men—Rural Radicalism in Norfolk 1870–1923.* Routledge & Kengan Paul.

Gillard, D. (2011). *Education in England: a brief history.* Available at: http://www.educationengland.org.uk/history/chapter04.html p.1. Date Accessed: 19 January 2017.

1. 'Nonconformists considered it an unfairness. . .' *Education in England,* p.1.

2. 'Though very few labourers were involved. . .' *Poor Labouring Men—Rural Radicalism in Norfolk 1870–1923,* p. 84.

3. 'This filled them with unhealthy ambitions. . .' *The Victorian & Edwardian Schoolchild,* p.106.

4. 'In accordance with the Board's resolution. . .' *The Burston School Strike,* p.94.

5. 'Would buy dog biscuits and fed any dogs. . .' Letter from Violet Turner (Potter) to Bert Edwards.

6. '16 April 1902: Visited by the attendance officer. . .' W.D. School logbook entry for date.

7. '1 July: Yesterday Albert Cottrell. . .' W.D. School logbook entry.

8. 'The Reverend Vicars was a funny man. . .' Interview with Tom Barnes by Mr B. Edwards.

9. 'Mixed school. There has been a complete. . .' W.D. School logbook entry for date.

10. 'The present staff, however, is quite inadequate. . .' Government Inspectors report quoted by Mrs.Higdon in the school logbook, 1902.

11. 'When it rained she would feel the. . .' Interview with Tom Barnes.

12. 'Jim Bussens' boy was playing about his watch. . .' Interview with Tom Barnes.

13. 'Tom wouldn't come into school. . .' Ibid.

14. 'The magistrates' surprise at Higdon's behaviour. . .' *The Burston Rebellion,* p.14.

15. 'Not a very good sport' Interview with Mr T. Williams by Mr B. Edwards.

16. 'She was very strict over the girls' hair. . .' Interview with Tom Barnes.

17. 'The Wood Dalling children won the schools. . .' Ibid.

18. 'Give any old tramp a good meal' *The Burston School Strike,* p.83.

19. '27 January, 1903: Mistress took first class for. . .' W.D. School logbook entry for date.

20. 'go and preach another sermon in the Chapel. . .' Interview with Tom Barnes.

21. '17 May, 1904: The question of change of. . .' Letter from Mr Blades to Norfolk Education Committee.

22. 'Mr.T.G.Higdon has shown much interest. . .' Testimonial by Rev. R. Vicars, June 1904.

23. '14 September, 1904: Attendance is excellent. . .' Government Inspectors Report for year ending, quoted by Mr B. Edwards.

24. 'sweeping and dusting having to be finished. . .' W.D. School logbook entry, 5 Feb 1906.

25. 'After considering them they formed. . .' *The Burston School Strike* p.63.

26. 'period of intense political activity. . .' *Poor Labouring Men*, p.84.

27. 'If you make the effort, I will make the. . .' Charlotte Edwards. *Sharpen the Sickle*, p.105.

28. 'Upstairs in the 'assembly rooms'. . .' *Poor Labouring Men*, p. 87.

29. 'That this conference composed of delegates. . .' Motion quoted in *Poor Labouring Men*, p.86.

## Chapter Eight: The Clatter and Clumper

1. 'though his original and interesting. . .' T.G. Higdon's account, as carried in *Sharpen the Sickle*, p.109.

2. 'spare figure bent over the handlebars. . .' *Sharpen the Sickle*, p.108.

3. '"Sure enough," Higdon commented. . .' Ibid., p.109.

4. 'They always stuck together. . .' Interview with Tom Barnes by Bert Edwards.

5. 'Repairs. Mrs. Higdon wrote calling. . .' W.D. School logbook entry, 16 May 1907.

6. 'bad state of the Girl's Playground. . .' Ibid., 17 May 1907.

7. 'H.M. Inspector having advised freer. . .' Ibid., 25 November 1908.

8. 'trouble and annoyance in the matter. . .' Tom Higdon's account of the W.D. affair, as reproduced in Appendix 1, p.1.

9. 'used bad language towards him' Ibid.

10. 'Closing School without permission. . .' Ibid.

11. 'They said nothing to Mrs. Higdon. . .' Ibid.

12. 'unmistakable evidence of the way. . .' Norfolk Education Committee confidential report.

13. 'Another chance' Reference to Tom Higdon's account reproduced in Appendix 1.

14. 'there would be two lots in a year. . .' Interview with Tom Barnes.

15. 'no infectious disease.' *The Burston School Strike*, p.66.

16. 'visited the School, tested the registers. . .' Ibid., p.67.

17. 'the agricultural labourers' movement. . .' *Joseph Arch* by Pamela Horn, p.69.

18. 'Arch, with old-fashioned peasant. . .' Ibid., p.210.

19. 'work continued in the 1890's and 1900. . .' *Poor Labouring Men*, p.105.

20. 'established a pattern of urban working men. . .' Ibid., p.105.

21. 'the ILP had over 500 members. . .' Ibid., p.105.

22. The local knowledge of the Wood Dalling. . .' Tom Higdon's own unpublished account of the Wood Dalling affair, p.2.

23. 'And there the matter could have rested.' Ibid., p.2.

24. 'Thus Mr.Bussens was reinstalled. . .' Ibid., p.3.

25. 'something was going to happen. . .' Ibid., p.105.

26. 'having made the most searching. . .' W.D. School logbook entry, 30 June 1910.

27. 'he having doubtless had his say. . .' Tom Higdon's own unpublished account of the Wood Dalling affair, p.8.

28. 'Headmistress absent one hour. . .' W.D. School logbook entry, 21 July 1910.

29. 'The usual farce of a Local Enquiry. . .' *The Burston Rebellion*, pp. 6–7.

30. 'find it undesirable for the Teacher to. . .' Norfolk Education Committee confidential report, January 1917, quoted in *The Burston School Strike*, p. 45.

31. 'as the most prejudicial form of removal' Ibid.

32. 'since regret for my lack of discretion. . .' Ibid.

33. 'resigning their position as Managers. . .' Ibid.

34. 'All these efforts, however, have not. . .' Tom Higdon's own unpublished account of the Wood Dalling affair, p.10.

## Chapter Nine: Two Pedestrian Strangers

From the time that the Higdons arrived in Burston, the amount of archival material charting their time and actions increases considerably. Tom Higdon's own short book, *The Burston Rebellion*, is a detailed memoir of events. The book also happens to be widely quoted in other accounts (though all now out of print) such as Edwards, B. (1974) *The Burston School Strike*. Lawrence & Wishart, London. The Norfolk Record Office holds a variety of materials, some of which have not been widely used or circulated before, which have been used to provide narrative detail. These have been supplemented with details from the following newspaper articles and studies:

British Newspaper Archive (1904). *Essex County Chronicle—Vicar of Felsted's Deal in Union Pacifics*, p.8. Date accessed: 14 April 2016.

British Newspaper Archive (1905). *The Newsman—Conservatives at Felsted*, p.3. Date accessed: 14 April 2016.

British Newspaper Archive (1906). *The Essex Newsman—Felsted*, p.? Date accessed: 14 April 2016.

British Newspaper Archive (1906). *The Essex County Chronicle—Felsted Water Question*, p.6. Date accessed: 14 April 2016.

British Newspaper Archive (1907). *The Essex County Chronicle—Felsted Results & Felsted Water Supply*, p.6. Date accessed: 14 April 2016.

British Newspaper Archive (1907). *The Essex County Chronicle—Summer Chaplaincies on the Continent*, p.6. Date accessed: 14 April 2016.

British Newspaper Archive (1908). *The Diss Express, And Norfolk And Suffolk Journal—New Vicar at Burston*, front page. Date accessed: 14 April 2016.

British Newspaper Archive (1908). *The Diss Express, And Norfolk And Suffolk Journal*—Mission Report, p.? Date accessed: 14 April 2016.

British Newspaper Archive (1908). *The Diss Express, And Norfolk And Suffolk Journal*—School Treat, p.2. Date accessed: 14 April 2016.

British Newspaper Archive (1908). *The Essex Newsman*—Dunmow, front page. Date accessed: 14 April 2016.

British Newspaper Archive (1909). *The Essex Newsman*—Felsted Children's Christmas Treat, front page. Date accessed: 14 April 2016.

British Newspaper Archive (1909). *The Diss Express, And Norfolk And Suffolk Journal*—Mrs Green Resigns, p.? Date accessed: 14 April 2016.

British Newspaper Archive (1910). *The Essex County Chronicle*—New Essex Vicar and His Wife, p.2. Date accessed: 14 April 2016.

British Newspaper Archive (1910). *The Newsman*—Church News—New Vicar at Felsted, front page. Date accessed: 14 April 2016.

British Newspaper Archive (1911). *The Essex County Chronicle*—Presentation to the Vicar of Felsted, p.3. Date accessed: 14 April 2016.

British Newspaper Archive (1911). *The Diss Express, And Norfolk And Suffolk Journal*—Clerical Appointments, p.? Date accessed: 14 April 2016.

Unknown (n.d.). A Walk through Felsted—A Trip Down Memory Lane. Available at: http://www.recordinguttlesfordhistory.org.uk/felsted/A%20Walk%20through%20Felsted%20in%201901.pdf. Date accessed: 6 February 2017.

1. 'with its windmill, its bridge over the. . .' *The Burston Rebellion*, p.1.

2. 'it was not for want of money. . .' Ibid., p.2.

3. 'the sweet bit of common land. . .' Ibid., p.1.

4. 'as their names had been sent as. . .' Ibid., p.13.

5. 'friend in the Wood Dalling district. . .' Ibid., p.14.

6. 'They had the heart knocked out of them. . .' Ibid., p.3.

7. 'there were no Labourers' Union Branches. . .' Ibid., p.13.

8. 'The school premises were ill-lighted. . .' Ibid., p.13.

9. 'this was a story discreditable. . .' Vicar of Felsted's Deal in Union Pacifics.

10. 'At a meeting of the managers of the Felsted.' *The Essex Newsman*, p.6.

11. 'That in the opinion of this Council. . .' Ibid.

12. 'The new Rector, after the words of. . .' The *Diss Express* report, p.?

13. 'the number was fairly good considering. . .' Ibid.

14. 'Large congregations attending the services. . .' Ibid.

15. 'With help of many kind friends and. . .' Ibid.

16. 'That while rector of Burston. . .' *The Newsman* report, p.?

17. 'He also had 54 acres of glebe land. . .' *The Burston Rebellion*, B. Zamoyska, p.22.

18. 'peremptorily demanded the Registers. . .' *The Burston Rebellion*, T. Higdon, p.14.

19. 'therefore absented herself and went to Chapel. . .' Ibid., p.15.

20. 'The place of the Schoolmistress is at Church. . .' *The Burston School Strike*, p.14.

21. 'The parson soon had his grievance. . .' *The Burston Rebellion*, T. Higdon, p.15.

22. 'let it be clearly understood. . .' Ibid., p. 14.

23. 'She would send out and buy children sweets. . .' *The Burston Rebellion*, B. Zamoyska, p.24.

24. 'on a Thursday, once a fortnight. . .' Ibid., p.25.

25. 'was very particular with the poor little children. . .' Ibid., p.26.

26. 'she organised a flower show in the school playground. . .' Ibid., p.26.

27. 'she bought a book, and sent eight of the older children. . .' Ibid., p.27.

28. 'The present Mistress had had charge. . .' *The Burston School Strike*, p.21.

29. 'I have much pleasure in testifying to. . .' Ibid., p.15.

30. 'I think Mr. Higdon most eligible for the post. . .' Ibid., p.14.

ENDNOTES

## Chapter Ten: The Road to Revolution

1. 'For two years they steered a clear course. . .' *The Burston Rebellion*, T.G. Higdon, p.15.
2. 'They had been talking about the need for some. . .' Ibid.
3. 'with the aid of the labourers there. . .' Ibid., p.16.
4. 'A rare type of old rustic Radical. . .' Ibid., p.16.
5. 'much to the surprise, apparently, of the old Council. . .' Ibid., p.17.
6. 'One elector was anxious to proceed. . .' *The Diss Express, and Norfolk And Suffolk Journal*—Burston, p.?
7. 'Surprise and consternation were plunged. . .' *The Burston Rebellion*, T.G. Higdon, p.18.
8. 'It was the "Skulemaster" who had done this thing. . .' Ibid., p.18.
9. 'many ominous gestures, lip curls. . .' Ibid., p.18.
10. 'swore a little more dreadfully than usual. . .' Ibid., p.18.
11. 'fresh from the Creed, the Ten Commandments. . .' T.H quoted in *The Burston Rebellion*, B. Zamoyska, p.41.
12. 'The Education Committee was authorised. . .' Ibid., p.41.
13. 'the line was thus made clear for the carrying-out. . .' *The Burston Rebellion*, T.G. Higdon, p.26.
14. 'A clergyman's holiday has two good points. . .' *The Burston School Strike* by Casey, p.5.
15. 'that the committee took a very serious view. . .' Ibid., p.5.
16. 'A surprise visit is the most modern form of torture. . .' *The Burston School Strike* by Casey, p.7.
17. 'will kindly remove Mrs Higdon to. . .' Letter from NEC to Mrs Higdon.
18. 'that this is the second place in which.' Ibid., p.7.
19. 'received a certain sum of money from. . .' *The Burston Rebellion*, B. Zamoyska, p.44.
20. 'surprising charge to bring against a woman. . .' Ibid., p.45.
21. 'The girls themselves, when questioned at School. . .' *The Burston Rebellion*, T.G. Higdon, p.31.
22. 'A clear day prior to one of these Managers' Enquiries. . .' Ibid.

23. 'She had not punished them at all. . .' Ibid., p. 36.

24. 'in the eyes of these gentlemen, Labourers' Union. . .' Ibid., p.23.

25. 'The Sub-Committee then found that the alleged. . .' Ibid., p. 37.

26. 'two old women, one of whom was the mother or. . .' Ibid., p. 42.

27. 'lamenting the fact that she had been forced. . .' Ibid., p. 42.

28. 'That two respectable teachers should be hounded. . .' *The Burston School Strike* by Casey, p.11.

29. 'The letters written by the Higdons to Dr. Barnardo's Homes. . .' *The Burston School Strike*, p.27.

30. 'who was the organisation's official paymaster. . .' Ibid., p.27.

31. 'Almost the whole village, except. . .' *The Burston Rebellion*, B. Zamoyska, p.55.

## Chapter Eleven: The Village in Revolt

1. 'Mr. Higdon saw no reason why a cheque in lieu. . .' *The Burston School Strike*, p.112.

2. 'similar warning was to be found on a. . .' *The Burston Rebellion*, T.G. Higdon, p.52.

3. 'with the slogans "We Want Our Teachers". . .' *The Burston School Strike*, p.114.

4. 'augustly and severely there the Inspector. . .' *The Burston Rebellion*, T.G. Higdon, p.60.

5. 'a more subversive explanation for the school. . .' *Hooligans or Rebels?* p.93.

6. 'another way in which pupils and parents. . .' Ibid., p.110.

7. 'led by one precocious boy, they armed. . .' *Birmingham Gazette*, 3 Feb 1914, front page.

8. 'a handsome, sturdy girl with some Irish blood. . .' *The Daily Mirror*, 4 Feb 1914, p.5.

9. 'One girl then secured a large school bell. . .' *Birmingham Gazette*, 3 Feb 1914, front page.

10. '"Strike boys, strike", and various other. . .' *Birmingham Daily Mail*, 3 Feb 1914, p.?

11. 'Virtually all the teachers involved were. . .' *The Victorian & Edwardian Schoolchild*, p.174.

12. 'of more significance was the gradual move. . .' *Poor Labouring Men*, p.103.

13. 'parliamentary committee of the TUC for a grant. . .' Ibid., p.111.

14. 'in most rural areas the only unionised workers' Ibid., p.111.

15. 'If you bought a ticket to Burston at Liverpool Street. . .' Interview with Mr G.C.T. Giles by Bert Edwards.

16. 'February 1914 the Essex Farmers had decided. . .' Country Standard blog—Essex Agricultural Labourers.

17. 'But the largest meeting was to hear Sylvia Pankhurst. . .' Ibid.

18. '"The proceedings," reported the *East Anglian Times*. . .' Ibid., p.64.

19. 'Thus the Magistrates appear to have only been. . .' *The Burston Rebellion*, T.G. Higdon, p.70.

20. 'when we got half-way home we all sat down. . .' *Our School Strike*, E. Wilby, p.1.

21. 'it was the next day that the mothers thought. . .' Ibid.

22. 'found it necessary to leave the Primitive Methodist. . .' Ibid., p.58.

23. 'Burston Flock in the Strike School. . .' Ibid.

24. 'in the open air, upon the village green. . .' *The Burston Rebellion*, T.G. Higdon, p.52.

25. 'The Committee think a fortnight sufficient time. . .' Letter to Headmistress.

26. 'men, women, girls, and boys, miller's cart. . .' *The Burston Rebellion*, T.G. Higdon, p.54.

## Chapter Twelve: Long Past Moonshine

1. 'The appointment and dismissal of teachers' Reply by Mr J.A. Pease recorded in Hansard: HC Deb 11 May 1914 vol. 62 c734W.

2. 'The Strike School was visited by County Councillors. . .' *Sharpen the Sickle*, p.157.

3. 'the room was warm and comfortable. . .' *The Burston Rebellion*, T.G. Higdon, p.76.

4. 'Instead they hit upon another place which caused. . .' *The Burston Rebellion*, B. Zamoyska, p.92.

5. 'He took some Glebe land from three poor men. . .' *Our School Strike*, by Emily Wilby.

6. 'Harry was the father of Marjory Ling. . .' *The Burston Rebellion*, B. Zamoyska, p.93.

7. '"That's how it went," Marjory recalled. . .' Ibid., p.94.

8. 'The *Eastern Daily Press*, July 28th, 1915. . .' *The Burston School Strike*, Casey, p.18.

9. 'Of victimisations and evictions there have been no end' *The Burston Rebellion*, T.G. Higdon, p.77.

10. 'by the Rector and his committee was the dismissal. . .' Ibid., p.75.

11. 'To this Mrs. Higdon gave a conditional agreement. . .' *The Burston School Strike*, p.31.

12. 'the last thing heard from the Education Committee. . .' *The Burston Rebellion*, T.G. Higdon, p.77.

13. 'His act in asking for an obtaining a Warrant. . .' Ibid., p. 80.

14. 'The facts concerning the Burston School Strike. . .' Report in *The Railway Review*.

15. 'When victory has come the building. . .' Appeal letter by Fredrick O' Roberts.

## Chapter Thirteen: War and Consequences

1. 'The Norfolk Nabobs of the County Education. . .' *Herald* report 16 Sept. 1914, p.7.

2. 'Burston folk are made of different stuff.' Ibid.

3. 'Burston is not heard of nowadays as much. . .' *Herald* report, 7 November, 1914, p.2.

4. 'who was "walking out" with Violet Potter. . .' *The Burston Rebellion*, B. Zamoyska, p.97.

5. 'Time and space forbids one to tell of a. . .' *The Burston Rebellion*, T.G. Higdon, p.78.

6. The New Year had come and had brought' New Year address, *Landworker*, 1917.

7. 'the available workforce had dropped by 7. . .' *Poor Labouring Men*, Howkins, p. 116.

8. 'The Selbourne Committee did for the labourer. . .' Ibid., p121.

9. 'embodied most of the union's pre-war aspirations. . .' Ibid., p.122.

10. 'Dear Mr. Higdon i thank you very much. . .' Letter from George Durbidge to Tom Higdon, March 1916.

11. 'there were German Zeppelins over. . .' Letter from Violet Potter to Bert Edwards.

12. 'She could speak German. One evening. . .' Ibid.

13. 'they had not been consulted on the matter. . .' *Diss Express* Court Report, 20 April 1917, p.?

14. 'That a good deal of friction was due to. . .' Ibid., p.?

15. 'Mr. Higdon, well-known in connexion with the. . .' *Diss Express* Court Report, 22 June 1917.p.?

16. 'The Rector, Alfred Johnson, & William Ling. . .' *The Burston Rebellion*, Zamoyska, p.101.

17. 'she came at full speed at him, just missing his. . .' *Diss Express* Court Report, 2 November 1917.p.?

18. 'Earlier, on a show of hands. . .Tom and his group. . .' *The Burston School Strike*, p.146.

19. 'He thought he might still be alive so he. . .' *Diss Express*, 2 November 1917.

20. 'no blame attaches, as our opinion is that. . .' Inquest Report quoted in the *Diss Express*, 2 November 1917.

## Chapter Fourteen: The Burston Strike School

1. 'that the principal witnesses were no longer. . .' *Adventures in Education*, Eyken & Turner, p.81.

2. 'absolutely filthy. The place was full of cats. . .' Mr. Giles interview with Bert Edwards, *The Burston School Strike*, p.155.

3. 'His body was not taken into the church. . .' Win Potter interview with Bert Edwards, *The Burston School Strike*, p.157.

4. 'She kept looking at me but she did not recognise. . .' Ibid.

# Bibliography

Arch. J. (1966). *The Autobiography of Joseph Arch*, Edited by John
   Gerard O'Leary; with a Preface by Frances Countess of Warwick.
   Hardcover. (Ed. 2). John Gerard O'Leary.
Author: Anonymous (2010). *Infant Baptism (Adapted from W.P. 'On
   Infant Baptism' under the G.N.U free documentation licence,
   2010)*. Global Oneness. Available at: http://www.
   experiencefestival.com/a/infant_baptism/id/1895554.
BBC. Potter, V. (1974). *Yesterday's Witness—The Burston Rebellion*.
   Documentary.
British History (1848). 'Thornton—Thornton, West', *A
   Topographical Dictionary of England* (1848), pp. 337–41.
   Available at: http://www.british-history.ac.uk/report.
   aspx?compid=51337. Date accessed: 31 March 2008.
British Newspaper Archive (1849). 'Births, Deaths, & Marriages',
   *The Westmoreland Gazette and Kendal Advertiser*, p.? Date
   accessed: 1 April 2016.
British Newspaper Archive (1849). 'The Explosion at Aldingham
   Hall', *The Westmoreland Gazette and Kendal Advertiser*, p.8. Date
   accessed: 1 April 2016.
British Newspaper Archive (1850). 'District Intelligence—
   Ulverston, Joseph Miller Vs. E.J.Schollick', *The Lancaster
   Gazette*, p.? Date accessed: 1 April 2016.
British Newspaper Archive (1853). 'Local Intelligence—Patents
   Sealed', *The Westmoreland Gazette and Kendal Advertiser*, p.5.
   Date accessed: 1 April 2016.
British Newspaper Archive (1853). 'Re-Baptism of an Infant',
   *Leicester Journal*, p.7. Date accessed: 30 November 2016.
British Newspaper Archive (1856). 'Register of Patents', *The London
   Gazette*, Registration No. 1218 & 1249. Date accessed: 1 April
   2016.

British Newspaper Archive (1857). 'Notice of Improvements', *Chester Chronicle and Cheshire and North Wales Advertiser*, p.? Date accessed: 1 April 2016.

British Newspaper Archive (1860). 'District Intelligence— Ulverston, Narrow Escape', *The Lancaster Gazette*, p.? Date accessed: 1 April 2016.

British Newspaper Archive (1860). 'Lonsdale North of the Sands— College of Surgeons', *The Kendal Mercury*, p.5. Date accessed: 1 April 2016.

British Newspaper Archive (1861). 'Apothecaries' Hall', *Bells Weekly Messenger*, p.3. Date accessed: 1 April 2016.

British Newspaper Archive (1861). 'Apothecaries' Hall', *Bells Weekly Messenger*, p.5. Date accessed: 1 April 2016

British Newspaper Archive (1861). 'Lonsdale North of the Sands— Aldingham', *The Kendal Mercury*, p.6. Date accessed: 1 April 2016.

British Newspaper Archive (1861). 'Poulton-cum-Seacombe', *The Liverpool Mercury*, p.3. Date accessed: 1 April 2016

British Newspaper Archive (1862). 'Ulverston and the Lakes— Launch', *The Preston Chronicle and Lancashire Advertiser*, p.7. Date accessed: 1 April 2016.

British Newspaper Archive (1866). 'Fleetwood—Improvement Commissioners', *The Preston Chronicle and Lancashire Advertiser*, p.2. Date accessed: 1 April 2016.

British Newspaper Archive (1866). 'Local Board of Health', *The Surrey Advertiser*, p.? Date accessed: 1 April 2016.

British Newspaper Archive (1866). 'Local News—Accident at Birkenhead Float', *The Liverpool Mercury*, p.? Date accessed: 1 April 2016.

British Newspaper Archive (1866). 'Valuable Freehold Property at Seacombe', *The Cheshire Observer*, p.4. Date accessed: 1 April 2016.

British Newspaper Archive (1867). 'Curious Action Against The Liverpool Shipwrights Association', *The Observer*, p.? Date accessed: 1 April 2016.

British Newspaper Archive (1867). 'Police Intelligence—Liverpool Police Court, Yesterday—Claim Against a Friendly Society', *The Daily Post*, p.7. Date accessed: 1 April 2016.

British Newspaper Archive (1869). 'Conservative Banquet at Ulverston', *The Lancaster Gazette*, p.4 Date accessed: 1 April 2016.

British Newspaper Archive (1872). 'Mr. Joseph Arch at Hoxne', *The Ipswich Journal, And Suffolk, Norfolk, Essex & Cambridgeshire Advertiser*, p.10. Date accessed: 1 March 2016.

British Newspaper Archive (1872). 'The Agricultural Labourers', *The Western Times*, p.2. Date accessed: 1 March 2016.

British Newspaper Archive (1872). 'The Agricultural Labourers', *The Bridport News, And Dorsetshire, Devonshire And Somersetshire Advertiser*, p.? Date accessed: 1 March 2016.

British Newspaper Archive (1872). 'The Farm Labourer Agitation', *The Western Times*, p.2. Date accessed: 1 March 2016.

British Newspaper Archive (1872). 'The Somersetshire Agricultural Labourers', *The Bridport News, And Dorsetshire, Devonshire And Somersetshire Advertiser*, p.? Date accessed: 1 March 2016.

British Newspaper Archive (1881). 'Local and District News—East Pennard—The Wesleyan Chapel', *The Western Gazette*, p.6. Date accessed: 8 April 2016.

British Newspaper Archive (1883). 'Local and District News—East Pennard—A Gospel Temperance Blue Ribbon Meeting', *The Western Gazette*, p.6. Date accessed: 8 April 2016.

British Newspaper Archive (1883). 'Local and District News—East Pennard—Huxham Sunday school', *The Western Gazette*, p.6. Date accessed: 8 April 2016.

British Newspaper Archive (1883). 'Local and District News—East Pennard—Huxham School Treat', *The Western Gazette*, p.6. Date accessed: 8 April 2016.

British Newspaper Archive (1885). 'Local and District News—East Pennard—Huxham Band of Hope', *The Western Gazette*, p.7. Date accessed: 8 April 2016.

British Newspaper Archive (1885). 'The Yeovil Division of Somerset,' *The Western Daily Press*, Bristol, p.6. Date accessed: 8 April 2016.

British Newspaper Archive (1886). 'Mr Joseph Arch and Mr. George Mitchell', *The Nottinghamshire Guardian*, p.5. Date accessed: 8 April 2016.

British Newspaper Archive (1887). 'Local and District News—East Pennard—Jubilee Celebrations', *The Western Gazette*, p.6. Date accessed: 8 April 2016.

British Newspaper Archive (1889). 'Local and District News—East Pennard—Presentation to the Vicar', *The Western Gazette*, p.6. Date accessed: 8 April 2016.

British Newspaper Archive (1890). 'Evercreech Agricultural Association', *The Western Daily Press*, p.7. Date accessed: 30 November 2016.

British Newspaper Archive (1890). 'Surrey Local News—Croydon', *The Sussex Express, Surrey Standard, Weald of Kent Mail, Hants & County*. p.3. Date accessed: 1 April 2016.

British Newspaper Archive (1890). 'The Huxham Tragedy Funeral for the Victims', *The Western Times*, p.3. Date accessed: 15 November 2016.

British Newspaper Archive (1891). 'Somerset Labourers—Forming a Union', *The Western Times*, p.3. Date accessed: 30 November 2016.

British Newspaper Archive (1892). 'Butlers, Coachmen, Gardeners, &c.', *The Western Daily Press*, p.2. Date accessed: 30 November 2016.

British Newspaper Archive (1892). 'Butlers, Coachmen, Gardeners, &c.', *The Western Daily News*, p.8. Date accessed: 30 November 2016.

British Newspaper Archive (1892). 'Distinguished Men And The Somerset Labourers', *The Western Daily Press*, p.8. Date accessed: 15 November 2016.

British Newspaper Archive (1892). 'East Lydford—Influenza', *The Western Gazette*, p.7. Date accessed: 30 November 2016.

British Newspaper Archive (1892). 'The Agricultural Labourers' Union', *The Western Daily Press*, p.8. Date accessed: 1 December 2016.

British Newspaper Archive (1893). 'Village Schoolmistresses', *Supplement to The Cheltenham Chronicle*, p.? Date accessed: 15 November 2016.

British Newspaper Archive (1894). 'East Pennard—School Board', *The Shepton Mallet Journal*, p.8. Date accessed: 30 November 2016.

British Newspaper Archive (1894). 'Somerton Petty Sessions—Disorderly Boys', *The Western Gazette*, p.3. Date accessed: 30 November 2016.

British Newspaper Archive (1895). 'School Board Accounts', *Advertiser for Somerset*, p.8. Date accessed: 30 November 2016.

British Newspaper Archive (1895). 'The Schoolmistress at Home', *The Shepton Mallet Journal*, p.8. Date accessed: 30 November 2016.

British Newspaper Archive (1899). 'Huxham Wesleyan Sunday School', *The Shepton Mallet Journal*, p.3. Date accessed: 30 November 2016.

British Newspaper Archive (1902). 'Sancreed School Board', *The Cornishman*, p 7. Date accessed: 7 April 2016.

British Newspaper Archive (1904). 'Vicar of Felsted's Deal in Union Pacifics', *Essex County Chronicle*, p.8. Date accessed: 14 April 2016.

British Newspaper Archive (1905). 'Conservatives at Felsted', *The Newsman*, p.3. Date accessed: 14 April 2016.

British Newspaper Archive (1906). 'Felsted Water Question', *The Essex County Chronicle*, p.6. Date accessed: 14 April 2016.

British Newspaper Archive (1906). 'Felsted' *The Essex Newsman*, p.? Date accessed: 14 April 2016.

British Newspaper Archive (1907). 'Felsted Results & Felsted Water Supply', *The Essex County Chronicle*, p.6. Date accessed: 14 April 2016.

British Newspaper Archive (1907). 'Summer Chaplaincies on the Continent', *The Essex County Chronicle*, p.6. Date accessed: 14 April 2016.

British Newspaper Archive (1908). 'New Vicar at Burston', *The Diss Express, And Norfolk And Suffolk Journal*, front page. Date accessed: 14 April 2016.

British Newspaper Archive (1908). 'Mission Report', *The Diss Express, And Norfolk And Suffolk Journal*, p.? Date accessed: 14 April 2016.

British Newspaper Archive (1908). 'School Treat', *The Diss Express, And Norfolk And Suffolk Journal*, p.2. Date accessed: 14 April 2016.

British Newspaper Archive (1908). 'Dunmow', *The Essex Newsman*, front page. Date accessed: 14 April 2016.

British Newspaper Archive (1909). 'Mrs Green Resigns', *The Diss Express, And Norfolk And Suffolk Journal*, p.? Date accessed: 14 April 2016.

British Newspaper Archive (1909). 'Felsted Children's Christmas Treat', *The Essex Newsman*, front page. Date accessed: 14 April 2016.

British Newspaper Archive (1910). 'New Essex Vicar and His Wife', *The Essex County Chronicle*, p.2. Date accessed: 14 April 2016.

British Newspaper Archive (1910). 'Church News—New Vicar at Felsted', *The Newsman*, front page. Date accessed: 14 April 2016.

British Newspaper Archive (1911). 'Clerical Appointments', *The Diss Express, And Norfolk And Suffolk Journal*, p.? Date accessed: 14 April 2016.

British Newspaper Archive (1911). 'Presentation to the Vicar of Felsted', *The Essex County Chronicle*, p.3. Date accessed: 14 April 2016.

British Newspaper Archive (1914). 'Eighty Schools Closed. Teachers' Strike Opens', front page', *Birmingham Gazette*. Date accessed: 21 April 2016.

British Newspaper Archive (1914). 'Strike of School Teachers', *Evening Despatch*, p.5. Date accessed: 21 April 2016.

British Newspaper Archive (1914). 'Norfolk Nabobs—Villagers Vigorously Resisting', *Daily Herald*, p.7. Date accessed: 28 April 2016.

British Newspaper Archive (1914). 'Strike of English Teachers', *The Aberdeen Daily Journal*, p.7. Date accessed: 21 April 2016.

British Newspaper Archive (1914). 'Teachers' Strike', *The Birmingham Daily Mail*, p.? Date accessed: 21 April 2016.

British Newspaper Archive (1914). 'School Children Go On Strike', *The Daily Mirror*, p.5. Date accessed: 21 April 2016.

British Newspaper Archive (1914). 'On Strike', *The Devon And Exeter Gazette*, p.12. Date accessed: 21 April 2016.

British Newspaper Archive (1914). 'Burston—Parish Meeting', *The Diss Express, And Norfolk And Suffolk Journal*, p.? Date accessed: 28 April 2016.

British Newspaper Archive (1914). 'Burston—Strike of School Children', *The Diss Express, And Norfolk And Suffolk Journal*, p.? Date accessed: 28 April 2016.

British Newspaper Archive (1914). 'School Teachers' Strike', *The Evening Express*, p.? Date accessed: 21 April 2016.

British Newspaper Archive (1914). 'Burston', *The Herald*, p.2. Date accessed: 28 April 2016.

British Newspaper Archive (1914). 'The School Strike', *The Western Daily Press*, p.? Date accessed: 21 April 2016.

British Newspaper Archive (1914). 'Strike of Teachers', *The Western Times*, p.? Date accessed: 21 April 2016.

British Newspaper Archive (1915). 'Burston Children Must Win', *The Herald*, p.3. Date accessed: 28 April 2016.

British Newspaper Archive (1915). 'Burston Outdoor Meeting', *The Diss Express, And Norfolk And Suffolk Journal*, p.? Date accessed: 28 April 2016.

British Newspaper Archive (1915). 'The Burston School Strike', *The Burston Daily Mail*, p.2. Date accessed: 28 April 2016.

British Newspaper Archive (1915). 'Burston Parish Meeting', *The Diss Express, And Norfolk And Suffolk Journal*, p.? Date accessed: 28 April 2016.

British Newspaper Archive (1915). 'Death of an Aged Parishioner', *The Diss Express, And Norfolk And Suffolk Journal*, p.? Date accessed: 28 April 2016.

British Newspaper Archive (1915). 'The Burston School Strike—Henderson's Letter', *The Diss Express, And Norfolk And Suffolk Journal*, p.? Date accessed: 28 April 2016.

British Newspaper Archive (1915). 'A Far Country—The Burston School Strike', *The Herald*, p.12. Date accessed: 28 April 2016.

British Newspaper Archive (1915). 'The Burston School Strike', *The Herald*, p.13. Date accessed: 28 April 2016.

British Newspaper Archive (1915). 'The Children's School Strike at Burston', *The Herald*, p.13. Date accessed: 28 April 2016.

British Newspaper Archive (1915). 'Things That Matter—The Burston School Strike', *The Herald*, p.2. Date accessed: 28 April 2016.

British Newspaper Archive (1916). 'The Burston Glebe Lands Dispute', *The Diss Express, And Norfolk And Suffolk Journal*, p.? Date accessed: 28 April 2016.

British Newspaper Archive (1916). 'Diss and Eye Courts', *The Diss Express, And Norfolk And Suffolk Journal*, p.? Date accessed: 28 April 2016.

British Newspaper Archive (1916). 'Sequel to Burston Glebe Land Dispute', *The Diss Express, And Norfolk And Suffolk Journal*, p.? Date accessed: 28 April 2016

British Newspaper Archive (1916). 'Straying Charge Dismissed', *The Diss Express, And Norfolk And Suffolk Journal*, p.? Date accessed: 29 April 2016.

British Newspaper Archive (1916). 'Fundraising notice', *The Herald*, p.15. Date accessed: 29 April May 2016.

British Newspaper Archive (1916). 'National Agricultural Labourers And Rural Workers' Union', *The Herald*, front page. Date accessed: 29 April May 2016.

British Newspaper Archive (1916). 'Passing Comment—The Burston Strike', *The Herald*, p.? Date accessed: 29 April May 2016.

British Newspaper Archive (1916). 'The Burston Battle', *The Herald*, p.10. Date accessed: 29 April May 2016.

British Newspaper Archive (1916). 'The Burston School Strike', *The Herald*, p.? Date accessed: 29 April May 2016.

British Newspaper Archive (1916). 'The Way of the World—Burston School Strike', *The Herald*, front page. Date accessed: 29 April May 2016.

British Newspaper Archive (1917). 'A Burston Memorial—School Strike And Family Feuds', *The Diss Express, and Norfolk And Suffolk Journal*, p.? Date accessed: 1 May 2016.

British Newspaper Archive (1917). 'Burston—Opening of the News Strike School', *The Diss Express, And Norfolk And Suffolk Journal*, p.? Date accessed: 1 March 2016.

British Newspaper Archive (1917). 'Charges Against Clergyman Dismissed', *The Diss Express, and Norfolk And Suffolk Journal*, p.? Date accessed: 1 May 2016.

British Newspaper Archive (1917). 'Farmers' Wages', *The Yorkshire Post*, p.8. Date accessed: 1 May 2016.

British Newspaper Archive (1917). *Labour Leader*, 17th May 1917, 'Burston Strike School Opened—Big Trade Union Demonstration', reproduced in Edwards, B. (1974). *The Burston School Strike*. Lawrence & Wishart, London, p.143.

British Newspaper Archive (1917). 'Labourers' Union Meetings', *The Western Gazette*, p.? Date accessed: 8 May 2016.

British Newspaper Archive (1917). 'Labourers' Union Meeting', *The Western Gazette*, p.3. Date accessed: 1 May 2016.

British Newspaper Archive (1917). 'Sunday Scene in Burston Church', *The Diss Express, and Norfolk And Suffolk Journal*, p.? Date accessed: 1 May 2016.

British Newspaper Archive (1917). The Burston School Dispute—*The Diss Express, and Norfolk And Suffolk Journal*, p.? Date accessed: 1 May 2016.

British Newspaper Archive (1917). 'The Burston Tablet Case—Judgement Against The Defendants', *The Diss Express, and Norfolk And Suffolk Journal*, p.? Date accessed: 1 May 2016.

British Newspaper Archive (1917). 'Burston School Dispute—County Council's Decision', *The Diss Express, and Norfolk And Suffolk Journal*, p.? Date accessed: 29 April 2016.

British Newspaper Archive (1917). 'The Depwade Union', *The Diss Express, and Norfolk And Suffolk Journal*, p.? Date accessed: 29 April 2016.

British Newspaper Archive (1917). 'A Parish Meeting', *The Diss Express, and Norfolk And Suffolk Journal*, p.? Date accessed: 29 April 2016.

British Newspaper Archive (1917). 'Burston—Encroachment on the Village Green', *The Diss Express, and Norfolk And Suffolk Journal*, p.? Date accessed: 29 April 2016.

British Newspaper Archive (1917). 'N.U.T and the Burston Case', *The Diss Express, and Norfolk And Suffolk Journal*, p.? Date accessed: 29 April 2016.

British Newspaper Archive (1917). 'The Opening of the New Strike School', *The Diss Express, and Norfolk And Suffolk Journal*, p.? Date accessed: 29 April 2016.

British Newspaper Archive (1917). 'An Interpleader Case', *The Diss Express, And Norfolk And Suffolk Journal*, p.? Date accessed: 29 April 2016.

British Newspaper Archive (1917). 'Sunday Scene in Burston Church', *The Diss Express, And Norfolk And Suffolk Journal*, p.? Date accessed: 1 May 2016.

British Newspaper Archive (1917). 'Burston', *The Herald*, p.? Date accessed: 29 April 2016.

British Newspaper Archive (1917). 'Events in Burston', *The Herald*, p.13. Date accessed: 29 April 2016.

British Newspaper Archive (1917). 'How the School was Opened', *The Herald*, p.18. Date accessed: 29 April 2016.

British Newspaper Archive (1918). 'Meeting of Agricultural Labourers' Union', *The Diss Express, And Norfolk And Suffolk Journal*, p.? Date accessed: 8 May 2016.

British Newspaper Archive (1919). 'Burston Cycle Accident', *The Diss Express, And Norfolk And Suffolk Journal*, p.9. Date accessed: 8 May 2016.

British Newspaper Archive (1919). 'Burston—The Housing Question', *The Diss Express, And Norfolk And Suffolk Journal*, p.? Date accessed: 8 May 2016.

British Newspaper Archive (1919). 'Echo of A School Strike', *The Northampton Mercury*, p.9. Date accessed: 15 May 2016.

British Newspaper Archive (1920). 'A Terror to the Neighbourhood', *The Diss Express, And Norfolk And Suffolk Journal*, Date accessed: 8 May 2016.

British Newspaper Archive (1920). 'I Have Shot my Father', *The Bury Free Press*, p.2. Date accessed: 8 May 2016.

British Newspaper Archive (1921). 'Burston School Strike', *The Diss Express, And Norfolk And Suffolk Journal*, p.? Date accessed: 8 May 2016.

British Newspaper Archive (1930). 'Agricultural Workers' Union', *The Diss Express, And Norfolk And Suffolk Journal*, p.? Date accessed: 15 May 2016.

British Newspaper Archive (1930). 'The Late Mr. Ambrose Sandy of Burston', *The Diss Express, And Norfolk And Suffolk Journal*, p.? Date accessed: 15 May 2016.

British Newspaper Archive (1937). 'Where to go! Burston', *The Diss Express, And Norfolk And Suffolk Journal*, p.? Date accessed: 8 May 2016.

British Newspaper Archive (1939). 'The Late Mr. T.G. Higdon', *The Diss Express, And Norfolk And Suffolk Journal*, p.? Date accessed: 8 May 2016.

Brook, C. (2007). *The Internet Surname Database*. Available at: http://www.surnamedb.com/Home/About#ixzz452Hame2yg. Date accessed: 1 April 2016.

Collins, K.J. (2007). *The Theology of John Wesley: Holy Love and the Shape of Grace*. Nashville: Abingdon Press.

Country Standard (blog), 2007. 'Essex Agricultural Labourers'. Date accessed: 11 March 2017.

Cumbria Amenity Trust Mining History Society (2004). *Edward Jones Schollick, Polymath, 1825–1908*. Available at: http://www.catmhs.org.uk/wp-content/uploads/2015/11/NEWSLETTER–077—November–2004.pdf. Date accessed: 20 November 2016.

Dale, I. (2003). *The Story of Bilston Wesley*. Harold Dale.

Edwards, B. (1974). *The Burston School Strike*. Lawrence & Wishart, London.

Eyken, W.V.D. and Turner, B. (1969). *Adventures in Education*. Penguin. Hazell Watson & Viney Ltd.

Gillard, D. (2011). *Education in England: a brief history*. Available at: http://www.educationengland.org.uk/history/chapter04.html p.1. Date Accessed: 19 January 2017.

Groves, R. (1949). *Sharpen the Sickle! The History of the Farm Workers Union*, Merlin Publications.

Guyatt, A.R. (2013). *History of the School*. Taken from 'A Village School in Soho: A history of Soho Parish School (St. James's and St. Peter's)'. Available at: http://www.sohoparish.co.uk/History—of-the-school. Date Accessed: 4 January 2017.

Hasbach, W. (1908). *A History of the English Agricultural Labourer*. Translated by Ruth Kenyon (1st Ed. English). S. King & Son.

Heath, F.G. (1872). *The "Romance" of Peasant Life In the West of England*. Cassell, Petter & Galpin.

Heitzenrater, R.P. (2005). *Wesley and The People called Methodists*. Nashville: Abingdon Press.

Higdon, T. (1903). *To the Departed*. Jarrod & Sons, Ltd. Norwich & London.

Higdon, T.G. (1916). *The Burston Rebellion*. National Labour Press. Manchester.

Horn, P. (1971). *Joseph Arch (1826–1919): the farm workers' leader*. Published Kineton: Roundwood Press.

Horn, P. (1989). *The Victorian & Edwardian Schoolchild* (Ed. 2010). Amberley Publishing.

Howkins, A. (1985). *Poor Labouring Men—Rural Radicalism in Norfolk 1870–1923*. Routledge & Kengan Paul.

Humphries, S. (1983). *Hooligans or Rebels?: An Oral History of Working Class Childhood and Youth*, 1889–1939. Published by Blackwell Publishers.

Keating, J. (2010). *Pupil-Teacher Training* [DOC]. Available at: https://www.history.ac.uk/history—in . . . in . . . /teacher_training_-_up_to_the_1960s.doc University of London. Date Accessed: 6 December 2016.

Mann, T. (1923). *Tom Mann's Memoirs*. The Labour Publishing Company Limited.

McCarthy, T. (1988). *Great Dock Strike of 1889*. Weidenfeld & Nicolson.

McKeever, R. and Layfield, J. (2006). *The Industrial Archaeology of South Ulverston* (2nd Ed.). Furness Peninsula Press, pp.91–3.

Mendip District Council (2008). 'Conservation Area Appraisal—East Pennard', PDF. Mendip District Council. Downloaded: 13 December 2016.

Norgate, J. and M. (2012), *Old Cumbria Gazetteer*, courtesy of English Heritage—ALDINGHAM HALL / / A5087 / ALDINGHAM / SOUTH LAKELAND / CUMBRIA / II / 75779 / SD2824271048. Geography Department, Portsmouth University. Available at: http://www.geog.port.ac.uk/webmap/thelakes/html/lgaz/lk04849.htm. Date accessed: 5 December 2016.

*North West Mail* (2009). 'Ulverston Canal'. Available at: http://www.nwemail.co.uk/news/Ulverston—Canal–93748a9f–041b–4633-b08e-aaa1b277d0f9-ds. Date accessed: 5 December 2016.

*North West Mail* (2010). 'When Canal Was a Hive of Shipbuilding Trades'. Available at: http://www.nwemail.co.uk/news/millom/When-canal-was-a-hive-of-shipbuilding—trades–441b91af-ed29–4710-a561–8b58d9a9246f-ds. Date accessed: 5 December 2016.

*North West Mail* (2011). 'Chance Discovery in a Rewriting History'. Available at: http://www.nwemail.co.uk/news/ulverston/Chance-discovery-results-in-a-rewriting-of—history-f77164d7-d027–4452-a283–3cbd637611f0-ds. Date accessed: 5 December 2016.

*North West Mail* (2011). 'Fortunate Butler'. Available at: http://www.nwemail.co.uk/news/ulverston/Fortunate-butler-f4adce2d-a078–4298—be7b–0b92a79e3e01-ds. Date accessed: 5 December 2016.

Owen, B. (2002). *One From the Plough—The Life and Time of George Mitchell* (1826–1901). Gazebo Press.

Pankhurst, S. (1917). 'The Woman's Dreadnought', reproduced in Zamoyska, B. (1985). *The Burston Rebellion*. Ariel Books, London.

Rack, H.D. (2002). *Reasonable Enthusiast: John Wesley and the Rise of Methodism*. (Ed. 3, 2002), Epworth. London.

Sandbach, P. (n.d.). *E.J. Schollick, Ulverston Shipbuilder*. Through Mighty Seas. Available at: http://mightyseas.perso.sfr.fr/articles/schollick.htm, pp.1–3. Date accessed: 1 March 2016.

Scarth. B. (1998). *We'll All Be Union Men: The Story of Joseph Arch and his Union*.

Scurr, J. (1917). 'How the School was Opened'. *The Herald*, p.8.

Shardlow, B. and Penney, D. (n.d.). 'Dockyard Shipwrights'. Available at: http://freepages.genealogy.rootsweb.ancestry.com/#slpenney/shipwrights%20trades%20etc/s_wrighw%20trade.htm. Date Accessed: 15 December 2016.

Simkin, J. (1997). 'The Dock Strike'. Available at: http://spartacus-educational.com/TUdockers.htm. Spartacus Educational Publishers Ltd. Date Accessed: 23 December 2016.

Stonard, D.D.J. (1840). 'Dissertation on the Discourse delivered by our Blessed Saviour in Answer to the Questions of his Apostles, touching the Destruction of the Temple and the End of the Worlds—The Church Quarterly Review'. *The Church of England Quarterly Review*, VOL. VIII, London, William Edward Painter. Rivingtons.

Tillett, B. (1910). *A Brief History of the Dockers' Union: Commemorating the 1889 Dockers' Strike* (6th Ed.). London: Dock, Wharf, Riverside, and General Workers' Union.

Trustees of the Burston Strike School (1984). *The Burston Strike School—The Story of the Longest Strike in History*. Rapide, Watton.

Unknown (n.d.). *A Walk through Felsted—A Trip Down Memory Lane*. Available at: http://www.recordinguttlesfordhistory.org.uk/ felsted/A%20Walk%20through%20Felsted%20in%201901.pdf. Date accessed: 6 February 2017.

Wilby, E. (1915). *Our School Strike*.

Wilson, M.W. (1872). *Imperial Gazetteer of England and Wales (1870–72)*—East Pennard, available at: http://www. visionofbritain.org.uk/place/13139. University of Portsmouth, 2009–2014. Date Accessed: 15 December 2016.

Wilson, M.W. (1872). *Imperial Gazetteer of England and Wales (1870–72)*—Colton, Lancashire. Available at: http://www. visionofbritain.org.uk/place/10055. University of Portsmouth, 2009–2014. Date Accessed: 15 December 2016.

Wilson, M.W. (1872). *Imperial Gazetteer of England and Wales (1870–72)*—Egton with Newland. Available at: http://www. visionofbritain.org.uk/place/10198. University of Portsmouth, 2009–2014. Date Accessed: 15 December 2016.

Wilson, M.W. (1872). *Imperial Gazetteer of England and Wales (1870–72)*—Montacute. Available at: http://www. visionofbritain.org.uk/place/13108. University of Portsmouth, 2009–2014. Date Accessed: 15 December 2016.

Wilson, M.W. (1872). *Imperial Gazetteer of England and Wales (1870–72)*—East Lydford. Available at: http://www. visionofbritain.org.uk/place/13088. University of Portsmouth, 2009–2014. Date Accessed: 15 December 2016.

# Index

# About the Author

Shaun Jeffery, the author of *The Village in Revolt: The Story of the Longest Strike in History*, was born in the market town of Beccles, Suffolk. Nestled on the southern bank of the River Waveney, he would spend his formative years exploring the surrounding countryside. It would be in Beccles – part defined by its active community spirit, and part by its surprisingly rich industrial heritage – that he would develop a passion for the natural world and social issues. Since leaving university, where he studied environmental science and management, he has worked in the horticultural sector, and is an active trade unionist and trustee of the Burston Strike School. He lives in the UK and India.

The author can be contacted at:

Email: burstonstrikeschool1917@gmail.com

Twitter: @Burston1917

Fb: https://www.facebook.com/shaun.jeffery.773